THE HARPERCOLLINS VISUAL GUIDE TO THE NEW TESTAMENT

THE HARPERCOLLINS VISUAL GUIDE TO THE NEW TESTAMENT

WHAT ARCHAEOLOGY REVEALS ABOUT THE FIRST CHRISTIANS

JONATHAN L. REED

HarperOne

A Division of HarperCollins Publishers

FOR
NATANIA
AND LEVI

Bible references are from the NRSV.

THE HARPERCOLLINS VISUAL GUIDE TO THE NEW TESTAMENT: *What Archaeology Reveals about the First Christians.* Copyright © 2007 by Jonathan L. Reed. All rights reserved. Printed in the U.S.A. No part of this book may be used or reproduced in any manner whatsoever without written permission except in the case of brief quotations embodied in critical articles and reviews. For information address HarperCollins Publishers, 10 East 53rd Street, New York, NY 10022.

HarperCollins®, ®, and HarperOne™ are trademarks of HarperCollins Publishers.

ISBN: 978–0–06–084249–9

ISBN-10: 0–06–084249–0

Book Club Edition

CONTENTS

PREFACE VI

1

ARCHAEOLOGY AND THE NEW TESTAMENT 2

2

WHAT ARCHAEOLOGISTS DO 16

3

JEWS AMONG GREEKS AND ROMANS 34

4

GALILEE AND
THE WORLD OF JESUS'S MINISTRY 54

5

THE ARCHAEOLOGY OF
JERUSALEM AND JESUS'S PASSION 78

6

PAUL AND THE CITIES
OF THE ROMAN EMPIRE 100

7

THE FIRST CHRISTIANS
AND THE JEWISH WARS 122

8

THE CHRISTIAN WORLD AFTER
THE NEW TESTAMENT 140

APPENDICES 156

GLOSSARY OF
ARCHAEOLOGICAL AND ARCHITECTURAL TERMS 160

ILLUSTRATION CREDITS 164

INDEX 165

PREFACE

Twenty years ago I volunteered for what was supposed to be a six-week excavation season at Capernaum. But those six weeks along the shore of the Sea of Galilee turned into a lifelong passion for archaeology. That passion has taken me back year after year to the lands of the New Testament; I have excavated for over a decade at Sepphoris, Galilee's one-time capital and neighbor of Jesus's hometown of Nazareth, and have returned summer after summer to the Albright Institute of Archaeological Research in Jerusalem, as well as spending some summers at the American School of Classical Studies in Athens and the American Academy in Rome. What archaeology can tell us about Jesus himself and his first followers has consumed my academic career. It has also changed my life.

The bulk of my university responsibilities have been dedicated to teaching undergraduates about the Bible. The way I am interested in teaching the New Testament is not as philosophy or theology, nor doctrinally or dogmatically, but as a window onto the lives of real people. When I teach my New Testament courses, I try to take my students back in time and away in space, two thousand years ago and ten thousand miles from here. The only way to do that successfully is with archaeology. If my students can't accompany me on a study tour to Israel, Greece, Turkey, or Italy, then I must bring that ancient world's topography, artifacts, and architecture excavations to them. I try to impress upon my students with slides that we are dealing with real communities from the past, whose members lived their lives with struggles similar to those in the modern world, including economic oppression, political dissent, and racial and gender discrimination. That is the goal of this book: to share with the reader the world of the New Testament as archaeology brings it to life.

Unfortunately, too much of the available archaeological studies fall into two categories: popular quackery and scholarly esotericism. Web sites by rogue "experts" clutter the Internet with absurdly spectacular claims, while shelves of impenetrable site reports laden with technical vocabulary sit unread in university libraries. All professors caution against the excesses of the Internet. But many of us also worry about drubbing the joy of discovery out of the curious. I have stood with groups of sweaty students under the hot Mediterranean sun in front of a maze of beige stones, lines of rocks zig-zagging though grayish beige dirt, and explained how Adan-Bayewitz Cooker 4B helps delineate subphase ER II here. We have a tendency to nuance ad nauseam. This book cuts through some of the nuances yet still attempts to be archaeologically responsible and accurate. The goal of this book is to provide those curious about Christian origins with a survey of the key discoveries, excavations, and artifacts that relate to the New Testament. I trust my colleagues will forgive me for simplifying some issues and ignoring others, but foremost in my mind is helping a wider audience — intelligent but not yet initiated into the technical vocabulary of scholars — envision the world of the New Testament as archaeology brings it to light.

Studying and teaching the archaeology of early Christianity has forced a certain amount of self-reflection about my own beliefs. I no longer have the same faith I did when I first set foot on the excavation site at Capernaum. That faith needed some challenges. After looking in great detail at the world of Jesus and Paul, I am convinced that Christian origins are more social than personal, more concerned with this life than the next, more politically subversive than politically acquiescent. This book is not intended to lead the reader along the same path that archaeology showed me, but I do hope it challenges the reader in similar ways, and generates both interest in the people behind the New Testament and an appreciation for their struggles. No particular Christian faith, no one religious tradition or even any religious inclination at all is presumed for this book — only curiosity. After two introductory chapters, the book unfolds the way most students approach the New Testament. It begins with a brief survey of the Greco-Roman world in chapter 3. Chapters on Galilee and Jerusalem accompany a reading of the Gospels. A chapter on the archaeology of Roman cities accompanies Acts and the letters of Paul. What excavations tell us about the two Jewish wars with Rome go alongside a reading of the remaining books of the New Testament. Finally, a concluding chapter deals with the period after the New Testament and touches on early Christianity's diversity and competitors.

This book owes a debt of gratitude to numerous people, especially Vassilios Tzaferis, John Wilson, and John Laughlin, who took me under their wings at Capernaum. Your first dig is always special. Second, I owe a debt of gratitude to Eric and Carol Meyers, who mentored me at Sepphoris, and put me in touch with scholars and now friends on that excavation's staff. This work has benefited from dig directors, archaeologists, and architects too numerous to mention. I thank the American Academy in Rome, the American School of Classical Studies in Athens, and especially Sy Gitin and his staff at the Albright Institute for Archaeological Research in Jerusalem for their kind assistance. Generous support for my travels was provided by the University of La Verne. Kenneth Atkinson, Byron McCane, Milton Moreland, Morten Hørning Jensen, and John Gingrich looked over various drafts and provided valuable help in shaping this book. Thanks are also due to Eric Brandt, Kris Ashley, and Terri Leonard at HarperOne; and the book's designer, Mark Ong; and Lisa Zuniga. But I owe the greatest thanks to my wife, Annette, for putting up with physical and mental absences while working on this project, and to my daughter, Natania, and son, Levi, to whom this book is dedicated.

— Jonathan L. Reed

THE HARPERCOLLINS VISUAL GUIDE TO THE NEW TESTAMENT

1

ARCHAEOLOGY AND THE NEW TESTAMENT

Archaeology is imperative for the study of the New Testament. There is no chance of understanding Jesus or Paul, Peter or Mary, without understanding their world. And there is no way to reconstruct that world without archaeology. Over the past century, hundreds of excavations and thousands of archaeologists have turned up coins and pots, statues and architecture from ruins all across the Mediterranean.

These finds revolutionize our understanding of the New Testament. Most people are drawn to archaeological discoveries because they provide a tangible link to the past. Holding a storage jar found in Galilee from the time of Jesus or walking on a mosaic from a Roman city visited by Paul is a powerful experience. It provides an intimate glimpse into the past and helps us imagine the lives of people who were once real, not just names in a book.

People are fascinated with what archaeologists do and envious of their travels to places described in the Bible. But they are also confused by archaeologists' technical terms and perplexed by competing claims regarding matters that seem irrelevant. Laypersons have to dig through layers of jargon to access a newly discovered artifact or put up with academic bickering about the artifact's interpretation, which kills the novice's enthusiasm. The goal of this book is to cut through those scholarly layers and take the reader on a visual tour of archaeology that relates to the New Testament. This book is intended to be a guide unencumbered by technical and theoretical terminology. Its ambition is to nurture enthusiasm and pique curiosity, and to do so in an intellectually responsible and archaeologically credible manner. This *Visual Guide to the New Testament* presents a picture of the most important artifacts, buildings, sites, and excavations relating to the world of Jesus and his first followers.

The illustrations in this book are not merely visual aids that accompany New Testament passages. Instead, they provide a window onto the ancient Mediterranean world that will transform the reader's understanding of the New Testament. For example, it is only after looking at the kinds of houses in which Jesus's Galilean disciples grew up that we can understand their awe at the Temple in Jerusalem. Only by examining shipwrecks at the bottom of the Mediterranean can we appreciate Paul's dogged commitment to spread his message. And only by surveying the numerous temples, statues, and inscriptions that proclaimed the Roman caesars to be sons of god can we comprehend the perils of proclaiming Christ the Lord.

CAN ARCHAEOLOGY CONFIRM THE NEW TESTAMENT?

We begin by looking at common expectations of archaeology. The most pressing question asked of archaeologists is whether their discoveries confirm the truth of the New Testament. Sometimes proof seems tantalizingly close, and other times frustratingly far. But even if finds cannot convincingly confirm a New Testament passage, archaeological artifacts can nevertheless profoundly affect our understanding of the New Testament's message. Archaeology may not be able to prove — or disprove, for that matter — the accuracy of the New Testament, but it teaches us much about the lives and beliefs of those earliest Christians.

opposite page

Registered Ceramic Fragment
Roman Disc Lamp (1st C. CE)
Galilean Jar (1st C. CE)
Mosaic (Pisidian Antioch, 4th C. CE)

this page

Ossuary (Jerusalem, 1st C. CE)
Inscription (Modern Forgery)

The paraphernalia of everyday life is a main concern of archaeologists. From thousands of fragmentary shards, archaeologists piece together aspects of ancient life without which the New Testament cannot be understood. The bulk of that time is consumed with carefully gathering, recording, washing, and registering tiny potsherds from such common household wares as this Galilean pot and Roman lamp. These provide the matrix in which more spectacular finds can be placed and are the archaeological glue that holds together a reconstruction of the ancient world.

The greatest archaeological discovery ever turned out to be a hoax. A forger inscribed this ossuary, or bone box, with "James, son of Joseph, brother of Jesus" in the Aramaic language used by first-century Jews. If authentic, it would have been the earliest evidence for Jesus.

Our first example is a hyped archaeological find that failed to prove anything. Hailed as the greatest archaeological discovery ever, this limestone box was inscribed with the words "James, the son of Joseph, the brother of Jesus." These boxes are common around Jerusalem; they are called ossuaries and were used by Jews during Jesus's time to deposit the bones of the dead, but this ossuary, purchased in an antiquities shop in Jerusalem, was notable for its inscription. Written in Aramaic, the language of Jesus and other Jews in the first century, it was thought to have contained the bones of James, another son of Joseph the carpenter. According to the New Testament's book of Acts, as well as the Jewish historian Josephus, James was an important leader in the early church who was stoned to death in 62 CE, right about the time to which the ossuary was dated. Initially, some experts authenticated the inscription based on the style of the Aramaic letters, and some geologists confirmed the box's antiquity with scientific tests. But their expert advice only ruled out a clumsy forgery.

This was a crafty forgery. Investigation by the Israel Antiquities Authority exposed the inscription as a fake. The Authority's Theft Unit linked the owner of the ossuary to a warehouse that served as a forger's workshop, with dental drills, chemicals, and soils from various archaeological sites, and scores of fake artifacts and inscriptions in various stages of production. A scientific panel concluded that though the box was ancient, the inscription was modern; it cut through the ancient surface, disturbing what geologists call biovermiculation, the bacterial erosion that takes place over centuries and looks like tiny, coral-like pits under magnification. The patina, a thin weathering that forms over time on stone surfaces, covered most of the ossuary with a crystalline sheen and a cauliflowerlike appearance, including parts of the inscription. But microscopic examination revealed that areas around and within the inscription had been carefully coated with a fake patina. The James ossuary, it turned out, was a hoax. It did not prove anything about

James or Jesus. But hoaxes do not disprove anything, either.

In the end, the ossuary was not a direct archaeological link to a New Testament figure; it only served as a reminder that none of the main characters of the New Testament left traces in the archaeological record. There are links to tangential figures mentioned in the Gospels and Acts, however. Archaeologists in Israel found a plaque inscribed by Pontius Pilate, the governor who condemned Jesus to crucifixion, and an ossuary that belonged to Caiaphas, the Jewish high priest who participated in Jesus's trial. And excavators in Greece uncovered an inscription naming Gallio, the procurator who tried Paul, according to Acts 18, and a pavement stone naming Erastus, whom Paul mentions in his letter to the Romans. Archaeology confirms that these people really existed, but none of these discoveries can affirm the New Testament's spiritual, moral, or religious claims. These discoveries may make those claims more plausible, but they certainly do not prove them true. These four names written in stone and discovered by archaeologists — Pilate, Caiaphas, Gallio, and Erastus — belonged to powerful and wealthy people. But no inscriptions mentioning Jesus, John the Baptist, Mary the mother of Jesus, Mary Magdalene, Peter, or Paul have been found, nor will they be found. That does not mean these people did not exist. It means that they lived like most people throughout history, without political power, unable to commission an inscription or even write. They vanished without leaving a trace in the archaeological record. The lack of proof need not be disappointing, but it does point to Christianity's humble beginnings.

Our second example concerns the location of holy sites. As early as the fourth century CE, Helena, the mother of the first Christian emperor, Constantine the Great, sought with prayer, intuition, or miracle to locate the events of Jesus's life. She constructed monuments to mark these sites; later Christian pilgrims brought an economic boom to the new Holy Land, as holy sites sprang up everywhere. But can modern archaeology authenticate these ancient holy sites? And would that identification confirm the New

Testament? To address this question, we turn to the village of Cana, where, according to John's Gospel, Jesus turned water into wine. Two sites in Galilee have been suggested as candidates, one Arabs call Kafr Cana ("the village of Cana"), located four miles northeast of Nazareth, the other Khirbet Cana ("the ruins of Cana," often called Cana of the Galilee to distinguish it from another Cana in Lebanon), nine miles north of Nazareth. The first is the traditional site, where a small Franciscan church commemo-

"... there was a wedding in Cana of Galilee ... now standing there were six stone water jars for the Jewish rites of purification ..."

JOHN 2:1-6

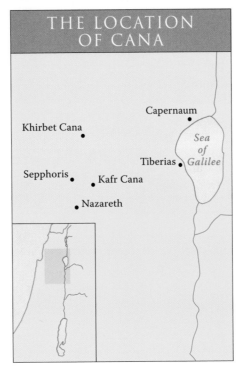

THE LOCATION OF CANA

Khirbet Cana

Capernaum

Sea of Galilee

Sepphoris

Tiberias

Kafr Cana

Nazareth

rates the miracle. But excavations date that church to the Byzantine period (fourth to seventh centuries CE), and no remains from the earlier, Roman period were found under it. So archaeologists favor the second site, Khirbet Cana, where recent excavations uncovered ample evidence from the time of Jesus. Excavators there also found a few fragments from small stone vessels, of note because John says that Jesus made wine from water in "six stone water jars for the Jewish rites of purification, each holding twenty or thirty gallons" (John 2:6).

But was Khirbet Cana really the site of the miracle? Maybe not. The Israel Antiquities Authority more recently conducted salvage excavations at Kerem al-Ras, on the outskirts of the traditional site of Kafr Cana. They found evidence of a large Jewish settlement from the time of Jesus, as well as fragments from large stone vessels like those mentioned by John — and

that have not yet been found at Khirbet Cana.

No one can be sure where the miracle is supposed to have happened. But if the debate only concerns which Cana is the New Testament Cana, we have missed the most important contribution archaeology offers for understanding the story. Archaeology sheds important light on those stone vessels and what they contribute to understanding Galilee at the time of Jesus. Excavations all across Israel uncover such stone containers in first-century CE layers. They are distinctly Jewish and

were an important part of Jewish purification practices during Jesus's time. But large stone vessels are typically found only in wealthy homes and at urban sites. The mention of "large stone jars" in John 2 tells us not only that the author describes it as a Jewish wedding, which is obvious in the text, he also characterizes it as an upper-class affair, a point that is not so obvious. That, of course,

opposite page

Scanning Electron Microscope

Patina over Inscription

Magnified Coccoliths

this page

Khirbet Cana (Galilee)

Excavations at Khirbet Cana (Galilee)

Stone Vessel Fragment (1st c. CE)

Microscopic examination of the patina by experts from the Israel Antiquities Authority determined that the inscription on the James ossuary was forged. The patina, a filmlike crust that forms on stone over centuries, was applied to the inscription, and upon close microscopic inspection was shown to contain many coccoliths, tiny shell-like creatures that exist in great numbers in limestone but not in the patina that forms on limestone.

The biblical site of Cana, where Jesus turned water into wine, according to John's Gospel, has yet to be located with certainty. There are two possibilities: Khirbet Cana (seen here from the northeast), just off the main route in antiquity, and Kafr Cana, site of a later church. Excavations at both sites have yet to definitively determine which is the *real* Cana. But excavations at each site and many others in Galilee have shown how widespread Jewish use of stone jars was during the first century CE.

contrasts with Jesus's more usual company of the down-and-out, as found in other Gospel stories.

These excavations of the possible Canas illustrate that archaeology should not be limited to locating holy sites. Regardless of whether an excavation is in the "right" site, what it tells archaeologists about rural, village, or city life in the Galilee of Jesus's time is important. A basic principle of this book is to examine sites that help us understand the New Testament, even if they are never mentioned in the New Testament. While this book is a visual guide, it is not limited to illustrating *where* Jesus, Paul, or the first Christians walked, but seeks to understand *how* they walked by sketching their first-century world using archaeological evidence.

300 BCE	**Hellenistic Period**
	Ptolemies & Seleucids
200 BCE	
	Maccabean Revolt
100 BCE	Hasmonean Expansion
	Roman Period
0	Herod the Great
	Jesus's Life
	Paul's Ministry
	James's Death
	First Jewish War
100 CE	
	Second Jewish War
200 CE	
	New Testament Canon
300 CE	
	Byzantine Period
	Constantine the Great
	Helena's Church-Building

In most academic circles, the terms BC (before Christ) and AD (*Anno Domini*, Latin for Year of our Lord) have been replaced by BCE (Before the Common Era) and CE (Common Era). So, BCE is BC and AD is CE.

> "See what large letters I make when I am writing in my own hand!"
>
> GALATIANS 6:11

Another example of archaeology's surprising contributions is its discovery of new texts. Great manuscript discoveries were made in the mid-twentieth century at Nag Hammadi and the Dead Sea. They revolutionized our understanding of the New Testament. The Nag Hammadi Codices, a set of thirteen books found in 1945 near the Nile River by two farmers, included many early Christian texts, such as the *Gospel of Thomas,* that provide insights into the great diversity of early Christianity and especially Gnosticism. The Dead Sea Scrolls — the first of which were discovered by a bedouin in the winter of 1946–47 in caves near the ruins of Qumran — included not only the oldest copies of the Hebrew Bible, which Christians call the Old Testament, but a remarkable library of previously unknown texts from a Jewish sect called the Essenes who lived in the

nearby settlement from the second century BCE through most of the first century CE.

But few archaeologists go into the field intending to unearth texts like the Gospel of Judas, which recently made its way through the antiquities market. Finding a codex or scroll on an excava-

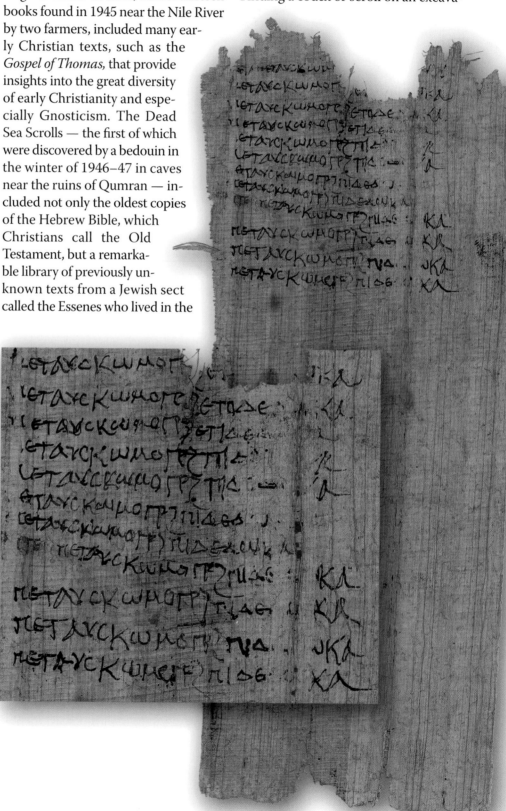

tion is like finding a needle in a haystack. Texts survive only in the most arid of climates. Though excavators do not expect to find that one sensational manuscript that will unlock the past's secret knowledge, all archaeologists examine the thousands of mundane papyri from ancient archives discovered in Egypt to help them reconstruct daily life in antiquity. Hundreds of thousands of papyrus documents survive from Egypt; though they may seem of little relevance to the New Testament, among them are itineraries, receipts, accounts, and letters, all of which unlock previously hidden aspects of everyday life and bear directly on New Testament passages.

We know from these papyri that most writing was done by professional scribes; literacy rates were notoriously low in antiquity. Probably only 10 percent of the population could read and write. That means, of course, that most people *heard* the New Testament but did not *read* it. It also implies that ancient texts are dominated by the interests of upper-class men, who were the most likely to be literate. The pages of ancient historical texts are filled with political concerns, long speeches by great men, and heroic battles. The masses are mentioned only when they cause unrest. Women are described only from the perspective of male interests. Archaeology, however, allows us to uncover aspects of the daily routines of people of the lower classes and women, whose voices are often silent in literary texts. That is as crucial as any manuscript discovery for our understanding of the New Testament.

Finally, archaeologists are often asked to find evidence for the first Christians, but nothing has been found

opposite page
Petaus Papyrus (Egypt, 2nd c. CE)

this page
Coin of Helena (324/25 CE)
Inside Holy Sepulcher (Jerusalem)

An ancient secret is preserved on this Egyptian papyrus, which dates from around 180 CE. In the village of Hormu, a man named Petaus had obtained the important position called the village scribe, something akin to the village mayor. He was functionally illiterate, a fact we know from this exercise tucked away among the other papyri. On it, he practiced his signature over and over again, the only line he would ever have to write: "I Petaus, the village scribe, have entered" (*Petaus komogrammateus epidedoka*). He misspells it repeatedly after the fifth line in his somewhat large and clumsy hand, and eventually tires of the exercise.

The patron saint of archaeologists is Queen Helena, the mother of Constantine the Great, who conducted the first archaeological excavation in search of a holy site. In the fourth century CE, she allegedly located the site of Jesus's crucifixion and resurrection, where the Church of the Holy Sepulcher now stands, by digging through later layers. Legend holds that she found three crosses and knew that one was the true cross when its touch revived a corpse.

from first-century CE Christians. None of the Christian symbols etched in walls or chiseled in stone go back farther than the late second century CE.

Surprisingly, the cross was not commonly used by Christians before the fifth century CE, though several "crosses" have been suggested as evidence for first-century Christians. In southern Italy at Herculaneum, one of the Roman cities covered by Vesuvius's eruption in 79 CE, a cross-shaped mark on a painted white background was discovered above a now-carbonized wood cabinet in what excavators call the House of the Bicentenary. Excavators initially described it as the earliest Christian cross inside an early Christian house church, with a kneeler before the crucifix. But that is impossible. Crosses appear elsewhere as a Christian symbol only after the Roman Empire became Christian in the fourth century CE. Closer examination of the cross at Herculaneum revealed it to be the imprint of a device for suspending a chest from the wall, most likely (and ironically) a shrine to pagan household gods. This was not a Christian house.

The absence of distinctly Christian archaeological evidence before the late second century CE is a reminder that the first followers of Jesus were Jewish. Neither his followers in Galilee nor those in Jerusalem developed a material culture apart from Judaism. And the earliest Gentile converts in the first century did not display any signs, art, or architecture that marked them as Christian. Until almost two centuries later, there is simply no way to distinguish Christian from Jew in the archaeological record. In fact, often it is only the absence of pagan images that distinguishes Jew from pagan.

Thus I will not be too concerned with finding inscriptions, sites, texts, or symbols from the original Christians in first-century Galilee, Jerusalem, Greece, or Rome. Instead I will sketch what can be known archaeologically about Judaism there, and the impact of cultural influences emanating from Greece and political power coming from Rome. Archaeologists will probably never find evidence for Jesus and his first followers in Galilee or from Paul of Tarsus and his first communities across the Mediterranean. But an examination of their context will profoundly affect how we understand them.

ARCHAEOLOGICAL DISCOVERIES AND NEW TESTAMENT TEXTS

Archaeologists distinguish themselves from relic hunters of the past by

opposite page
"Cross" (Herculaeneum, 1st c. CE)
Fresco of Fish (Ephesus, 1st c. CE)
Looted Site in Iraq (2004)

this page
Miletus Gate (Berlin Museum)
Broken Pot in Situ (Capernaum)
Excavation Square (Sepphoris)
Mosaic in Situ (Pisidian Antioch)

The first Christian symbols date to the late second century CE, when Christians developed a set of cryptic signs. One of the earliest was the fish, perhaps a combined reference to Jesus's first followers being fishermen, the common food for their communal meals, and the Greek word *ichthus,* which was an acrostic for "Jesus Christ God's Son Savior." But not every fish is Christian; fish were popularly displayed in mosaics and frescos, as in a dining room in Ephesus. Likewise, not every cross is Christian, like this one from Herculaeneum, which simply held a chest to the wall.

The world's archaeological heritage is being destroyed at an alarming rate by looting. In the chaos that followed the invasion of Iraq, sites were looted with backhoes, metal detectors, and shovels, as seen here in 2004. Tragically, we lose not only artifacts but also their context, their associated layers, and nearby objects, upon which archaeologists rely to reconstruct history. In the past, the most appealing artifacts were carted off to European museums, like the entire Miletus Gate, which was taken from Turkey to Berlin.

The magic words are *in situ*, Latin for "in place," which describes how archaeologists encounter artifacts during meticulous excavation. Whether this mosaic from Pisidian Antioch in Turkey or this broken pot from Capernaum in Israel, artifacts in situ are recorded and associated with soil layers, which archaeologists use to trace a site's occupation layers.

insisting on the importance of in situ artifacts. This Latin phrase, meaning "in place," refers to finds made by excavators in the spot where ancient history had left the item until it was unearthed by archaeologists. This is an archaeological ideal because it ensures the object's authenticity. Unlike the James ossuary, which came to the public through the shady world of private collectors and antiquities dealers, the authenticity of in situ finds is guaranteed.

Archaeologists do not look to any single discovery to reveal the ancient

world; instead they rely on the accumulation of finds anchored in situ, each of which has a specific known relationship in space and time to others. No single artifact helps us understand the New Testament as much as the web of artifacts connected in space and time by carefully recorded scientific excavations. Four examples illustrate the importance of cumulative evidence over single artifacts.

The Caiaphas ossuary, a rare archaeological witness to a New Testament figure, was found in 1990 by construction workers south of Jerusalem's Old City when they broke through a Jewish burial cave sealed since the Roman War in 70 CE. The Israel Antiquities Authority's salvage archaeologists were called immediately, but they were not allowed to complete their work on the tomb. Following protests and pressure by ultra-

orthodox Jews, the tomb was resealed and the human remains handed over to the Ministry of Religious Affairs for reburial on the Mount of Olives. However, the archaeologists had had enough time to examine and photograph most of the tomb and its ossuaries in situ. The burial chamber had a 5.5-foot ceiling that made it hard to stand upright; four shafts, each large enough to lay out a body, extended like fingers from the main chamber. In one of those shafts was an ornately decorated ossuary, one of most beautiful ossuaries ever found, with the name *Yehosef bar Qafa* (Joseph, son of Caiaphas) crudely etched on one side in Aramaic. The rarity of that name combination left little doubt (though not absolute proof) that this was the final

resting place and ossuary of the high priest known as Caiaphas in the Gospels, who was infamous for his role in Jesus's arrest and trial.

This alone makes it an exciting discovery. It affirms that there was a person named Caiaphas in Jerusalem around the time of Jesus's crucifixion. But no serious scholar had doubted Caiaphas's existence, since he is mentioned in other ancient sources, such as writings of the Jewish historian Josephus. And the ossuary's discovery could not determine if the Gospels accurately reported his presence and role in Jesus's trial.

But the discovery had additional, often neglected, significance because of what was found alongside it. The forensic archaeologist was able to identify sixty-three other skeletons in the burial chamber, several of which were inside the Caiaphas ossuary. The demographic distribution of the dead is a grim reminder that even a wealthy high-priestly family was not immune to premature death or infant mortality. Of those buried with Caiaphas in the tomb, some 40 percent never made it past their fifth birthday. An additional 20 percent never reached puberty. Those statistics are shocking, especially when one considers that high-priestly families ate more meat than other groups, since they received a share of the animal sacrifices, and as we will see in chapter 5, they lived in a neighborhood with ample flowing water and underground sewage. We can be sure that Jerusalem's urban poor

Mortality Rates in Caiaphas's Tomb	
Age	Skeletal Remains
0 – 1 years	10
2 – 5 years	16
6 – 12 years	14
13 – 18 years	3
19 – 25 years	1
26 – 39 years	1
40 +	6
Adult, age unknown	13

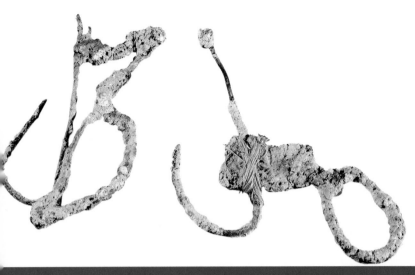

"...and after having dug through the roof, they let down the mat on which the paralytic lay."

MARK 2:4

and Galilean peasants were worse off. The accumulation of artifacts in Caiaphas's tomb underscores the fragility of life in antiquity. It's no wonder, then, that stories of Jesus's healings resonated with its inhabitants. Curing the sick was an urgent concern. The context of Caiaphas's ossuary shows why students of the New Testament must look beyond the obvious connections between artifact and Gospel,

and broadly examine the world of the New Testament.

The second example is the archaeological attempt to locate the House of Saint Peter at Capernaum in northern Israel. A fifth-century CE pilgrim talks about being shown the "House of the Prince of the Apostles" near the Sea of Galilee. This house was discovered early in the twentieth century, when Franciscan excavators uncovered an octagonal shrine there. Later excavations distinguished three distinct stratigraphic phases on that site: three architectural layers, one atop the next. The uppermost and most recent was the fifth-century CE shrine; underneath was a fourth-century CE courtyard complex centering around a single room; and under that, dating to the time of Jesus, was a simple house like so many in Galilee. One room of that earliest house had been plastered, and what looks like Christian graffiti had been etched into its walls by the end of the second century CE. This room later became central to the fourth-century CE complex and, still later, the foundation for the shrine.

As we will see in detail in chapter 4, connecting that late second-century CE evidence to early first-century CE gospel stories is frustratingly tenuous. A century after Jesus, some people venerated this room, and it is reasonable to connect it with Jesus or Peter. But we cannot know beyond a reasonable doubt wheth-

er it was the room where Peter lived or where Jesus healed.

Did archaeology fail here? If the goal is to locate a holy place, then yes. But if the cumulative finds of the excavations in and around that one house are examined, a pattern emerges that is of enormous relevance for understanding the Gospels. The excavators found some roof tiles from the octagonal

The resting place of Caiaphas, the high priest mentioned in the Gospels for his role in Jesus's arrest and trial, has been discovered in Jerusalem. Dating to the first century CE, the ossuary contained the bones of several deceased, including those of a man in his sixties, presumably Joseph Caiaphas, whose name was crudely etched onto the box's left side in Aramaic (*Yehosef bar Qafa*).

The House of Saint Peter at Capernaum may have been found on the northwestern shore of the Sea of Galilee. Franciscan archaeologists uncovered an octagonal church from the fifth century CE built over a first-century CE private house. What were originally thought to be the fisherman's hooks, however, turned out upon closer examination to be chains used in a later century for hanging lamps.

The houses in Jesus's Capernaum had beaten earth floors, walls made of field stones packed with mud, straw, and dung for insulation, and thick reed-and-mud thatched roofs, which had to be periodically resealed using a heavy cylindrical roof-roller. In contrast, the houses in Roman cities and later times were covered with roof tiles connected by inverted half-pipes, which could be easily removed and repaired when broken.

"... Sergius Paul[l]us, an intelligent man, who summoned Barnabas and Saul and wanted to hear the word of God."

ACTS 13:7

and kept rainwater running off its gentle slope. This kind of construction is exactly what we find in Mark's story of Jesus healing the paralytic: when his friends could not enter the house, "they removed the roof above him, and after having dug through it," lowered him down to Jesus (Mark 2:4).

The archaeology of Capernaum may not demonstrate that the later church was built over Peter's house, but it does shed light on the otherwise awkward phrase in Mark's Gospel, that they "dug through" the roof. Even more interesting, when Luke's Gospel tells the same story, it says that the friends "went up on the roof and let him down with his bed through the tiles" (Luke 5:19). Luke's friends do not *dig* through the roof but *remove* its tiles. Does the absence of roof tiles in first-century CE Capernaum disprove Luke? That's not the point. The archaeology of Capernaum simply shows that Mark is more familiar with Jesus's original Galilean context, while Luke is less familiar and tells this story as he imagines it happening in his urban context, where roof tiles were the norm and thatched mud roofs unheard of. The excavations at Capernaum may have proved little about the holy site, but they offer insights into the lives of the Gospel writers.

The third example concerns the discovery of inscriptions. While papyrus or parchment manuscripts are rarely found in excavations, texts chiseled in-

church's fifth-century CE strata, but none at all from the earliest layer in the Early Roman period (50 BCE–135 CE) in that house or any of the houses around it. The absence of roof tiles in-

dicates that Capernaum's roofs were made by layering reeds over wood beams and packing on mud above. Cylindrical stone roof-rollers compactly sealed a one- or two-foot-thick roof

to stone are common. What archaeologists call *epigraphic* remains (Greek for "written upon") are of great importance to archaeologists interested in the New Testament, especially their cumulative impact. One inscription from the Turkish town of Yalvaç, ancient Pisidian Antioch, contains the lines "To Lucius Sergius Paullus the younger, son of Lucius, one of the four commissioners in charge of the Roman streets, tribune of the soldiers of the Sixth Legion styled Ferrata." From other inscriptions found in Rome and on the island of Cyprus, we suspect that the father of Lucius Sergius Paullus was transferred from Pisidian Antioch and appointed as Roman governor on the island of Cyprus, at the time when the book of Acts tells of Paul converting a Roman official named Sergius Paullus (Acts 13:6–12).

These inscriptions seem to corroborate the account in Acts. The inscriptions may also explain why Paul's first journey took him straight from Cyprus to Pisidian Antioch, where the elder Sergius Paullus could recommend hospitality, and may explain the apostle's name change from Saul to Paul in Acts 13, if he adopted the family name of this important Roman official. But considering the other inscriptions found at Pisidian Antioch, a more disturbing question arises. Alongside the Sergius Paullus inscription were found many fragments of the so-called *Res Gestae Divi Augusti* (The Achievements of the Divine Augustus). This autobiographical eulogy was composed by the emperor Augustus, placed in his mausoleum in Rome, and copied and distributed across the empire during his lifetime. The title alone proclaims him to be a god. And most inscriptions discovered across the Mediterranean and the New Testament world, at some point or another, declare Caesar's divinity. Julius Caesar, Caesar Augustus, and their successors bore the titles *God* and *Son of God, Lord and Savior*. The messianic language used for the emperors is remarkably similar to what the Gospels and Paul use for Jesus, a phenomenon apparent in the *Res Gestae Divi Augusti* and other inscriptions, such as one from Priene in western Turkey that reckons time from the year of Augustus's birth. Similar to the Christian calendar based on Jesus's birth, the much earlier Priene inscription has remarkable parallels to later Christian language about Jesus: "The birthday of the most divine Caesar . . . the beginning of everything . . . Caesar was born . . . a common blessing to all . . . he is the beginning of life and living . . . Caesar, who by his epiphany exceeded the hopes of those who prophesied good news [*euaggelia*]."

"Since Providence, which has ordered all things and is deeply interested in our life, has set in most perfect order by giving us Augustus, whom she filled with virtue that he might benefit humankind, sending him as a savior, both for us and for our descendants, that he might end war and arrange all things, and since he, Caesar, by his epiphany [exceeded even our anticipations], surpassing all previous benefactors, and not even leaving to posterity any hope of surpassing what he has done, and since the birthday of the god Augustus was the beginning of the good news for the world that came by reason of him."

Sergius Paullus was converted by the apostle Paul, according to the book of Acts. This inscription found at Pisidian Antioch in central Turkey is one of several that mention this prominent Roman family.

The divinity of the Roman caesars is one of the most ubiquitous claims in epigraphic remains. Though fragmentary and badly in need of conservation, *The Achievements of the Divine Augustus* is on display at a museum near Pisidian Antioch, where Paul once ministered. Similar messianic language describing the caesars is found on this inscription from Priene, which declares that Asia Minor's calendar will begin with the birth of Augustus, which brought "good news."

The inscription uses the same word that the New Testament uses for its good news or gospel. The proximity of that Sergius Paullus inscription to the *Res Gestae* at Pisidian Antioch raises a startling question: how could Sergius Paullus or any Roman official convert to Christianity and serve the imperial god *and* the Christian God? Imagine the political and psychological conflict. How could any Christian proclaim Jesus to be the Son of God in a world that was already ruled by a Roman son of God? These collective epigraphic discoveries help us understand why

Paul was persecuted and, according to tradition, beheaded by the emperor Nero for proclaiming that Christ (and not Nero) was Lord and Savior.

The final example comes from underground Rome. Underneath that city there are over fifty known catacomb complexes stretching some three hundred miles. Many of them bear Christian decorations and inscriptions, mostly from the third century CE and later. Excavations under Saint Peter's Basilica in the Vatican, however, uncovered a second-century CE tomb that many think belongs to Peter, who

was martyred in the first century CE and buried under the spot where Constantine the Great built the basilica in the fourth century CE. In the second century CE, one tomb in a mostly pagan cemetery was reconfigured with a second-rate column-and-roof edifice along a shared wall. Controversial excavations in the mid-twentieth century identified some bones as belonging to a strongly built man who died in his sixties; they were said to be Peter's. But later examination showed that they belonged to three people, one of whom was a woman, as well as to a pig, a

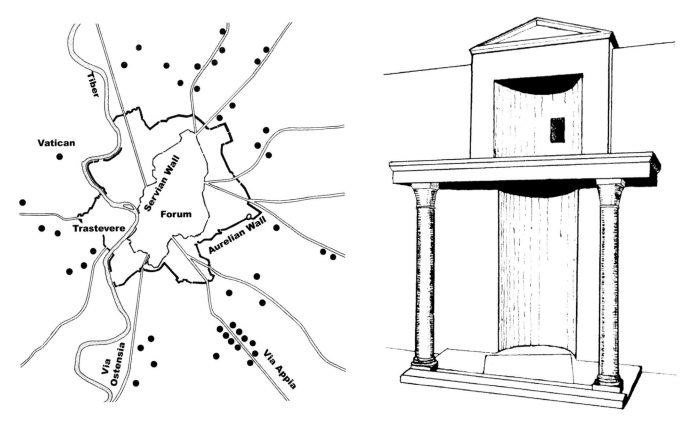

chicken, and a mouse. A few years later, another set of bones, tinted purplish (perhaps from the robe in which the first pope was buried) and belonging to an elderly man, were discovered. They were tied to a graffito that was — some would say questionably — reconstructed as *Petros Eni*, Greek for "Peter inside." Although this location is hotly disputed, some still suggest that Peter's final resting place has been found, even though the evidence dates to nearly a century after his death.

By focusing on that one tomb, however, one misses the significant revelations offered by archaeological studies of the catacombs. When all the Christian catacombs are plotted on a map of Rome, it is clear that they lie along particular roads *outside* the city, thus providing an indication of where the first Christians lived *inside* the city, since people buried their dead along the radial roads nearest their neighborhoods. The earliest and most prominent Christian burials were south of the city along the Via Appia or west of the city along roads leading from the neighborhood of Trastevere.

The neighborhoods through which these roads passed were in many ways similar. They were outside the old city wall, where most Jews of Rome lived, a reminder that the earliest Christian

communities arose within Judaism. These areas were heavily populated with other immigrants also. The main industries were brick-making and tanning, the latter of which used urine collected from public latrines. The neighborhood stank. Sailors and longshoremen worked Trastevere's docks and warehouses, and traders and transport workers carted their wares on the streets, by law only at night. It was noisy and boisterous. Judging from the names of several neighborhoods, there were also textile industries there that employed weavers, dyers, and tent-makers. That is exactly the kind of place where one would expect to find the apostle Paul's associates, Prisca and Aquila, the Jewish tent-making couple who earlier lived with him at Corinth and Ephesus, according to the New Testament. In short, the archaeology of the catacombs in Rome cannot conclusively prove that Saint Peter's tomb and bones have been located, but it can locate the first Christians in the hardworking neighborhoods of Rome. The archaeology of the early Christian catacombs provides important clues about the first Roman Christians' class and socioeconomic status.

These examples show that archaeology may not prove the truth of the

New Testament's teachings, but its discoveries nevertheless dramatically increase our understanding of the New Testament. They show that archaeologists rely not on any one artifact but on a body of evidence whose cumulative effect opens our eyes to demographic and socioeconomic issues, as well as political and religious tensions, that are not apparent from reading the New Testament alone. This book seeks to guide the reader visually through aspects of the New Testament world that are crucial for understanding the spoken words of Jesus, the written letters of Paul, and the lives of the first Christians.

opposite page

Catacomb of Priscilla (Rome)

this page

Map of Christian Catacombs (Rome)
Reconstruction of Peter's Tomb

The underground world of Christians in Rome has been intensely studied. A popular misunderstanding is that Christians hid underground from Nero's great persecution in the sixties CE. But there is no evidence before the second century CE, and Christians simply buried their dead underground alongside pagans and Jews, who likewise began to construct underground tombs on the edge of the city. Christians did not hold regular worship services in the catacombs, but met there for a commemorative meal on the anniversary of their leaders' death like at the burial site of Saint Peter.

2

WHAT ARCHAEOLOGISTS DO

Each year archaeologists and thousands of volunteers share the exhilaration of digging up artifacts. The work is painstaking and meticulous, involving early morning wake-up calls, manual labor in the Mediterranean sun, hours of washing and registering pottery, and absolute exhaustion after weeks of digging. It's no wonder that field archaeologists become possessive about their finds and seem to resent anyone who speaks about them without having endured the expeditions' hardships. But the truth is that those who have never been on an excavation are envious. Everyone would love to work on a dig, and those of us who have had that opportunity bear the responsibility not only of describing, analyzing, and interpreting the finds but also of sharing the joy of discovery.

To appreciate how those discoveries ultimately relate to the New Testament, some familiarity with what archaeologists do is necessary. Archaeology has three tightly interwoven aspects: field archaeology, analytical archaeology, and interpretive archaeology. Field archaeology extracts the artifacts from the ground and is absolutely foundational; analytical archaeology analyzes those artifacts with the help of highly trained specialists; and interpretive archaeology sifts through site reports and articles, sites and museums, and then presents an interpretation of one or more aspects of ancient life or history, usually after consulting ancient literary texts. This book is primarily interpretive archaeology, as it offers a survey of how excavations and artifacts relate to the New Testament and illuminate the world of the first Christians. Some familiarity with field methods and analytical tools, however, will help us to appreciate the potential as well as the limitations of bringing together archaeology and the biblical text.

FIELD ARCHAEOLOGY: RECOVERING THE PAST

Current excavation techniques vary slightly from site to site, depending on geographical location, geological features, historical period, and site type, but all excavations adhere to the basic principles of *stratigraphy* and *typology*, employing tightly supervised workers in a manageable space, usually five-by-

to top with the sequence of ceramic types from oldest to most recent, that archaeology became a serious discipline. After Petrie, soil layers and their accompanying shards became as important as monumental architecture and museum pieces.

Tiny pottery shards preoccupied biblical archaeologists in Palestine for much of the twentieth century. The American William F. Albright refined pottery typologies from the Bronze Age through the Roman period, and biblical archaeologists focused on dating their sites' layers using these shards. Wedged between the Egyptian and Mesopotamian superpowers, Palestinian sites were more frequently destroyed and rebuilt, creating the characteristically

five-meter squares. Stratigraphy refers to the sequential occupational layers of site, in which the most recent layers are found at the surface, and then older and older layers are exposed as archaeologists dig deeper. Typology refers to the dating of artifacts found in those layers based on stylistic changes over time. Slight variations in pottery styles are used to date a site's layers, so archaeologists collect small ceramic pieces called shards (or potsherds). These shards, and all other artifacts, are tagged to the soil layers where they are found, which archaeologists call a locus (plural *loci*). A locus can be any discreet three-dimensional unit of soil or architecture, of which there may be hundreds or thousands after a site has been excavated. In essence, archaeolo-

gists first physically disassemble the site like a kind of three-dimensional jigsaw puzzle, analyze the pieces — the loci — then reassemble the site in their imagination to understand its history and character.

That meticulous work clearly differs from the "excavations" of earlier centuries. Before the twentieth century, archaeologists dug through the soil to uncover buried treasures. They looked for artifacts to stock museums, used poorly supervised workers, did not record where items were found, and tossed away thousands of shards. It was not until the end of the nineteenth century, when the British archaeologist Sir Flinders Petrie carefully observed the successive layers of a mound in Palestine and correlated them from bottom

high artificial mounds that were once ancient cities (called a *tell* in Arabic or *tel* in Hebrew). Rectangular hewn stone blocks, called ashlars by archaeologists, were reused in later buildings, making dating by architectural style unreliable. By necessity, then, biblical archaeologists concentrated on how soil layers related to architecture and dated both by the small pieces of pottery in them.

Preoccupied with dating layers, biblical archaeologists excavated sites with deep vertical shafts of four by four meters set into a five-by-five-meter grid. These squares were limited in number, but painstaking attention was devoted to tracing the sequence of layers in the face of the balk, the one-meter strip between the squares. The balk's vertical face is called a section; this cross section reveals the history of a tell, as though someone had sliced a cake with a knife to see what kind it is. The focus was intensely on the vertical — that is to say, the relationship of the balk's layers to events in biblical history. The burning questions revolved around whether cities like Jericho and Hazor were destroyed by the Israelites when the book of Joshua claimed they were, or whether the gates excavated at Gezer and Lachish were part of King Solomon's fortifications as described in the book of 1 Kings. But there were no similar questions for the New Testament, because the likes of Jesus, Paul, and James lived within the short period of a few decades. It is almost impossible to distinguish archaeologically a stratum associated with Jesus in the thirties from a stratum of James in the sixties, or Paul between the two. But more important, unlike the ancient Israelites, Jesus and his followers never built or destroyed cities. They were from the lower classes, and they lived and died without leaving a trace in the archaeological record.

But as archaeology was transformed in the 1970s, the door was opened for those interested in the New Testament. The New Archaeology (in no way related to the *New Testament*) advocated a more anthropological and scientific approach to archaeology (sometimes labeled "processual archaeology," although aspects of the *New* Archaeology are already old, and most archaeologists now consider themselves "post-processual"). Aspects other than their historical sequence were considered important, such as a society's diet, environmental adaptations, settlement patterns, and gender relations. Excavation teams not only focused on dating pottery but became more interdisciplinary, drawing upon geologists, paleobotanists, zoo-archaeologists, and metallurgists, who used new scientific techniques to analyze artifacts. The volume of information on an excavation became so immense that computer specialists had to manage, update, and run inquiries on sophisticated databases.

Although these developments were advanced by archaeologists with no particular interest in the New Testament, they were ironically of great relevance to it. The vertical approach of biblical archaeology, digging deep in a few squares and correlating the stratigraphy to biblical events, was really only relevant to the Old Testament and the history of Israel. But the new horizontal

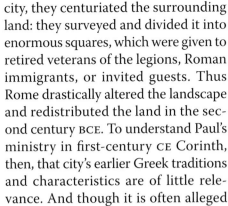

approach — digging more squares across a wider area at a site and correlating them with excavations at nearby sites and regional surveys — had great relevance to the New Testament. It provided ample evidence, for example, of the differences between village life and urban life in Jesus's Galilee; it shed light on the complex interaction between country and city and how it may have affected Jesus's ministry; and it could trace differences between Jewish Galilee and the surrounding pagan regions that help us assess Jesus's audience.

The advances in archaeological method include sophisticated surveys to reveal the historical trends of a re-gion. Surveys on the ground involve teams of archaeologists walking an area along a preassigned grid and picking up all ancient shards that have worked their way to the surface. In this way, smaller farmsteads, hamlets, or villages, which are not as obvious as the ruins of a city, can be mapped. This is especially important for identifying Galilean sites associated with Jesus's ministry, since these sites were often small and lacked inscriptions, making them hard to identify.

Modern surveys often include the use of aerial photography or satellite imaging. At Corinth, for example, surveys have shown that this Greek city, destroyed by the Romans in 146 BCE, was rebuilt as a Roman colony. When the Romans rebuilt the city, they centuriated the surrounding land: they surveyed and divided it into enormous squares, which were given to retired veterans of the legions, Roman immigrants, or invited guests. Thus Rome drastically altered the landscape and redistributed the land in the second century BCE. To understand Paul's ministry in first-century CE Corinth, then, that city's earlier Greek traditions and characteristics are of little relevance. And though it is often alleged that Paul's letters to the Corinthians must be read in light of that city's history of temple prostitution and the Athenians' condemnation of Corinthian licentiousness, these date to the earlier classical Greek period (sixth to fourth centuries BCE), well before Rome's newfound colony. The character of the old Greek Corinth has little bearing on the new Roman Corinth that Paul knew.

In addition to surveys, aerial photography, and satellite imaging, archaeologists also consult geologists to help them identify sites, as in the case of Bethsaida. The New Testament describes this site as the home of several

opposite page

Heinrich Schliemann (1892)

Sophia Schliemann (1873)

Excavation Trench at Troy

Square on Modern Excavation

this page

Diagnostic Shards

Galilean Pottery (1st C. CE)

Jerusalem Pottery (1st C. CE)

Treasure-hunting at Troy was done by the German entrepreneur and archaeologist Heinrich Schliemann when he cut a trench in the 1870s to find evidence of Homer's Trojan War. Like biblical archaeologists, he linked Troy's layers with the city's destruction by the Greeks, but his dating was off by centuries. He was later accused of "salting" the site with forged gold treasures, worn by his Greek wife, Sophia, and planted for later "discovery" as Priam's Treasure.

Modern excavations dig in squares, like this site in Israel. This allows the occupational layers to be seen in the balk and dated by small pottery shards. Especially important are what archaeologists call diagnostic shards, including rims, bases, and handles, which are easiest to date.

Pottery from Jesus's Galilee and Jerusalem has been scrutinized by archaeologists. Although similar, the Galilean assemblage is functional and utilitarian, whereas Jerusalem's similar forms show more variety and include some imports.

of Jesus's disciples, but because Bethsaida simply means "fisherman's house," it could refer to any number of places on the Sea of Galilee or along the Jordan River. Around the time of Jesus, the local ruler Herod Philip renamed the town Julias in honor of the mother of the current Roman emperor, so one presumes it was a larger site. But of the likely candidates on the northeast side of the Sea of Galilee, the largest, called et-Tell, was almost a mile from the Sea of Galilee and a quarter-mile from the Jordan River — too far for a fishing village. But recent core samples by geologists and excavations by archaeologists suggest that this town was in fact the biblical Bethsaida. Excavations uncovered ample pottery from the time of Jesus at the site, and geologists detected traces of major tectonic movements sometime after the first century CE, which caused the Jordan River to alter its course to a path farther from et-Tell and to deposit silt south of the site, so that the

shoreline receded over the centuries. Although today it is far from the river and lake, in antiquity it was next to the river and not far from the lake. And residents could well have been fishers, as indicated by numerous fishing weights and hooks found there. The lost city of Bethsaida appears to have been found. And that is important not only because a New Testament city has been located but also because it helps assess the extent of that site's wealth, Hellenization, and Romanization at the time of Jesus.

ANALYZING THE FINDS

Once excavated, finds are recorded by locus, tagged, boxed, and then analyzed by specialists. Ceramics are traditionally the most intensely studied artifacts. Diagnostic shards, including pottery rims, bottoms, and handles, are initially "read" during fieldwork and correlated to architectural remains as a guide to further digging and initial interpretation of the stratigraphy. Af-

ter each excavation season, diagnostic shards or whole pots from key loci are drawn in cross section by professional artists in a standardized style that can be examined by other experts as well as future generations of archaeologists. Ceramic typologies are thus continually refined as more excavations increase the pool of evidence; in turn, pottery from older reports is reexamined and buildings are redated.

But shards are not only used for dating. They also serve to assess the function of a space, the cooking habits of a people, and the extent of trade at a site. Counting the proportions of pottery forms in a given locus, such as the ratio of cooking pots to serving vessels or of storage jars to lamps, helps determine the function of rooms. One study of relevance to the New Testament was conducted at Banias in northern Israel, which the New Testament calls Caesarea Philippi. Near here, according to the Gospels, Peter proclaimed Jesus to be the

Messiah (Mark 8:27). Archaeological surveys and excavations reveal that for over one hundred years, this region had been inhabited by a group of Gentiles called Syro-Phoenicians, who came to the grotto and waterfall at Banias, named after the woodland god Pan, to worship, eat sacred meals, and offer wine and food to the god. Large numbers of shards were found there, dating from the Early Hellenistic through Middle Roman periods. Those from the Late Hellenistic period (second to mid-first century BCE) were almost entirely locally made serving and cooking vessels, many of which had fire marks. Without any accompanying architecture, this evidence shows that visitors congregated around the cave for what archaeologists call ritual dining. We might think of this as a holiday picnic. Around the time of Jesus (first century CE), however, several pagan temples were built in front of the grotto. In addition to serving dishes and cooking vessels, shards from this period include oil lamps,

suggesting that some visitors simply stopped to leave a burning oil lamp as a votive gift at the temple, much like Catholics today might light a candle in a church. By the Middle Roman period (second to third centuries CE), however, almost all the shards were from lamps. The preparation of meals had ceased at Caesarea Philippi's temples. When the temple architecture was most impressive — funded by wealthy families who held priestly positions, according to several inscriptions — the common people ceased to dine there with their families.

The ceramic evidence at Banias gives a clear picture of an all too common phenomenon. Lower-class, simple, and even disorganized religious activities

opposite page

Aerial Photograph (Omrit, Israel)

this page

Underwater "Dig" (Bozburun, Turkey)

Pottery with Locus Tag (Bethsaida)

Aerial Photograph (Bethsaida)

Archaeology in sky and sea helps examine the ancient world. Aerial photography at Omrit in northern Israel gives an important perspective on a recently excavated Roman temple. This is done with a balloon; two ropes are visible on the sides of the photo. Underwater archaeologists work much like those on land, though shifting sands and short dive periods make the task more arduous.

The lost New Testament city of Bethsaida was found with the aid of archaeology and geology. It was difficult to locate because of the Sea of Galilee's shifting shoreline, which had receded nearly a mile from the site. Bethsaida means "House of Fishers" in Aramaic.

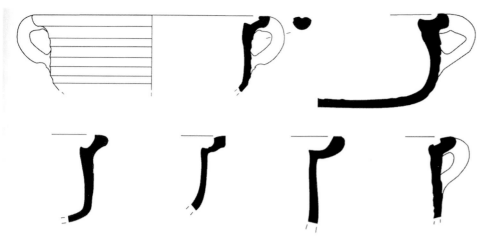

are often pushed aside as wealthy elites gain control. They build temples as a stage to display the social hierarchy. That is a common path in Greek and Roman paganism. As we will see in chapter 6, Paul stubbornly resisted this at Corinth; however, Christianity ultimately succumbed to this temptation, as we will see in chapter 8. Lower-class or egalitarian communities gravitate toward hierarchy.

Archaeologists also use pottery to trace ancient trade patterns and to discern the extent of a site's participation in international trade. Storage jars called amphorae are easy to trace, and lend themselves to what archaeologists call provenance studies. Used especially in the Hellenistic and Roman periods, when trade in wines flourished, amphorae had the manufacturer's name, date, and location stamped on the handle. Although after their initial use they were typically reused and redistributed, their presence at a site indicates its participation in the wider economy. We find these amphorae all across the eastern Mediterranean, in each of the cities visited by Paul, but they are noticeably absent from Galilee before and during Jesus's time. Galileans drank their own wine rather than importing. Fine wine from Greek or Italian vineyards never made it to Galilee, perhaps because it was too expensive, or perhaps because they deemed it ritually impure having been made by Gentiles.

There are also more sophisticated — and expensive — techniques for provenance studies. One is Neutron Activation Analysis, a scientific process that can match the chemical makeup of a pot or the clay in a lamp to the geographical region where the clay originated. Neutron Activation

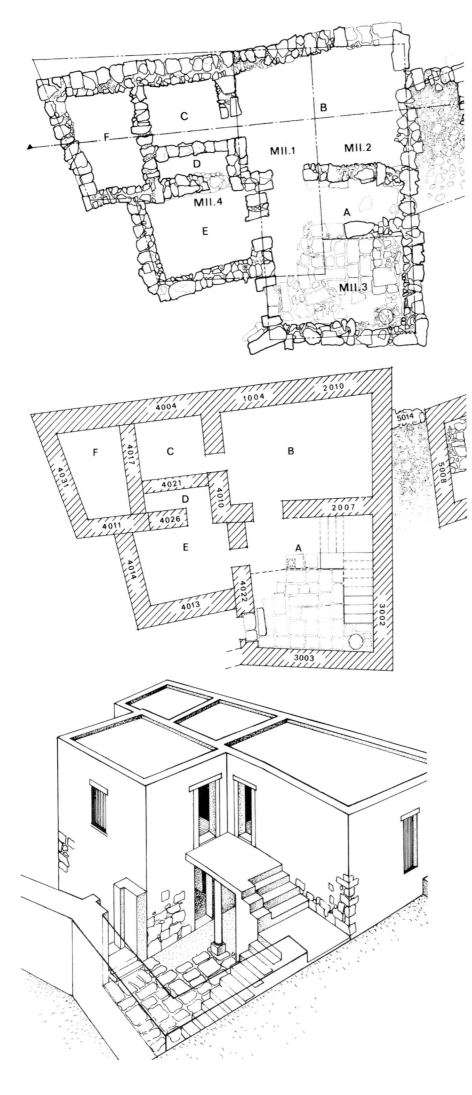

Analysis has helped archaeologists establish a link between the Dead Sea Scrolls and a site called Khirbet Qumran, strongly suggesting that the texts were written there. Most scholars believe that the scrolls, many of which were found in large jars and hidden in caves, belonged to a conservative Jewish religious sect called the Essenes, who lived in what looks like a monastic complex on the northwest shore of the Dead Sea. Jars similar to those that held the scrolls have been found there. Neutron Activation Analysis demonstrated that jars from the site had the same chemical makeup as those holding the scrolls, both made of clay from the nearby spring of Ein Feshkha. Significantly, similar-looking jars found at other sites in the region were from a different clay source. Thus the Qumran jars and the jars holding the scrolls were probably produced by the same community, very likely the Essenes.

Artifact analysis is not restricted to ceramic material. Excavations regularly employ paleobotanists and zooarchaeologists, who study floral and faunal remains. Zooarchaeologists look at the animal bones found at a site. In addition to determining whether a site was inhabited by Jews (by whether pig bones are found there), they also examine harvesting techniques and patterns. They

opposite page

Ceramic Drawings (Tel Anafa, Israel)
Pan Grotto (Caesarea Philippi)
Syro-Phoenician Bowl (2nd C. BCE)
Roman Disk Lamps (2nd C. CE)

this page

Stone, Block, and Isometric Plans (Galilee)

Ceramic plates are included in each archaeological publication. They are drawn by professional artists and show the cross section on the right-hand side and the outside view on the left-hand side; the diameter can be reconstructed from a small shard. This pottery is from the Gentile site of Tel Anafa in northern Israel, not far from Caesarea Philippi.

Pottery from Caesarea Philippi in front of a grotto and temples tells archaeologists that pagans once ate here and poured libations to the god Pan. In later periods, devotees simply left oil lamps as votive offerings in front of the temple.

Reconstructing a Galilean house is a step-by-step process. After drawing a stone-by-stone top plan, a block plan is then drawn with locus numbers on the walls assigned as they were excavated. Finally an architect makes an isometric reconstruction, here of the Patrician's House from Meiron in Upper Galilee.

can tell from the blade- or break-marks on bones whether the butchers were professionals or just family members who slaughtered their own animals. For example, the large cities of Galilee, Sepphoris and Tiberias, employed skilled professionals, whereas the bones from Galilean villages show signs of inferior butchering techniques. This suggests that the Galilean villages had a subsistence economy. This was Jesus's context, where the father of the house in a place like Nazareth carved up a goat on occasion, and the village priest slaughtered a lamb on holidays. Zooarchaeologists can also determine animals' age and sex from the size and shape of their bones, indicating whether sheep and goats were raised for food, wool, or milk. Faunal analysis of tiny fish bones, which can only be recovered by sifting or flotation, reveals a population's appetite for exotic foods, and whether fish were imported from the sea. The wealthy inhabitants of the city of Sepphoris, for example, were not content to dine on local fish from the nearby Sea of Galilee, as were the inhabitants of the village of Capernaum, but preferred and could afford to dine on saltwater fish caught in the Mediterranean.

Paleobotanists examine the kinds of wood used in the construction of homes, boats, and in one case even crucifixion. They also examine the seeds found in an excavation using a scanning electron microscope, which can reveal whether grapes were fermented (and hence used in winemak-

ing) or the kinds of grains used for daily bread — high-quality wheat or nearly inedible millet. At an even higher microscopic level, pollen can be counted to determine the ratio of cultivated and wild plants.

There are many other specialists who look at materials. Organic materials with carbon molecules can be dated using carbon-14, and inorganic materials can be dated using thermoluminescence, often to within a century. That is still not as accurate as dating by pottery typology or by the epigraphic styles on inscriptions, however. Geologists can determine the origins and distribution of marble from quarry to structure using isotope analysis in scientific labs. Metallurgists can examine the chemical makeup of coins and the extent to which a currency was debased; they can determine the heat at which tools were fired by blacksmiths and trace badly corroded shapes with X-ray photography. Unfortunately, cost is often the most important factor in deciding which objects to examine with which methods.

INTERPRETIVE ARCHAEOLOGY

Nonspecialists are often frustrated by the complexity of these analytical studies, as well as by the difficulty of reading reports of excavations. That frustration is often compounded by densely descriptive publications by archaeologists that contain impenetrable technical jargon and no readable inter-

pretive summary. Some archaeologists, however, conduct broader synthetic studies in a more holistic manner, integrating ancient texts as they interpret the evidence and ponder its relevance for reconstructing the ancient world. There are many such studies of relevance to the New Testament. The following three studies suggest the many ways archaeology connects to a study of early Christianity.

Our first example concerns the relationship between gender and labor in the Roman world. Archaeology is a key means of unlocking the world of ancient women, since they were mostly ignored in ancient literary texts or discussed only in relation to men. But archaeologists examining epigraphic and papyrological remains are beginning to understand the role of women in the ancient workforce. A study of funerary inscriptions from Rome shows a heavily gendered division of labor: there were no women at all in building, banking, and transportation, a few in sales and professional positions, and many who worked as barbers, masseuses, and entertainers. Notable, however, is the number of women listed on burial inscriptions as co-workers with their husbands. Most women who worked as barbers, for example, assisted their husbands, who were the head barbers. Given what we know about patriarchal Roman society, working alongside one's husband likely meant the wife's subordination to the husband, and that is of some relevance to

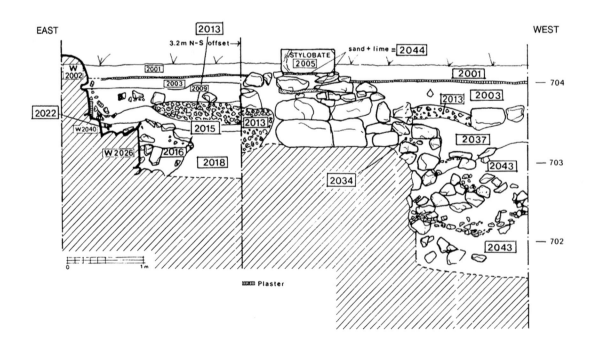

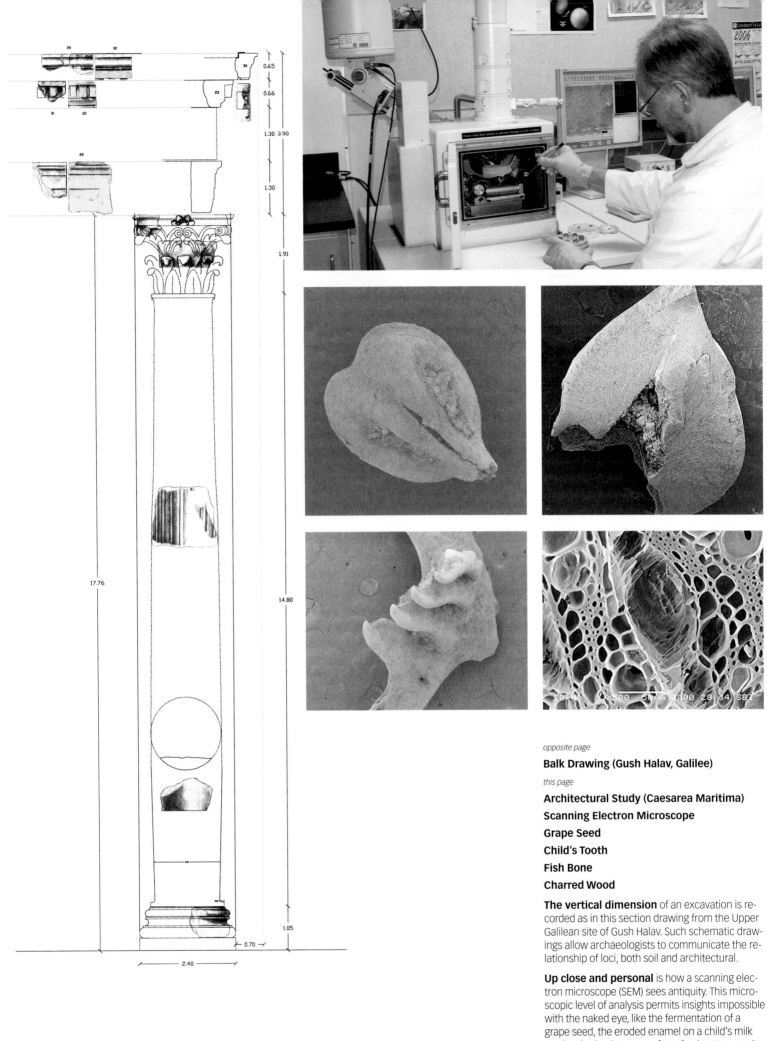

opposite page

Balk Drawing (Gush Halav, Galilee)

this page

Architectural Study (Caesarea Maritima)

Scanning Electron Microscope

Grape Seed

Child's Tooth

Fish Bone

Charred Wood

The vertical dimension of an excavation is recorded as in this section drawing from the Upper Galilean site of Gush Halav. Such schematic drawings allow archaeologists to communicate the relationship of loci, both soil and architectural.

Up close and personal is how a scanning electron microscope (SEM) sees antiquity. This microscopic level of analysis permits insights impossible with the naked eye, like the fermentation of a grape seed, the eroded enamel on a child's milk tooth, whether bones are from freshwater or saltwater fish, or the kind of wood used in an object.

the New Testament. Paul's co-workers, the husband and wife team of Aquila and Prisca from Rome, were tentmakers, like him. Based on those inscriptions, we would expect her to work *for* and *under* him. It is surprising, then, that Paul almost always refers to them with the wife's name first, as in Romans 16:3, "Greet Prisca and Aquila." That was countercultural.

Several papyri from the Roman period that were found in Egypt show the relationship between gender and apprenticeships in weaving, an activity often considered a woman's domestic work. These apprentice contracts stipulate an apprenticeship of between one and five years, with pay at the outset of only rations of wheat and oil, followed by modest wages as skill and output increase. But there is not a single contract for a freeborn woman. Instead, the majority are for freeborn boys, a few for slave boys, and only a couple for slave

Occupations on Roman Tombstones		
Occupation	Men	Women
Building	112 (100%)	0
Manufacturing	282 (85%)	49 (15%)
Sales	99 (92%)	9 (8%)
Banking	42 (100%)	0
Professional	101 (84%)	19 (16%)
Skilled Service	40 (53%)	35 (47%)
Domestic Service	235 (73%)	86 (27%)
Transportation	55 (100%)	0
Administration	296 (97%)	10 (3%)

"Year seventeen of Imperator Caesar Nerva Traianus Augustus Germanicus Dacicus, Hathyr 13 in Tebtunis in the district of Polemon of the Arsinoite nome. Protas, son of Petesouchos, about forty years old, with a scar on his right wrist, has apprenticed his son Harphaesis to Heron son of Orseus, weaver, about twenty-five years old with a scar in the middle of his forehead, so that he, Harphaesis, may learn the weavers' trade in its entirety as Heron himself knows it, for [?] years from the first of the month Choiak. . . ."

girls. Freeborn women simply did not engage in work outside the home and would not be subordinate to any male outside the home like a father, husband, or brother. When they learned a trade, like Prisca, they must have learned from their mothers or older sisters and did not leave the confines of the house. These archaeological finds, whether on Roman tombstones or Egyptian papyri, help us appreciate how radical Paul was when he spoke of and treated Prisca and Aquila as equals, even giving her name primacy of place. And we recognize how radical Jesus must have sounded when he invited Mary to join him at the table despite the protests of her sister Martha, who remained in the kitchen (Luke 10:38–42).

Women who lost the protection of husband, father, or brother, whether by death, divorce, or disowning, would have had few opportunities. If they were young, they could become prostitutes; if they were old, they could beg. There is abundant evidence for brothels in the city of Pompeii that we will

examine in chapter 6, but none at all in rural or village settings. Presumably women who sold themselves or begged in a rural context would have been chased from village to village. Those social outcasts might well have been among those attracted to Jesus's message, if we take seriously his statement that tax collectors and prostitutes will enter the kingdom of God ahead of religious leaders (Matthew 21:32).

A second kind of interpretive study involves demographics and population estimates. Population figures in ancient literary texts are notoriously unreliable and often wildly exaggerated. Ancient census counts are concerned more with tax-paying individuals than entire populations, so they ignore slaves and minors. But ancient sites' populations can nonetheless be assessed by multiplying the area of the city's ruins with the probable density of persons living there. Both variables, however, require scrutiny. For example, the ruins of ancient Capernaum, where Jesus spent a good deal of his ministry, look vast, but exca-

vations across that site show that the eastern half was not inhabited until centuries later. The density of living quarters depends on several factors, such as whether the site was walled, whether it

opposite page

Mummy Portrait (Egypt, ca. 60 CE)
Funerary Bust (Palmyra, 2nd c. CE)
Papyrus Contract (Egypt, 113 CE)

this page

Brothel (Pompeii, 1st c. CE)
Frescoed Room (Pompeii, 1st c. CE)

Bringing women to light is an important contribution of archaeology. Literary texts tend to ignore women, but archaeology provides occasional glimpses of them, such as this funerary mask from Roman Egypt. The first-century CE tombstone from Palmyra shows husband and wife — he holds a scroll and she holds weaving tools.

The frescoes of Pompeii come from wealthy houses as well as brothels. The abundance of frescoes at Pompeii has helped archaeologists to trace stylistic changes over time. The boxed fresco at the brothel is racy and suggests a sexual position available for a set price, a reminder that women in antiquity were often treated as objects. In spite of obvious male involvement, sexual immorality was seen as the archetypal female vice.

had large open spaces or gardens, and whether people lived in multistoried apartments like in some Roman cities, two-storied houses with atrium gardens like Pompeii, or single-storied courtyard houses like most Galilean villages. Excavations at Capernaum show that almost none of the walls could support a second story, and that most houses had large courtyards to keep animals in at night. Using census data from preindustrial villages across the Middle East, we can estimate that Capernaum had about 150 persons per hectare. It was spread over approximately 10 hectares, so the population at Jesus's time would have been no more than 1,500 and more likely about 1,000.

Such population estimates are important because they give a sense of scale. For example, we know that Jesus grew up in the Galilean hamlet of Nazareth of around 300 inhabitants; he centered his ministry in the larger village of Capernaum, with around 1,000 inhabitants; however, by all accounts, he did not minister in the Galilean cities of Sepphoris or Tiberias, which had populations between 8,000 and 12,000. Did Jesus not feel at home in these larger cities? Archaeology cannot answer that question, but it can pose it. Archaeology can also lead us to wonder about Jesus and his disciples' reaction to Jerusalem, which had a population of over 30,000 and perhaps three, six, or ten times that many pilgrims during festivals. And it helps us appreciate Paul's urban context in cities like Antioch, Corinth, and Ephesus, all with populations well over 60,000.

Those figures help us picture the places mentioned in the New Testament. But the ancient mind based a site's importance less on size and more on its architecture and aesthetics. Jesus's Capernaum was insignificant not so much because of its modest population but because it lacked the wealthy and powerful men who built urban structures and amenities like temples, baths, fountains, and colonnaded streets. The abundance of those kinds of urban structures made Antioch, Corinth, and Ephesus important. First-rate architecture in a particular

Comparable Population Densities	
Site	Density per Hectare
Roman Ostia	360–435
Bronze Age Aegean Walled Cities	ca. 300
Iron Age Palestinian Walled Cities	ca. 300
Medieval Walled Cities	ca. 250
Roman Pompeii	125–190
Unwalled Mesopotamian Villages	100–150
Unwalled 19th-Century Palestinian Villages	100–150

"To Heron from Sansneus, son of N.N., grandson of Patynis, his mother being N.N., daughter of Sansneus, public farmer from the village of Talei. In accordance with the orders, I register for the house-by-house census of the past 23rd year of Antoninus Caesar the Lord in the 3rd share of a paternal house, owned in common with my brothers, in the same village. And I am Sansneus the aforementioned, 3[.], with a scar on the small finger of my left hand; and my brother from the same father and mother, Apollonios [3?], scarless; Sochotes, another brother by the same mother, 33, scarless; the wife of Apollonios, 32, scarless; and Tamystha, daughter from both parents, — , scarless; and the wife of Sochotes, N.N., daughter of Hatres, granddaughter of N.N., her mother being Sarapous, — , scarless; and the daughter from both parents with a scar on her middle [?], and Sarapous, 3, scarless. And there belong [?] a house and courtyard in which [?] Year 24 of Antoninus Caesar the Lord, Pharmouthi 30."

style communicated the importance of the people who lived there and why they were important. Under the Roman emperor Augustus (31 BCE–14 CE), Roman rule was emphatically solidified by a standardized urban architecture and imagery. Right when Christianity was born of Judaism, Roman cities were transforming the Mediterranean basin from a collection of diverse provinces into a homogenous Roman Empire. Rome used urbanization as a kind of globalization, as cities everywhere were adorned with similar marble and columned facades, ordered along grids that highlighted imperial Roman structures, and filled with opportunities for bathing and entertainment. Cities provid-

ed the empire's citizens with a homogenized set of visual and social experiences that varied little from Spain to Syria, from the Alps to Armenia.

The transformation of cities under Augustus is evident in any excavation around the Mediterranean. It is perhaps clearest at Pompeii, where buildings are preserved from floor to roof, but it can also be traced in Jerusalem, which was clothed in the Augustan architectural vernacular by Herod the Great (40–4 BCE). Even Herod's greatest architectural achievement — the Temple Mount, which surrounded the Jewish God's sanctuary — adopted Roman-inspired styles. Though it is not obvious when one looks at the Temple's remains in Jerusalem today, meticulous archaeologi-

cal work around the Temple can help us see what it looked like in Jesus's time. Architectural fragments toppled from the upper courses by Roman soldiers

opposite page

Roman Theater (Miletus, Turkey)

Census Papyrus (Egypt 161 CE)

this page

Overview of Capernaum

Determining ancient populations is impossible from literary sources. Texts exaggerate, inscriptions are incomplete, and papyrus registers like this one from Egypt only concern one household. Some have suggested that the size of public buildings, like this theater at Miletus in Turkey, correlate with a city's population, but that has more to do with the city's wealth. Archaeologists estimate populations by assessing the extent of a site's ruins and multiplying that by the probable population density.

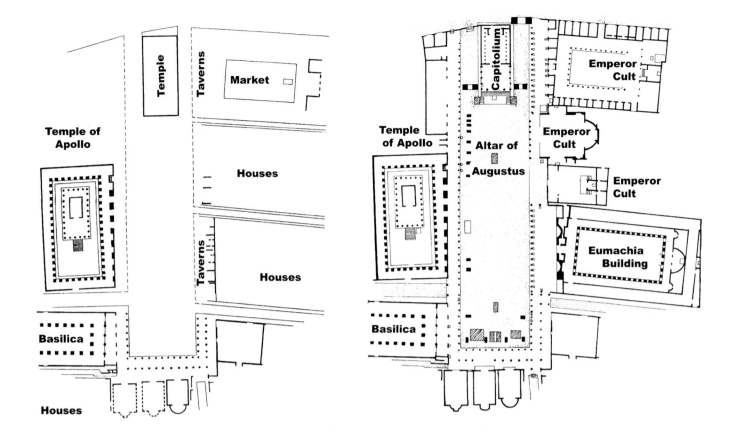

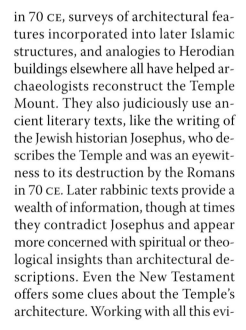

in 70 CE, surveys of architectural features incorporated into later Islamic structures, and analogies to Herodian buildings elsewhere all have helped archaeologists reconstruct the Temple Mount. They also judiciously use ancient literary texts, like the writing of the Jewish historian Josephus, who describes the Temple and was an eyewitness to its destruction by the Romans in 70 CE. Later rabbinic texts provide a wealth of information, though at times they contradict Josephus and appear more concerned with spiritual or theological insights than architectural descriptions. Even the New Testament offers some clues about the Temple's architecture. Working with all this evidence, scholars of architecture and archaeology, in concert with literary scholars, have provided a serious reconstruction of Herod's Temple at the time of Jesus. That reconstruction makes clear the extent to which Herod intended that the Temple dominate the cityscape: he wanted to impress his citizens and visitors alike with his power. But he also wanted to associate his kingdom with the larger Roman world: its facades, vistas, and techniques left an indelible Roman imprint on the Jewish city. Given that context, we may well wonder, what exactly was Jesus upset about when he condemned the temple? Did his anger go beyond religion to include how politics were shaping religion and how power was shaping the city? Archaeology is unable to answer that, but it can raise the question.

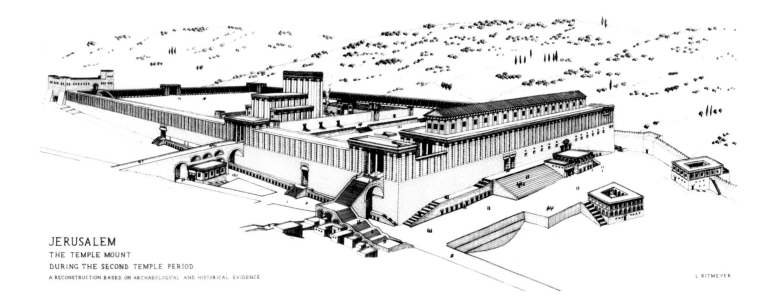

JERUSALEM
THE TEMPLE MOUNT
DURING THE SECOND TEMPLE PERIOD
A RECONSTRUCTION BASED ON ARCHAEOLOGICAL AND HISTORICAL EVIDENCE

L RITMEYER

These examples — gender relations, population size, and urban architecture — illustrate what this *Visual Guide to the New Testament* intends to achieve in subsequent chapters. Pictures of recent excavations or newly discovered artifacts are not simply illustrated alongside New Testament texts. The goal is not narrowly focused on what excavations have been conducted at which New Testament site, or whether this or that story is true. Instead, the pictures are designed to help tell archaeology's story and to help the reader envision the world in which Jesus and the first Christians lived.

opposite page

Pompeii, Before and After Augustus

Rubble from Temple (Jerusalem)

Tombs of the Patriarchs (Hebron)

this page

Architectural Reconstruction of Temple

Artist's Reconstruction of Temple

The Augustan revolution in urban architecture is clear in the archaeological record. Note how, on these maps, the entire focus of the city's forum shifts from a north-south to an east-west axis and onto monuments dedicated to the worship of the emperors, especially Augustus.

The Temple at the time of Jesus is a subject of considerable archaeological energy. Most excavations in Jerusalem have focused to the south and west of the Temple Mount; thus nearly all reconstructions show it from a southwestern perspective. The temple can be reconstructed based on the rubble excavated below and similar Herodian architecture, like the Tomb of the Patriarchs in Hebron. Architectural line-drawings differ from lifelike color reconstructions, which add another interpretive layer and accentuate a mood.

THE IMPORTANCE OF VOLUNTEERS

Pay your own way, sleep very little, wake up before dawn, work in the hot sun, and live in a tent or cramped room . . . but have the time of your life and memories to last a lifetime. Many excavations run digs as a field school, in which volunteers exchange labor for a first-rate learning experience. Volunteers commit to two- to six-week terms and are often the backbone of expeditions. Well-organized, credible excavations can be found by contacting the American Schools of Oriental Research, which accredits excavations in the Near East, many relating to the biblical world; the American Institute of Archaeology, which focuses on classical sites of the Greek and Roman world; or the Israel Antiquities Authority, which encourages volunteers.

The Dead Sea Scrolls rank perhaps as the greatest manuscript discovery ever. They were discovered by a Bedouin shepherd in a Judean Desert cave during the winter of 1946–47. After they sold on the black market, treasure-hunters scoured the nearby hills and caves, eventually compiling an unparalleled body of often-fragmentary manuscripts. They date to between the second century BCE and the end of the first century CE, and many are from the Hebrew Bible. Others are linked to a sect called the Essenes. The Essenes are one of three Jewish groups mentioned in ancient literary sources, along with the Pharisees and the Sadducees, who are also mentioned in the New Testament. The Essenes were a smaller, apocalyptic, baptismal group who held a worldview similar to that of John the Baptist. Beginning in 1951 at the site called Khirbet Qumran on the northwest shore of the Dead Sea, very close to where the scrolls were discovered, Roland de Vaux of Jerusalem's École Biblique et Archéologique Française began excavations that lasted until 1956. De Vaux hoped to uncover evidence for the monastic community that housed the Essenes, but he died in 1971 without having published the final report — it is still lacking to this day. For that reason, aspects of the site's stratigraphy, the complex's original function, and the function of some rooms are disputed.

By and large, it is fair to say that de Vaux and many archaeological interpreters after him excavated with a trowel in one hand and the Dead Sea Scrolls in the other, and so identified strata and rooms in accordance with their reading of the Dead Sea Scrolls' history and meaning. A rectangular room with a table was called the scriptorium and was thought to be where the scrolls were written. Abundant smashed pottery was said to have been from the refectory, where the scrolls said the Essenes ate in silence. But there was also puzzling evidence. For example, a hoard

of 561 silver coins stashed away in three pots were almost all Tyrian tetradrachmas, the coin with which adult male Jews paid the annual Temple tax. But the manuscripts are clear about the Essenes' contempt for the priestly regime that ran the Temple in Jerusalem. Did they still pay the tax? Maybe. Or did they simply store their cash in

The site of Khirbet Qumran is never mentioned in the New Testament, nor are the Essenes who settled there. But the sect described in the scrolls shows remarkable parallels to John the Baptist, whose fiery apocalyptic preaching of impending doom is not unlike what is found in the scrolls. And they, like him, were baptizers or practiced ritual immersion in pools or in the Jordan River. But both apocalyptic thought and ritual bathing were widespread in first-century Judaism, so it is pure speculation that either he or his disciples were Essenes.

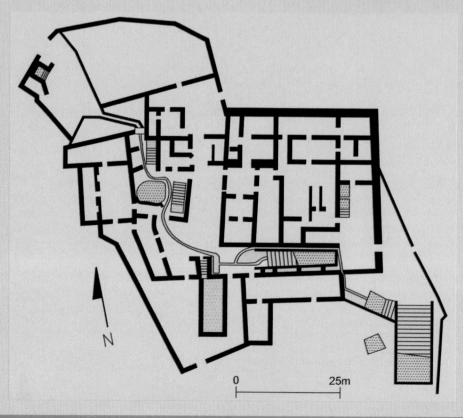

0   25m

Tyrian coinage, which was the least debased silver coinage?

Over the past decade, several archaeologists have challenged the widely accepted interpretation of Khirbet Qumran as an Essene settlement. They speculate that it could have been a country villa, a Hasmonean fort, or an industrial complex. These critics suggest that the real problem was de Vaux's preoccupation with excavating the site through the lens of the scrolls — an appropriate challenge and a valid criticism. One cannot dig to find what is in a text, as biblical archaeologists were prone to do for much of the twentieth century. That is a mistake. But at the same time, it is absurd to avoid consulting texts, especially when they can shed light on archaeological finds. At some point artifact and text must be brought to bear on each other; the trick is not to prejudge what the archaeology means because of preconceptions based on the text. And that does not seem to have happened at Qumran. Most of de Vaux's archaeological finds agree with the textual inferences: Qumran very likely was an Essene settlement. Similarly this book brings together archaeological discoveries and New Testament studies in a constructive dialogue. But in this conversation, archaeology talks first and does most of the talking.

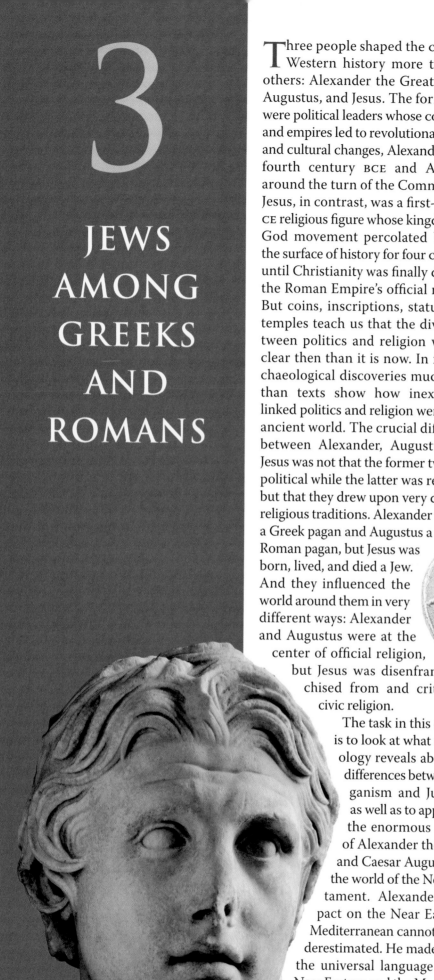

3

JEWS AMONG GREEKS AND ROMANS

Three people shaped the course of Western history more than any others: Alexander the Great, Caesar Augustus, and Jesus. The former two were political leaders whose conquests and empires led to revolutionary social and cultural changes, Alexander in the fourth century BCE and Augustus around the turn of the Common Era. Jesus, in contrast, was a first-century CE religious figure whose kingdom-of-God movement percolated beneath the surface of history for four centuries until Christianity was finally declared the Roman Empire's official religion. But coins, inscriptions, statues, and temples teach us that the divide between politics and religion was less clear then than it is now. In fact, archaeological discoveries much more than texts show how inextricably linked politics and religion were in the ancient world. The crucial difference between Alexander, Augustus, and Jesus was not that the former two were political while the latter was religious, but that they drew upon very different religious traditions. Alexander was a Greek pagan and Augustus a Roman pagan, but Jesus was born, lived, and died a Jew. And they influenced the world around them in very different ways: Alexander and Augustus were at the center of official religion, but Jesus was disenfranchised from and critical of civic religion.

The task in this chapter is to look at what archaeology reveals about the differences between paganism and Judaism, as well as to appreciate the enormous impact of Alexander the Great and Caesar Augustus on the world of the New Testament. Alexander's impact on the Near East and Mediterranean cannot be underestimated. He made Greek the universal language of the Near Eastern and the Mediterranean world; because of him, the New Testament was written in Greek, and hence was understandable everywhere. Caesar Augustus's rise to power in Rome reverberated across the Roman Empire: he brought peace and prosperity, which made extensive trade and travel safe. Because the region was peaceful and there was a network of Roman roads, Paul and others were able to spread the message of Jesus all over the Mediterranean. We will sketch Alexander's and Augustus's achievements in this chapter, revealing another difference from Jesus: they radically shaped the material culture of antiquity that archaeologists find today, whereas Jesus made no impact discernible to archaeologists.

ALEXANDER THE GREAT AND GREEK CULTURE

Twenty-year-old Alexander came to power at the right time. By the beginning of the fourth century BCE, the Greek city-states were worn down by fraternal wars, the Persian Empire was overextended and soft, and Rome still depended on farmer-warriors whose interests were confined to Italy. Alexander's father, Philip, ruled rugged Macedonia, later subduing the Greek city-states through political intrigue and military intimidation. He entrusted his son's education to the Athenian philosopher Aristotle, who provided Alexander with a proper Greek education. After Philip's assassination, Alexander cast himself as the liberator of Greece, vowing to free the Greeks of Asia Minor, in what is now the western shoreline of Turkey but was then the westernmost part of the Persian Empire. With daring tactics, brazen ambition, and youthful charisma, he defeated the Persian armies, swept through Egypt and Palestine, captured the Persian capital of Persepolis, and made an unbelievable but ultimately exhausting incursion into India. He returned to make Babylon his capital, but died there in 323 BCE at the young age of thirty-three. He changed the world and left an indelible mark in the archaeological record.

Ironically, the world-conquering Alexander himself left very little archaeological evidence behind. Only a few artifacts can be traced directly to him, but they are telling. One is a mar-

"As I was watching, a male goat appeared from the west, coming across the face of the whole earth. . . . The male goat is the king of Greece."

DANIEL 8:5, 21

ble inscription in western Turkey dating to 334 BCE, which honors his gift to the city of Priene and the temple of Athena Polias, the Greek goddess who won the Trojan War. That same year, he also paid homage to the greatest Greek warrior of the Trojan War when he visited Achilles' tomb. Early in his rule, he saw himself as a new Achilles.

Later in life, he saw himself as a god. A silver coin called a decadrachma that was minted after Alexander's return from India contains perhaps the only surviving image from his lifetime. Minted in Babylon, it depicts him on one side fighting an elephant and on the other wearing a Macedonian cloak and a Persian headdress, and bearing Greek armor. The symbolism powerfully captures the essence of Hellenism, which formed one new culture from several old ones. But more telling, Alexander holds a thunderbolt in his hand, symbolizing his divinity, in which he had come to believe by the end of his life.

These finds aptly capture two aspects of Alexander's rule that permeated the Hellenistic world and characterize subsequent periods. First, he had become the model for all rulers; his image symbolized for subsequent generations the conquering-hero-become-god. Even though the generals that succeeded him squabbled and carved up his kingdom, each claimed to be his rightful heir by striking Alexander's image on their coins, and like him, they claimed to be divine. His portrait was wildly popular and appeared on coins, statues, paintings, and mosaics that endured for centuries. Second, his language also endured, spreading across the Near East and the Mediterranean region, so that most inscriptions found by archaeologists are in Greek and not in indigenous languages. *Koine* Greek, or common Greek, became the standard language for governance, trade,

opposite page
Bust of Alexander (Pergamum, 3rd C. BCE)
Gold Coin with Alexander (281 BCE)

this page
Alexander Mosaic (Pompeii, 2nd C. BCE)

Antiquity's most popular image was no doubt Alexander the Great. Statues, such as this one from Pergamon, portray him with windswept hair, large eyes, and a broad brow. Coins from after his lifetime depict him in profile, often with a ram's horn, symbol of Zeus Ammon, a local Egyptian manifestation of the god Zeus that is worshipped at the oasis of Siwa. The mosaic is likely a copy of Philoxeneos's famous painting, which was praised by the Roman author Pliny the Elder. Found inside a Pompeiian house, this mosaic may have staked the owner's claim to Hellenistic culture or announced Rome as the new world-conqueror.

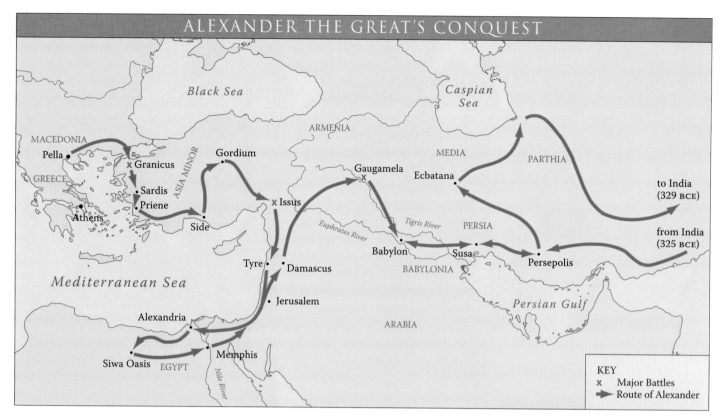

science, and education. Some familiarity with Greek filtered down to broad segments of the population, even in Galilee at the time of Jesus, though Aramaic was more commonly spoken. *Koine* Greek would become the overwhelming choice for public inscriptions and urban conversation, and would eventually become the language of the New Testament. Because of Alexander, the Greek New Testament could be read, heard, and understood all over the Mediterranean world.

In addition to his image and language, Alexander's conquest left an even larger artifact in its wake: the particularly Greek city called the polis (plural poleis). The Greek polis of the earlier Classical era (sixth to fourth centuries BCE) bore political connotations like self-autonomy, rule by the *demos* or land-owning adult males, and competition with other poleis for prestige. But under Alexander's successors, few pretensions of autonomy remained. Local elites still owned the

and Philadelphia, present-day Amman, east of the Jordan River; and Gaza and Marisa southwest of Jerusalem. These and other cities were located along the coastal plain, inland on fertile tracts of land, or along busy trade routes. Excavations at these sites point to thriving cosmopolitan populations, as previously distinct indigenous peoples shared features of Hellenistic urban life. Language and lifestyle were less of a hurdle than ever before; after Alexander, the world was on its way to becoming one universal city, which Greeks called the *cosmopolis.*

THE JEWISH REVOLT AGAINST HELLENISM

Hellenistic culture made city dwellers in and around Palestine more homogenous, but political control of the area alternated between two competing dynasties that arose among Alexander's successors (often called the *Diadochoi,* from the Greek word for "successors"). Jerusalem and Judea were on the southern border of the Seleucid Empire, ruled from Syrian Antioch, which would later be home to a large Christian community mentioned in the book of Acts, and on the northern border of the Ptolemaic Empire, ruled from Egyptian Alexandria. The Ptolemies ruled Palestine for most of the third

opposite page

Coin of Alexander (Babylon, 324 BCE)

Alexander's Inscription (Priene, 334 BCE)

this page

Rosetta Stone (Egypt, 196 BCE)

Artifacts from Alexander's life are exceptionally rare. This coin depicts him on his horse Bucephalos fighting a retreating Indian elephant; the other side suggests his claim to divinity, as he holds Zeus's thunderbolt in his hand. Also from Alexander's life is this four-foot-tall inscribed stone found among the ruins of Priene and dating to 334 BCE, which proclaims: "King Alexander dedicated the Temple to Athena Polias."

The world's most famous inscription is the Rosetta Stone, found in 1799 by Napoleon's army near the Egyptian town of el-Rashid (Rosetta). Written in three rows, with ancient Egpytian hieroglyphics above, demotic or alphabetic Egyptian in the center, and *koine* Greek below, it helped scholars decipher hieroglyphics. It also signals the shift from Pharaonic to Ptolemaic empires, when Greek became commonplace. The decree describes the priests' support for institutionalizing the worship of the Ptolemaic kings and was written on the anniversary of the coronation of thirteen-year-old Ptolemy V Epiphanes in 196 BCE.

land and set local policies, but they did so on behalf of a king who made sure the appropriate taxes went into the royal treasury. Poleis provided the setting for local culture to fuse with Greek culture into syncretistic Hellenism (from the Greek name for their land, *Hellas*). The physical characteristics of the polis have been excavated from North Africa to Turkey to Syria. They always include urban planning on a grid pattern; an area called the acropolis, or "upper city," where temples are found; an agora or public square around which markets and civic buildings are found; and a gymnasium, the complex where elite male youths were

educated and shaped as future leaders of the city. The gymnasium included military training, philosophical discourse, instruction in the arts, and physical exercise in the nude (in Greek, *gymnos,* from which the institution took its name). The youthful nude male body was considered, as we can tell from Greek and Hellenistic statues, the aesthetic ideal.

Archaeologists have uncovered evidence of such poleis, dating to the Hellenistic period, all around the traditional homeland of Jews in Galilee and Judea. This includes Scythopolis (earlier Beth-Shean), Ptolemais, Hippos, and Philoteria surrounding Galilee; Gerasa

century BCE; it changed hands several times at the end of the third century BCE; and by the beginning of the second century BCE, the Seleucids had taken control. These political changes had little impact on daily life, however, and there is no archaeological evidence that any cities were destroyed, as each side was eager to preserve the economic boom. The two empires used comparable coinage bearing Alexander's image, maintained Greek as the official language, and participated in the international trade of goods like wine, olive oil, and ceramic fine wares. Hellenized elites dominated civic and religious life in the poleis and functioned as tax collectors who sent on taxes to whichever king was in charge, either Seleucid or Ptolemaic. An inscription found in 1960 just outside Scythopolis indicates that local elites remained constant as Seleucids and Ptolemies alternated. Known as the Hefzibah Inscription, it records the correspondence between the Seleucid kings Antiochus III and Antiochus IV and a local military governor named Ptolemaios (who, incidentally, was also a high priest). The very name suggests connections to the southern Hellenistic kingdom, and perhaps he had earlier served in a similar capacity for the Ptolemies.

Several wealthy Jewish families administered Judea on behalf of the Hellenistic rulers. We know quite a bit about one of them, the Tobiads, from excavations on the east side of the Jordan, where they built a family estate at a site called Iraq el-Emir (Arabic for "Cave of the Prince," referring to a cave where some Tobiads were buried). Set in the midst of an artificial lake created by a 150-meter dam, its central palace was built with enormous rectangular stones and somewhat clunky Doric

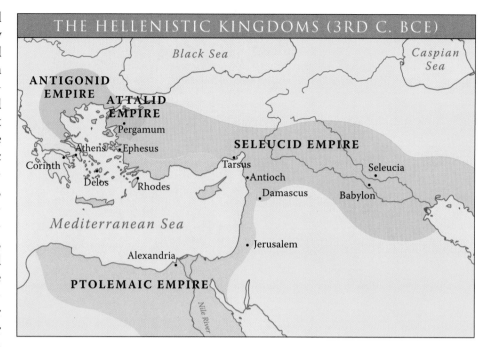

columns in the earliest Greek style, and its fountains and water channels created an air-conditioned oasis in hot summers. Archaeologists there found ample coins, amphorae once filled with expensive wine imported from the Greek islands, and most intriguingly, several relief sculptures of panthers and lions. Though artistically crude, they show that pagan styles were adopted by these Hellenized Jews at a time when most Jews frowned upon such depictions and complied with a strict interpretation of the Mosaic commandment against graven images.

At distant Iraq el-Emir, such Hellenistic inclinations drew little attention, but inside Jerusalem they were causing trouble in the early second century BCE. Some aspects of the Jewish tradition were simply antithetical to the Hellenistic spirit — in areas far more serious than representational art. In pagan Hellenism, civic religious duties were open to all rich males, but for Jews the high priesthood was limited to particular families — priests could not simply be appointed from outside by royal decree. Furthermore, Jewish monotheism was absolute: there was only one God. Alexander's claim to divinity was reluctantly tolerated, but the same claim by later and usually incompetent kings was abhorrent. Finally, Jewish aversion to nudity generally, and the dis-

tinctness of male circumcision particularly, created awkwardness in the gymnasium, where the polis's elite youths were acculturated to Hellenic life.

In the 160s BCE those tensions became violent. This is reflected in the archaeological record, but the full story is told in literary sources, especially the apocryphal book 1 Maccabees. Some highborn Jews were too rapidly adopting Hellenistic ways and shaping Jerusalem into a polis. They neglected their sons' circumcision, and to fit in with the cosmopolitan Hellenistic ethos, some even undid the marks of circumcision with a painful procedure. Appointment to the high priesthood was for sale to the highest bidder and had become a political tool (*Was there any other way?* pagan Hellenists would wonder). Tensions between Jewish Hellenists and Jewish traditionalists divided the city. Finally, to ensure the loyalty of his Judean subjects — and still smarting from a humiliating defeat in Egypt at the hands of the emerging Roman Empire — the Seleucid king Antiochus IV Epiphanes (Greek for "god manifest," a title that appears on his coins, where he is depicted sitting godlike on a throne) opened the Jewish Temple to Gentiles. Non-Jews instituted sacrifices there to Zeus. Antiochus wanted a more loyal population in Jerusalem, one that was Hellenized like those in his other poleis, and who would sacrifice (pigs!) to his favored god and even to himself as god. But his plan backfired.

The conservative Jewish reaction was led by the family of Mattathias. His son Judas Maccabee (Hebrew for "the hammer") used guerrilla tactics in the hills and then formed a small army that eventually defeated the Seleucids and established an independent Jewish kingdom in Judea. Judas's successors formed what scholars call the Hasmonean dynasty (named after Mattathias's grandfather, Asmoneos), who successively expanded Jewish territory south into Idumea, west toward the coastal plain, east along the Jordan Valley, and eventually north into Galilee. Jewish independence and expansion were won with God's help, according to ancient Jewish theological explanation, but modern geopolitical analysis explains it by a power vacuum: Rome was on the rise and both Ptolemies and Seleucids were on the run. Their empires were about to disintegrate.

opposite page

Dan Inscription (Israel, 2nd c. BCE)

this page

Venus di Milo (2nd c. BCE)
Bronze Herm (early 1st c. BCE)

Good Greek but sloppy Aramaic are inscribed on this plaque from Dan found in northern Israel and dating to the Early Hellenistic period. The first three lines' neat and professional Greek (which reads, "To the god who is among the Danites, Zoilos makes a prayer") contrasts with the irregular and less practiced Aramaic of the final line (which is fragmentary and may be a rough translation). Likely done by the same person, the difference is the result of having templates in and practice at Greek, but carving the Aramaic letters in free hand, even though the latter was probably his mother tongue. Referring to the deity as "the god among the Danites" might be a respectful way for a pagan (Zoilos) to avoid the unmentionable name of the Jewish God.

Hellenism viewed nudity very differently than Judaism. The famous Venus di Milo, a slightly larger-than-life marble statue of Greek Aphrodite found in 1820 on the island of Melos, dates to the late second century BCE and illustrates the Hellenistic attitude toward the body and nudity: nonchalant, appreciative, and inspiring. Male genitalia were even ascribed protective properties, which can be seen on herms, like this one from Asia Minor and dating to around 100 BCE. Herms had a god's bust atop a square pillar, originally only Hermes but later Dionysos was common; about midway down the pillar, male (uncircumcised) genitalia protruded. Herms were thought to magically protect boundaries, crossroads, and doorways.

"Forces sent by him shall occupy and profane the temple . . . and they shall . . . set up the abomination that makes desolate."

DANIEL 11:31

The Hasmonean expansion is readily apparent in the archaeological record. Sites across Palestine reveal either a conflagration or abandonment beginning in the late second century BCE. The poleis of the coast and coastal plain, with their thriving economies and cosmopolitan populations, were no more. Excavations at Ashdod, Dor, Gezer, Marisa, Straton's Tower, and Yavneh-Yam show destruction or desertion. In the north, the Hellenistic sites of Philoteria, Tel Anafa, and Kedesh were no more by the early first century BCE.

Archaeologists have traced a demographic shift under the Hasmoneans in which new settlement patterns appear across Palestine. By the mid-first century BCE, the Jewish population in the small Hasmonean kingdom lived along the hill country that runs north-south from Galilee through Samaria to Judea. They lived in villages with only one city to speak of — Jerusalem. Their artifacts bear little resemblance to those of the Hellenized poleis; they used locally made pottery for utilitarian purposes and imported no fine wares for dining or drinking. They did not import foreign wine amphorae, used little or no glass, and befitting Jewish law, avoided images of humans or animals. In contrast to the previous century, there is an almost complete absence of Greek inscriptions. In fact, there are almost no public inscriptions of any kind until the subsequent Roman period.

But there is an irony in the archaeological record. Half a century after rebelling against Hellenization, the Hasmonean kings minted coins with *Greek* letters, and they even adopted *Greek* names. Their small bronze coins, known from the Gospel story of the widow's mite, have both Hebrew and Greek letters, and one king was even named Alexander. Also called Jannaeus, his coins show that he combined the office of king and high priest, as was customary among Hellenistic pagans but in violation of Jewish tradition. This, along with other Hellenizing tendencies, was vigorously opposed by some Jews, including the Essenes, who fled Jerusalem and established a countercultural monastic community at Qumran near the Dead Sea. Disputes over Hellenistic acculturation continued for some time, and the Essenes at Qumran asserted a radically traditional approach until the community was destroyed by Roman legions in 70 CE at the end the first Jewish War.

THE JEWISH DIASPORA

The Maccabees managed to hold off the tide of Hellenization for a while, but their initial isolation could not be replicated by Jews living outside the land of Israel. Significant Jewish

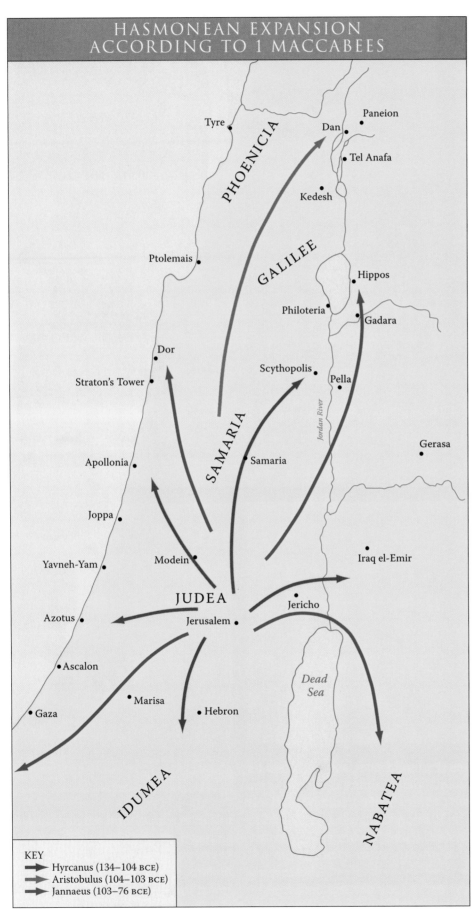

HASMONEAN EXPANSION
ACCORDING TO 1 MACCABEES

Tyre
PHOENICIA
Paneion
Dan
Tel Anafa
Kedesh
GALILEE
Ptolemais
Hippos
Philoteria
Gadara
Dor
Scythopolis
Straton's Tower
Pella
Jordan River
SAMARIA
Apollonia
Samaria
Gerasa
Joppa
Yavneh-Yam
Modein
Iraq el-Emir
JUDEA
Jericho
Azotus
Jerusalem
Ascalon
Dead Sea
Marisa
Hebron
Gaza
IDUMEA
NABATEA

KEY
➤ Hyrcanus (134–104 BCE)
➤ Aristobulus (104–103 BCE)
➤ Jannaeus (103–76 BCE)

opposite page

Tobiad Palace (Iraq el-Emir, Jordan)

Coin of Antiochus Epiphanes (175–164 BCE)

Lion Relief (Iraq el-Emir)

Violation of Jewish law is clear in this pagan coin and Jewish palace. Minted shortly before Antiochus Epiphanes ("god manifest") defiled the Jewish Temple, the coin portrays Zeus on his throne holding Nike on his hand. The Jewish Tobiad family served as tax collectors for Seleucid and Ptolemaic overlords during much of the Hellenistic period. They adopted pagan representational art, like the lion, which was frowned upon by most Jews.

The Maccabees and the Hasmonean Dynasty	
Judas Maccabaeus	died 160 BCE
Jonathan	152–142
Simon Thassis	142–134
John Hyrcanus	134–104
Aristobulus I	104–103
Alexander Jannaeus	103–76
Alexandra Salome	76–67
Aristobulus II	67–63
Hyrcanus II	63–40
Antigonus	40–37 BCE

communities had lived in Babylon and Egypt during the Persian period (sixth to fourth centuries BCE), and after Alexander redrew the world's political map in the late fourth century BCE, the number of Jews living abroad increased along with the areas they inhabited. Some became expatriates because of war, either as mercenaries on the winning side who retired and settled in foreign lands, or as soldiers on the losing side who were sold into slavery, some of whom were later freed. Other Jews migrated as merchants or traders along the busy trade routes made possible after Alexander.

Ironically, Jews living inside Ptolemaic Egypt in cities like Alexandria were called *Hellenes,* the official bureaucratic designation for Greek-speaking resident aliens, and they held a higher legal standing than did indigenous Egyptians. These Jewish *Hellenes* had learned Greek as their mother tongue, were active in commerce, and participated at various levels in civic life. In subsequent centuries, the impact on Judaism of diaspora Jews, such as the philosopher Philo of Alexandria, who was a contemporary of Jesus and Paul, is significant. Hellenized diaspora Jews also made Jerusalem more cosmopolitan with their many pilgrimages, whether they came from Alexandria, Antioch, or later even Rome, as mentioned in the book of Acts' account of Pentecost.

Jewish expatriates in Egypt and elsewhere gathered weekly in *synagogues,* a Greek term that could refer to a building but generally refers to the gathering itself. Jews met for prayer, scripture reading, and other communal activities, like the Gospels describe in accounts of some of Jesus's healings in Galilee, and like Acts describes in stories of Paul's preaching. For the most part, inscriptions discovered in Egypt refer to the meeting place itself as a *proseuche,* Greek for a place of prayer. Numerous *proseuche* inscriptions survive from Hellenistic Egypt and provide a glimpse into diaspora life. They are in Greek and often include dedications to the Ptolemaic king or members of the royal family; these dedications might be a Jewish way of circumventing the more common pagan practice of sacrificing to the king. The oldest known synagogue inscription dates to the late third century BCE: "On behalf of King Ptolemy and Queen Bernice his sister and wife and their children, the Jews dedicated the *proseuche.*" Another, from a later date and uncertain location, has the royal family officially

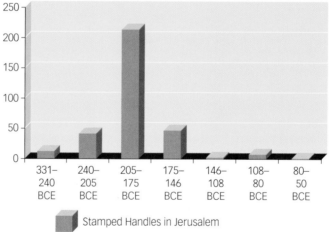

Stamped Handles in Jerusalem

declare a synagogue "inviolate" (Greek *asylos*) — that is to say, it was a place where accused persons could find asylum, a prized status typically granted only to significant temples.

In spite of the number of synagogue inscriptions, synagogue structures themselves are very rare in the diaspora. The oldest was discovered on the tiny Greek island of Delos and dates to before the first century CE. It was found in 1912 next to the island's gymnasium, nestled among houses in a domestic neighborhood. It had probably been a private house and was renovated as a synagogue by placing, along two walls, marble benches that could comfortably seat twenty-five. Another twenty-five to fifty could have sat on the floor or on portable benches, and a single thronelike seat, probably "Moses' Seat," the special chair from which the

> "The scribes and the Pharisees sit on Moses's seat ... but do not do as they do."
>
> MATTHEW 23: 2–3

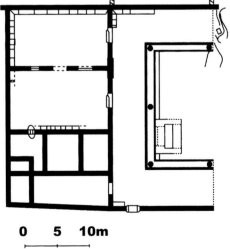

0 5 10m

opposite page

Stamp on Amphora Handle (2nd c. BCE)
Amphorae (Dor, 2nd c. BCE)
Coin of Alexander Jannaeus (103–76 BCE)

this page

Temple of Isis (Delos, Greece)
Roma Statue (Delos, 2nd c. BCE)
"Seat of Moses" (Delos, 1st c. BCE)
Plan of Synagogue (Delos)

Judaism's struggle against Hellenism is clear in one study of stamped amphorae found in Jerusalem. Wine from the Greek islands was ubiquitous in Hellenistic poleis along the coast and was eventually brought to Jerusalem in amphorae with handles stamped with their dates, like these found at Dor. This chart shows their frequency in late third- and early second-century Jerusalem, and their almost complete disappearance after the Maccabean Revolt.

His Hebrew and Greek names appear on this later Hasmonean coin of Alexander Jannaeus, or *Yehonatan,* who ruled from 103 to 76 BCE. One side has his name in paleo-Hebrew letters, which mimic an archaic style, around an eight-sided star, and the other side replicates the Seleucid anchor (ironically, since the Hasmoneans were notoriously landlocked) and has Greek letters spelling *Basileos Alexandros* (King Alexander).

The goddess Roma overlooks the activities of a religious group on the island of Delos. Set up in a fellowship of merchants and shippers who worshipped Poseidon, the statue of the Roman goddess made clear their support for Roman power and ensured that they continued to avoid suspicion.

This seat of Moses is from the oldest synagogue ever discovered, dating to the first century BCE. Found on the Greek island of Delos, Jewish scriptures were read from this ornate seat with a backrest, while the other seats were long, simple stone benches lining two sides of the room.

scriptures were read (mentioned in Matthew 23:2), faced the eastern entrance. A side room had a cistern and may have been a Jewish ritual bath (*mikveh*), and several inscriptions use the Greek term *Theos Hypsistos,* "the most high God," which Jews commonly used for their deity (also in Acts 7:48, 16:17). Another inscription explicitly calls the structure a *proseuche.*

The Jews on Delos were one of many ethnic or religious groups who met communally for worship. There is evidence for a synagogue where Samaritan immigrants met. Jews considered the Samaritans to be half-Jews and looked down on them, to judge from Jesus's parable of the Good Samaritan. There was also a group of Egyptians who met to worship the god Sarapis and goddess Isis, as well as a group of Syro-Phoenicians from Beirut who met to worship Poseidon. According to one inscription, the Poseidonists consisted mainly of shippers and merchants who lobbied for favorable civic policies toward their profession. In addition to worshipping the god of the sea, they also recognized the new power in the Mediterranean, by erecting a statue in honor of the goddess Roma.

ROME AND THE AUGUSTAN REVOLUTION

Five major wars between the Ptolemies and Seleucids left both drained at the end of the second century BCE. That is exactly when Rome emerged as the dominant power, having expanded beyond the banks of the Tiber to become masters of the Mediterranean. They won several successive wars against North African Carthage, and in the second of these Punic Wars (from the Latin *punici,* for Phoenicians), Rome began to meddle in the affairs of the eastern Mediterranean. In the third Punic War, Roman forces smashed the league of Greek cities, burnt its leading city of Corinth to the ground, and then rebuilt it as a Roman colony, where Paul would later live and minister for over a year. Rome built a road that extended from the Adriatic Sea all the way to the Black Sea, calling it the Via Egnatia after the Roman governor Gnaeus Egnatius, whose legions constructed it. Excavations all along

that road have found water and way stations, showing that Rome wanted to made troop movements quick and secure — and possible in the winter, when ships were anchored in ports.

Rome used that road to control heavily urbanized and wealthy Asia Minor, an area where New Testament Christianity flourished, to judge from Acts, Paul's letters, and the seven churches of the book of Revelation.

The Roman elite had a voracious appetite for Greek works of art, with bronze and marble statues moving at an amazing pace from east to west. They were copied, often by Greek craftsmen brought to Rome as slaves, and then put on display in Roman villas, in view of Roman youths being educated by hired Greek philosopher-tutors, often in *koine* Greek, which became the benchmark of a Roman's educational status. Paradoxically, even as Rome was conquering the Hellenistic world, aspects of Hellenistic culture deeply penetrated Roman life. In fact, from the second century BCE on, those two cultures have such a complex interaction and intermingle in such complicated ways that it's hard to distinguish Greek

from Roman in the first century CE. And that is important when we consider early Christianity, which made a remarkably fast transition from Jesus's Aramaic parables first spoken in Galilee, through Paul's Greek letters written mostly to cities in the eastern Mediterranean, and finally to Latin hymns and prayers offered in the city of Rome. Linguistic and cultural barriers were minimal at the time of the first Christians.

Rome expanded under a form of government and in a period scholars refer to as the Republic, when senators shared and competed for offices and honor. But the archaeological layers across Italy, Greece, and Turkey show that the republican system fueled factional and personal antagonisms that resulted in civil war, as legions turned

on each other for the better part of a century. As senators fought for control of the Republic, Pompey "the Great" campaigned in the East, dismantled the Seleucid Empire, and visited Jerusalem in 63 BCE to settle a dynastic dispute between the last two Hasmonean rulers, the brothers Aristobulus and Hyrcanus.

Julius Caesar eventually defeated Pompey in Alexandria, where he also had a liaison with the Hellenistic Egyptian queen Cleopatra and acquired the Nile's fertile valley, whose grain would feed Rome's masses for centuries to come. But Caesar was assassinated on the floor of the Senate by resentful senators in 44 BCE, and his right-hand man, Mark Antony, and eighteen-year-old grandnephew and adopted son, Octavian, would later vie for control of the empire. They met in a naval battle at the Bay of Actium on Greece's western coast in 31 BCE, where Octavian routed Mark Antony, who fled with Cleopatra and committed suicide in Alexandria, leaving Octavian with absolute control of the Mediterranean world.

Octavian's rule was revolutionary; historians call the era after he put an end to the civil wars in 31 BCE the Imperial period, or simply the Roman Empire. Augustus extended Rome's borders to their greatest extent, and brought about the *Pax Romana*, or Roman peace, with its unparalleled prosperity. He was named *princeps* by the senate, short for *primus inter pares*, "first among equals." But all other equals were dead in battle, any pretenders were murdered, and only those swearing allegiance to him survived. He nominally restored authority to the senate but ruled as an autocrat for forty years, until his death in 14 CE. In 27 BCE the Senate gave him the title *Augustus* ("the revered one"), which carried religious connotations suggestive of divinity. In 13 BCE he be-

came *pontifex maximus*, "supreme bridge-builder" and high priest of the state religion of Rome. He was allowed to wear the civic crown of laurel and

oak when he saw fit, an honor that had previously been granted only to conquering generals during their triumphal processions, when allegedly a slave held the crown *above* their heads and whispered continually, "Remember that you are a man." No whispering

opposite page

Bust of Pompey (1st C. BCE)
Bust of Julius Caesar (1st C. BCE)

this page

Statue of Cleopatra (1st C. BCE)
Lamp with Cleopatra (1st C. BCE)

Portrait busts of great men were ubiquitous in late Republican Rome. Whereas classical Greece preferred full-bodied statues of deities and the Hellenistic period saw some portrait busts of Alexander, wealthy Roman villas were saturated with realistic busts, like that of Pompey, which showed warts, puffy cheeks, a wrinkled forehead, and a double chin, while his windswept bangs resembled Alexander's, thus evoking world conquest. The gnarled face of Julius Caesar is emphatically lifelike, complete with wrinkles, receding hairline, and hollow cheeks. Hellenism idealized leaders in their twenties, but Romans valued seniority and idealized the mature man in his fifties, whose supposed wisdom was preferred to youthful ambition.

Two views of Cleopatra, one elegant and the other sleazy, can be seen in this black basalt statue and molded Roman lamp. Most busts of women often depict wives of leading men. These two depictions of Cleopatra, the last ruler of the Ptolemaic kingdom, who bore a son with Julius Caesar and later took Antony as a lover, illustrate very different responses to her. The Egyptian statue portrays Cleopatra as Isis, the Queen of Heaven and perfect wife, lover, and mother. The Roman lamp portrays her as the whore of Egypt, riding a crocodile with an exaggerated phallus. Similar contradictions occur later with Mary Magdalene, whose initial leadership was undermined by allegations of having been a prostitute.

CHAPTER 3 · JEWS AMONG GREEKS AND ROMANS

slaves for Augustus, as he tapped into the popular Roman belief that his peace and victories were divinely sanctioned. The initial impulse to consider him divine came, ironically, not from Rome but from the conquered Hellenistic world, where, after Alexander, ascribing divinity had become habitual. But Augustus did bring peace, security, and prosperity, and for this, well before Jesus's birth, he was called Lord, Savior, Redeemer, and Liberator, as well as Divine, Son of God, God, God from God.

Most of the people conquered by Rome ultimately came to believe that Rome and Augustus ruled by divine right and imperial divinity. For that reason, Augustus cannot be characterized as a tyrant or dictator, titles he eschewed. He was a staunch advocate of traditional Roman religion and piety. In his *Res Gestae Divi Augusti*, he recounted how he restored previously neglected temples in Rome. He was concerned with public morali-

ty, strengthening marriage (especially the father's control), encouraging procreation (by the Roman elite), and restricting immoral behavior (contaminations ascribed to eastern lands). On the latter point he was notably unsuccessful, eventually banishing his own daughter Julia for adultery. But on the whole, Augustus left Rome a cleaner, safer, and wealthier city. He covered it with marble, which jump-started an empirewide marble trade; he maintained its sewers and aqueducts, which other cities imitated; and he entertained the masses with spectacles that the world would learn to crave.

Augustus transformed Rome and shaped the provinces into a more cohesive empire. In part this was accomplished by making the city a more suitable capital for the provinces, and in part by making the provinces more Roman and akin to the city. At Augustus's death in 14 CE, he had outdone Alexander, having not only conquered the world but organized it

into an empire that his successors would rule for centuries to come, until Christianity ultimately triumphed in the fourth century CE. Much more than Alexander and his successors, Augustus used cities to pacify conquered subjects and urban life to unify diverse peoples into one "globalized" Roman Empire. Colonies, controlled by veterans but absorbing locals, were planted all across the Mediterranean, including the key New Testament sites of Corinth in Greece and Pisidian Antioch in Turkey. Existing cities, including poleis founded by Alexander and his successors, were reshaped into tools of Romanization. The ruins of those cities are, for sure, the single largest artifacts that archaeologists use to understand Roman rule. Excavations at ancient urban sites across the empire show their functional and ideological purposes. Cities were administrative centers for supervising the production and distribution of local and regional resources. That, of course, meant taxes flowing back to Rome. But Roman cities also built communities by creating, for the empire's urban population, a common form of civic life in which urban amenities seduced the populace into complicity. And that, of course, meant loyalty flowing back to Rome.

The Augustan revolution encompassed religion, culture, literature, and especially architecture. In all cities from the Roman period excavated by archaeologists, styles and materials conform to a basic pattern that Augustus had fashioned in Rome. These

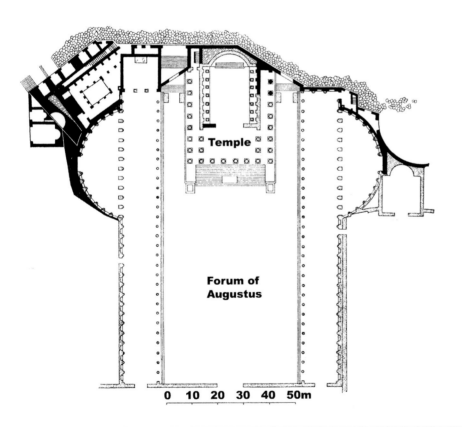

Temple

Forum of Augustus

0 10 20 30 40 50m

"In those days a decree went out from Emperor Augustus that all the world should be registered."

LUKE 2:1

opposite page

Prima Porta Statue (1st C. BCE)

this page

Coin of Augustan Temple (40–39 CE)

Plan of Augustan Forum

The god Augustus stands supreme in this statue found at Rome's Prima Porta. Riding a dolphin at his feet is Cupid, pointing to Augustus's mythological descent from Venus/Aphrodite, and the so-called hip-cloak stance and bare feet are iconographic references to divinity. The center of his cuirass, or breastplate, depicts the return of the Roman standards by a submissive Parthian.

The Augustan Forum in Rome was a spectacular architectural feat that focused on the Temple of Mars Ultor, dedicated by Augustus to the god of revenge, who aided him in defeating the murderers of Julius Caesar. This coin shows what that temple might have looked like, and includes an inscription of the Divine Augustus (*Divo Aug*).

styles showed a predilection for facades, such as frescoes on walls, mosaics on floors, or especially marble all over. They also featured urban planning that stressed regularity and order, and structures that reinforced the social hierarchy. And above all, the placement of structures and open spaces focused attention on monuments dedicated to or accentuating Roman rule.

Roman-style urban architecture spread all over the empire; it is found in Israel at places like Caesarea and Jerusalem, and to some extent in Galilee at places like Sepphoris and Tiberias. In addition to these styles, the content of Roman urbanization included the imperial cult and what might be called the cult of luxury. The omnipresent imperial cult, with its mix of temples, inscriptions, and statues, highlighted the divinity of Augustus and his successors. It was the physical and visible expression of local gratitude for the blessings of the *Pax Romana* as well as a demand for imperial allegiance. It homogenized the upper classes all across the empire, but in Jewish lands the imperial cult was remarkably restrained or altogether lacking. Rome by and large tolerated the uniqueness of Jewish monotheism, and its high priests were not required to sacrifice *to* Caesar as citizens were elsewhere. In a lenient compromise, their prayers *for* Caesar sufficed.

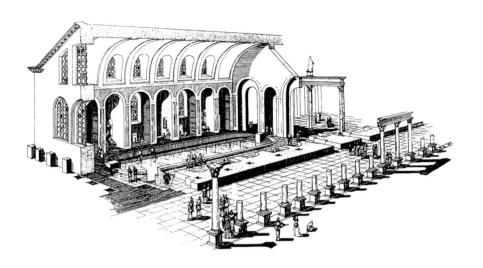

Accompanying the imperial cult is archaeological evidence for the Roman love of luxury. Daily comforts were brought to city-dwellers everywhere in the form of flowing water, maintained sewage, public latrines, and especially public baths. And weekly entertainment, whether music or plays in the theater, blood sports or spectacles in amphitheaters, or horse racing in hippodromes, gave inhabitants something to look forward to and relief from daily burdens. We will see later that metaphors from such Roman-style sports and games permeate even the letters of Paul.

The spread of the imperial cult and the pervasiveness of luxury owe much to Augustus's vision, which was never limited to the city of Rome but always extended to the broader Mediterranean world. Although he started ruling as the young Octavian just when Rome had conquered the world, at the time of his death he was the world's emperor who just happened to rule from Rome. During Augustus's lifetime, much more than under Alexander's Hellenizing successors, a cosmopolitan empire was forged; the cities of the world became one, and that made it possible for Christians like Paul to move from city to city with remarkable ease, and for Christians in one city to share a set of common concerns with Christians in another city. The Gospel of Luke, for example, would appeal equally to Corinthian

Christians and to Ephesian Christians and to Alexandrian Christians.

THE HERODIAN CLIENT KINGS

One way that Augustus governed outlying territories was through client kings — local nobles who ruled in his stead and on his behalf. They kept the peace, funneled taxes to Rome, and moved their people steadily into the Roman cultural orbit. They understood local customs better than any Roman official could; they could anticipate problems and avert tensions. One of Augustus's most trusted client kings was Herod the Great, who ruled from 40 to 4 BCE over what had been the Hasmonean kingdom, located between two key Roman provinces, Egypt and Syria. This, incidentally, is King Herod of Matthew's Christmas story and not the Herod (Antipas, the son of Herod the Great) who participated in Jesus's trial. Herod the Great's father was a convert to Judaism from Idumea who served as an official in the Hasmonean court and consistently favored Rome during the lengthy dynastic disputes among the Hasmoneans. In 40 BCE Herod petitioned the Senate to become king of the Jews, a title they granted him, but it took him another three years of fighting from northern Galilee to southern Judea to subdue resistance and take control of his kingdom. Rome had in him a reliable partner and friend who,

along with his descendants, would exert an enormous influence on the world of the New Testament.

Herod the Great became one of antiquity's most prolific builders, and his projects dominate Israel's archaeological landscape to this day. He combined architectural elements of his Hasmonean predecessors, aspects of the Hellenistic poleis that stood nearby, and especially Roman technology and style. Thanks to the careful archaeological dating of his buildings, we know much about how his rule over the Jews unfolded. Herod first built several fortress palaces, including the oasis compound at Jericho, the terraced palace at Masada, and an enormous palace and man-made mound called the Herodium that was to be his mausoleum. These sites show both his opulence and his paranoia, and were built as much with luxury as with security in mind.

After he was secure in his rule, Herod the Great embarked on two immense projects in the twenties BCE that absorbed his energies and have engaged archaeologists' efforts for years since: the port city of Caesarea and the Temple Mount in Jerusalem. Caesarea Maritima (as it is called today to distinguish it from the Caesarea of Herod's son Philip) opened Herod's kingdom to the wider Mediterranean world and oriented it geographically, culturally, politically, and commercially toward Rome. Later

opposite page

Aqueduct (Caesarea Maritima)

this page

Reconstruction of Baths (Ankyra, Turkey)
Coin of Herod the Great (40–4 BCE)

"What have the Romans ever done for us?" Plenty, most of its subjects would say. Rome seduced the urban inhabitants of newly conquered territories into compliance with Roman rule by building high-level aqueducts, as here at Caesarea in Israel, that brought fresh running water to city-dwellers who used it for fountains, sewage, and public baths. By the end of the first century CE, even cities like Ankyra, in the remote province of Galatia, had spectacular public baths, and citizens became accustomed to daily baths that alternated between hot, warm, and cold water.

The king of the Jews, Herod the Great, avoided putting his representation on coins. Instead of his own profile, Herod (40–4 BCE) preferred to represent his helmet, topped by a star and flanked by two palm branches, as a way to avoid offending the populace with an image of himself.

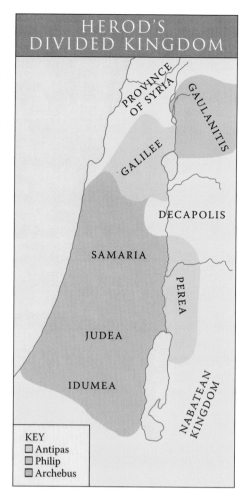

KEY
☐ Antipas
☐ Philip
☐ Archebus

kings, though he and later Roman governors, including Pontius Pilate, controlled that office through collaborating families of suitable lineage. The Temple was such an enormous undertaking that Herod did not finish it before his death in 4 BCE. In fact, it was not completed during Jesus's lifetime, a generation later, but only barely before the Romans destroyed it in 70 CE.

These two projects, Caesarea and the Temple Mount, point to Herod's schizophrenia as both Roman client-king and king of the Jews. That uneasy coexistence between pagan Rome and Jewish Jerusalem continued after Herod the Great's death in 4 BCE, around the time Jesus was born. But Jesus would live his adult life in the territory inherited by Herod's son Antipas, the northern district of Galilee. Herod the Great's kingdom was divided among three of his surviving sons — he had killed many others — with the eldest, Archelaus, inheriting Judea and Samaria, Philip receiving the Gentile areas to the north, and the younger son Antipas obtaining Jewish Galilee and Perea on the other side of the Jordan. It was in a Perean fortress called Machaerus, according to the Gospels, that Herod Antipas watched his step-daughter Salome dance and then beheaded John the Baptist.

Shortly after Herod the Great's death, Roman legions from Syria quelled minor rebellions and disturbances in his former kingdom. The oldest son, Archelaus, mismanaged his territories, so Augustus exiled him to Gaul in 6 CE and put Judea and Samaria under the direct control of a Roman procurator, who ruled from Caesarea and answered to the Roman governor in Syrian Damascus. From then on, the southern portion of Palestine would be occupied by Roman troops, though not by a full legion and probably not by many Italian-born soldiers. Italian-born soldiers were not permanently stationed in Galilee until after the Jewish Revolt in 66–70 CE, and were a rare sight in Herod Antipas's lands. Augustus did not cede Archelaus's lands to his brother Antipas, who had sought them as well as his father's title of king of the Jews. Antipas instead had to settle for a tetrarchy (literally, a quarter-

many Christians, including Paul, would set sail from this port to spread Christianity abroad. Herod named the city after his patron, Caesar Augustus, and he named the spectacularly engineered harbor Sebastos, Greek for Augustus or "the revered one." Built on an orthogonal grid, the master plan included a theater, an amphitheater, and a hippodrome to entertain his subjects. When ships entered the harbor, they faced an imposing temple dedicated to the goddess Roma and the god Augustus, to which all roads inside the city also led. Herod built similar temples in Samaria and at Banias, which would later become known as Caesarea Philippi.

But Herod the Great built these temples to the imperial cult in areas not heavily populated by Jews. For them, Herod enlarged the Temple complex in Jerusalem into one of the largest sacred precincts of the ancient world. (In chapter 5 we look in detail at the Temple Mount that Herod built and Jesus visited, with its imposing facade, which dominated Jerusalem's cityscape.) But Herod did not offend Jewish sensibilities by appointing himself high priest, as had the Hasmonean

kingdom) and the title tetrarch (quarter-king), which left him less wealthy than his father and less able to undertake building projects. He nevertheless inched his territory toward the Roman urban ideal, as he rebuilt at the beginning of his rule the city of Sepphoris, and founded in the middle of his rule a city on the Sea of Galilee that he named Tiberias, after Augustus's successor, Caesar Tiberius. Like his father, Antipas had to balance the demands of being a Roman client with ruling an overwhelmingly Jewish population. He balanced that by selectively adopting aspects of Roman urbanism at Sepphoris and Tiberias, such as facades, axiality, and order, but without any signs of the imperial cult.

That was the context for Jesus's life and ministry in Galilee. The region had been settled by Hasmonean Jews, who had resisted but could not quite overcome Hellenizing tendencies, and though Roman power loomed all around Galilee, no Roman troops occupied it, nor did Roman officials directly control it. But their client-tetrarch, Herod Antipas, who did

"But when [Joseph] heard that Archelaus was ruling over Judea in place of his father Herod, he was afraid to go there."

MATTHEW 2:22

directly control it, introduced Roman urban life, which in some ways was Hellenization repackaged as Romanization, into Jewish Galilee. Within the confines of tiny Galilee, Jesus crafted his message of the kingdom of God, ate and healed, taught and listened, and attracted an audience that would eventually change the world as much as either Alexander or Augustus had.

this page

Terraced Palaces (Masada, Israel)

Fresco in Northern Palace (Masada)

Herod the Great's spectacular terraced palace perches on the northern cliffs of his fortress Masada, overlooking the Dead Sea. On the lowest terrace, Herod built a triclinium, or dining room, with spectacular fresco panels and faux columns to mimic the grand banquet halls of Rome. Excavators there found jars once filled with the finest wine, along with elegant imported *terra sigillata* plates and cups.

MARITIMA: KING HEROD'S DREAM

The enormous ruins of Caesarea spread over an area of 250 acres along the western seashore of Israel. Once the site of a small Phoenician port named Straton's Tower, Herod the Great founded the city of Caesarea in construction lasting from 22 to 10 BCE, and the city reached its zenith in the Byzantine period. Its population later declined, and it was deserted after the Arab conquest in the seventh century CE. Crusaders disassembled much of the center city to build a moat and fort with the available ashlar blocks and columns, which has greatly frustrated archaeologists and made Herod's temple platform virtually indistinguishable.

Sporadic finds of sculptural fragments and scattered columns on the surface hinted at Caesarea's greatness, but the first systematic excavations were only undertaken in 1959 by the Italian Missione Archeologica. Working around the theater, whose semicircular cavity protruded from the sand, they found a Pontius Pilate inscription on the back of a stone turned upside down and used as a seat. In 1971 a consortium of North American universities formed the Joint Expedition to Maritime Caesarea, which excavated for twelve seasons across the site in an effort to trace the grid plan of the original Herodian city. Beginning in 1979, the Hebrew University in Jerusalem excavated a seaside palace on the southern shore that once belonged to Herod the Great and later to the Roman procurator. More recently, the Combined Caesarea Excavations have conducted semiautonomous but cooperative ventures on both sea and

land. This most recent work includes an examination of the construction and maintenance techniques of the original harbor, the warehouses along the harbor — one of which was converted into a shrine to the god Mithras — the Hippodrome inside the city, and the temple platform dedicated to Augustus and Roma.

The artifacts found at Caesarea fill storerooms and warehouses of the Israel Antiquities Authority, and many must be ignored in an effort to

Caesarea is mentioned in the New Testament only in the Acts of the Apostles. There it is described as the location of the apostle Philip's preaching (8:40; his home in 21:8), Peter's conversion of the centurion Cornelius (10:1, 24; 11:11), Herod Agrippa's death (12:19–23), and Paul's travels (9:30; 18:22; 21:8, 16) and imprisonment (23:23, 33; 25:1, 4, 6, 13).

convey some sense of the whole and give some sense of the site during the New Testament era. What is perhaps most clear is the pervasiveness of Roman urban architectural styles at Caesarea. An enormous number of mosaic floors, frescoed walls, and marble columns or veneers have been found there over the years. Although the rate at which marble was used accelerated in the second century CE, its use in the first century made Caesarea one of the earliest cities to mimic Roman preference for marble. Further, the orthogonal layout imposed by Herod the Great instilled a sense of order into visitors, and vistas highlighted propagandistic structures like the temple to Augustus and Roma, which was raised on a platform slightly off-grid to face ships coming into the harbor. Other evidence for the imperial cult includes the Pontius Pilate inscription, which records his dedication of a *Tiberium,* a structure to hon-

or Augustus's successor, Tiberius. Roman urban amenities also emerge from the ruins of Caesarea: an aqueduct brought ample freshwater from miles away, the public was entertained

with a theater and hippodrome inside an entertainment zone in the city's southern portion, and two amphitheaters outside the city walls have been discovered.

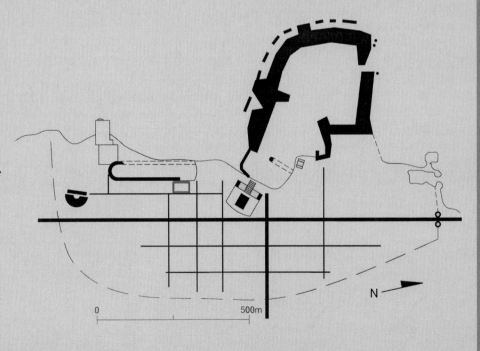

0   500m

N

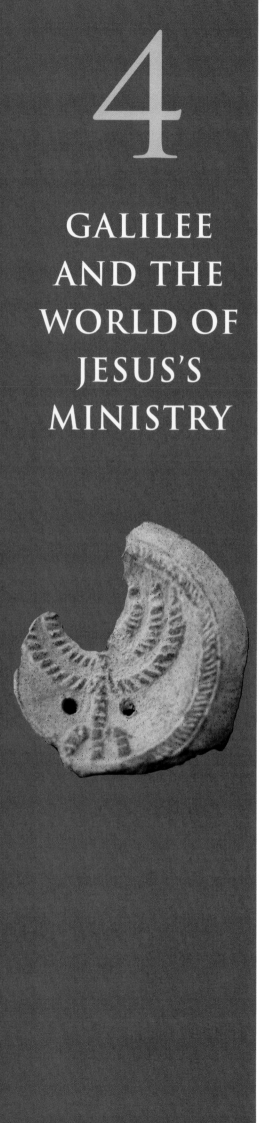

4

GALILEE AND THE WORLD OF JESUS'S MINISTRY

Alexander the Great was born in Macedonia, studied in Athens, and then sliced through the Persian Empire, all the way to the Himalayan Mountains. Augustus was born in Rome, fought in Greece, and sailed the Mediterranean from Spain to Syria. But Jesus was local. He lived his life in Galilee, an area some twenty-five miles across. He moved inside this region from the small hamlet of Nazareth in central Galilee to the larger village of Capernaum on the northwest shore of the Sea of Galilee. And though he occasionally crossed into neighboring territories, his only lengthy trip was the fateful journey to Jerusalem, about a week's walk away.

Jesus was a Galilean, and Galilean archaeology is the focus of this chapter. Excavations and surveys show that Galilee at the time of Jesus was overwhelmingly Jewish and just beginning to experience the effects of Hellenization and Romanization in a significant way. Herod the Great's son Antipas, who ruled Galilee from 4 BCE to 39 CE, adapted aspects of Hellenistic culture and Roman urban forms when he rebuilt the city of Sepphoris in 4 BCE and founded the city of Tiberias in 19 CE. But though excavations at each site show that he cautiously avoided overtly pagan elements that would offend Jewish sensibilities, the new economy that accompanied the construction of these cities made an impact on Galilee that is clearly reflected in Jesus's teachings. The overall population increased, as did agricultural production and small-scale manufacturing. But much of the wealth generated by that urbanization accumulated in the hands of the few Galilean elites connected with Antipas, who lived in the cities or large towns. The differences between the haves and have-nots increased, and Antipas's kingdom-building served as a foil for Jesus's proclamation of the kingdom of God.

THE TERRITORY AND TERRAIN OF JESUS'S GALILEE

Galilee was on the fringe of the Roman Empire, both geographically and politically. Herod the Great's territory was important by virtue of its position between two crucial Roman provinces — Egypt, which served as Rome's breadbasket, and Syria, whose legions kept the Parthian Empire in check. After Herod the Great's death, sixteen-year-old Antipas received the territory of Galilee, which did not yet have a city of consequence and had been neglected by Herod the Great's extensive building program.

The topography of Galilee fostered its marginality. In the centuries leading up to Jesus's birth, it lacked any sizeable site because there were busier trade routes and more arable land in neighboring regions. The major trade routes of antiquity had always skirted Galilee, with one, the Via Maris, running along the coast and connecting a series of port cities, including Ashdod, Ptolemais, and Tyre, and another, the King's Highway, running along the eastern side of the Jordan River through the caravan cities of Petra, Philadelphia, and Gerasa. Hills make north-south travel through Galilee cumbersome, but east-west valleys contained some minor roads in Jesus's time. Sturdy, well-constructed Roman-style roads dotted with mile-markers would not cross Galilee until the second century CE.

Topographically, Galilee is divided into three distinct regions, which to some degree shaped the social and cultural characteristics of their inhabitants. To the north, Upper Galilee is a hilly region. Some ancient texts call it

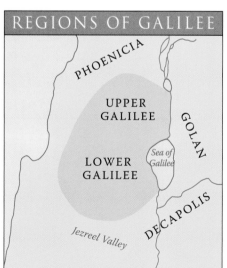

REGIONS OF GALILEE

PHOENICIA

UPPER GALILEE

GOLAN

LOWER GALILEE

Sea of Galilee

DECAPOLIS

Jezreel Valley

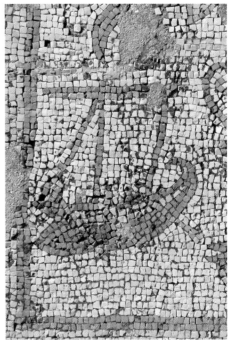

> "...he left Nazareth and made his home in Capernaum by the sea...[in] Galilee of the Gentiles."
>
> MATTHEW 4:13–15

Tetrakomia, Greek for "four villages" (though which four is uncertain), an indication that it was even more of a hinterland than the rest of Galilee. Trade and travel were arduous because of steep hills; in the absence of large fertile plains, the slopes were mostly used for vineyards and olive trees. The region produced much olive oil, sought after by Jews in the diaspora, who valued its production by Jews attuned to purity concerns. But olive oil was about the only export from Upper Galilee in the Roman period.

opposite page

Menorah on a Lamp (Sepphoris, 3rd c. CE)
Coin of Mattathias (40–37 BCE)

this page

Galilean Valley
Boat on Mosaic (Tabgha, 5th c. CE)
Plain of Ginnosar

"Galilee of the Gentiles" is a term used by the prophet Isaiah (9:1) and repeated by the Gospel of Matthew (4:15–16). But archaeological excavations in and around Galilee show that the Galileans were Jewish, not a mixed blend of Gentiles. Galilee was overwhelmingly Jewish at the time of Jesus, and the Hasmonean *prutot* is the coin most often found there, like this one minted by Mattathias Antigone (40–37 BCE). The menorah on this disk-shaped lamp from the Middle Roman period at Sepphoris is a reminder that even the cities were mostly inhabited by Jews, even though Gentile cities encircled Galilee.

The Sea of Galilee made fishing an important industry, one that was heavily taxed and controlled at the time of Jesus. Most boats looked like this depiction of a small sailboat from Tabgha, found on a mosaic in a church commemorating Jesus's multiplication of the loaves and fishes.

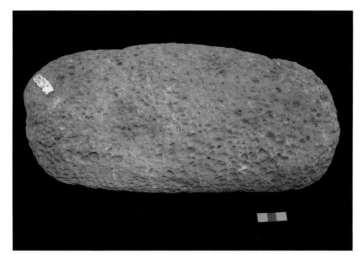

Lower Galilee is characterized by four valleys running east-west, with less imposing hills. The largest of those valleys, the Beth Netofa, had rich, fertile soil, was well watered after winter rainfalls, and produced the kind of high-yield crops from summer through fall that could support an urban population. A road ran along the Beth Netofa, connecting the Sea of Galilee with the Mediterranean port and pagan city of Ptolemais. Not surprisingly, Antipas located his first capital overlooking this valley at Sepphoris, where earlier the Hasmoneans had built a fortress and administrative center that served a modest population. The geological formations in Lower Galilee and especially around Sepphoris are mostly limestone, which is relatively easy to quarry into building blocks that harden with exposure to the sun, making it an ideal mate-

rial for large-scale construction projects. Just over the hill from Sepphoris, only four miles away, was Jesus's hometown of Nazareth. Since Lower Galilee tended to be more active with travel and trade, it was exposed to more outside influences, and more Greek appears in inscriptions discovered there than in Upper Galilee, though these influences should not be exaggerated at the time of Jesus.

The third region around the Sea of Galilee is volcanic, characterized by

basalt stones that are porous and harder to shape, making construction somewhat cumbersome as well as producing unattractive dark gray structures. The soil in this region is full of potato- to football-sized rocks and boulders that make plowing almost impossible. Arduous work over decades, if not generations, has cleared strips in terraces across portions of the slopes around the Sea of Galilee, many of which go back to the time of Jesus. The volcanic soil on these slopes, how-

Archaeological Periods in Galilee

Iron II	1000–733 BCE
Iron III	733–586 BCE
Persian	586–332 BCE
Early Hellenistic	332–167 BCE
Late Hellenistic	167–63 BCE
Early Roman	63 BCE–135 CE
Middle Roman	135–250 CE
Late Roman	250–363 CE
Byzantine	363–640 CE

These archaeological periods are based on a combination of historical events and archaeological phenomena. For example, the Hellenistic periods are delineated by Alexander's march through Palestine (332 BCE), Antiochus Epiphanes's rule (167 BCE) and Pompey the Great's visit to Jerusalem (63 BCE). Many scholars prefer to call the Early Roman period the Herodian period, since Herod left more of a mark in the archaeology, and they date it from 40 BCE to 70 CE. The Roman period in Galilee ended with a massive earthquake in 363.

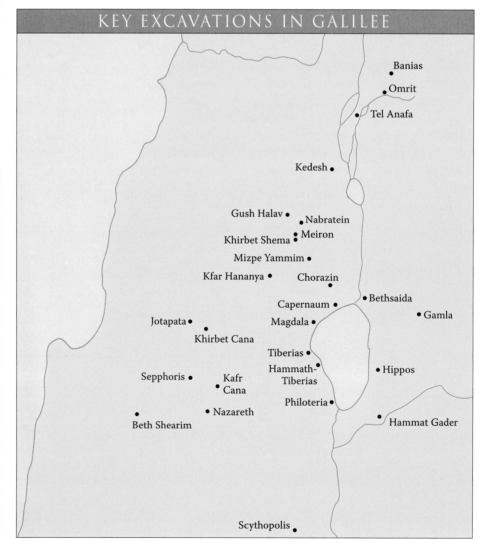

KEY EXCAVATIONS IN GALILEE

Banias
Omrit
Tel Anafa
Kedesh
Gush Halav • Nabratein
Khirbet Shema • Meiron
Mizpe Yammim
Kfar Hananya • Chorazin
Capernaum • Bethsaida
Jotapata • Magdala • Gamla
Khirbet Cana
Tiberias
Hammath-
Sepphoris • Kafr Tiberias • Hippos
Cana
Philoteria
Nazareth
Beth Shearim Hammat Gader

Scythopolis

by the Decapolis cities of Hippos, Gadara, and Gerasa.

Although not technically part of Galilee and never under Antipas's control, parts of the Golan just east of the Jordan and the Sea of Galilee were dotted with Jewish villages and towns, including Gamla, a site that has been extensively excavated, as well as Bethsaida-Julias on the eastern bank of the Jordan River. The latter site was home to several of Jesus's disciples, according to the Gospels, and archaeologists suggest it had a more cosmopolitan flavor as a result of its mix of pagans and Jews, but in all likelihood its more Hellenized character came only after Herod Philip renamed the village Julias in 30 CE, in honor of Caesar Tiberius's mother, Livia Julia. Herod Philip, whom the ancient Jewish historian Josephus considered a fair ruler, built a palace and administrative center just north of Galilee at Caesarea Philippi, which archaeologists have worked on for decades.

> "And you, Capernaum, will you be exalted to heaven? No, you will be brought down to Hades."
>
> LUKE 10:15

opposite page

Basalt Grindstone (Sepphoris, 1st c. CE)
Olive Press (Chorazin, 4th c. CE)

this page

Capernaum Synagogue Ruins (1838)
The Site of Magdala

The Mediterranean triad of olive oil, wine, and grains provided the basic sustenance for Galileans. One of the main activities in village courtyards was grinding grain into flour with dark stone grinders made of rough basalt. Upper Galilee was well known for its fine olive oil, which was produced in small industrial facilities or shared village presses.

"Desolate and mournful" is how the American explorer Edward Robinson described the site of Tell Hum, which he identified as Capernaum in 1838. Since then, Franciscan excavators have worked at the site for the better part of the twentieth century.

The ruins of Mary's Magdala lie on the western shore of the Sea of Galilee. In all likelihood, Mary Magdalene was from Migdal, Aramaic for "tower." The Jewish historian Josephus refers to the town as Taricheae in Greek — akin to "Village of Dried Fish." Excavations carried out at the site under Franciscan supervision suggest it was modest in size and wealth during Jesus's time.

ever, is acidic and produces excellent wines. A deep and rich alluvial soil covers a strip along the Sea of Galilee's northwest shore, called the Ginnosar Plain, and here the hot and humid climate — this is some two hundred meters below sea level — resembles a greenhouse. The Jewish historian Josephus called it the most productive patch of land in Israel. The lake also supplied ample water and fish to nearby inhabitants, and created some trade opportunities with the mostly Gentile areas across the lake, lands controlled

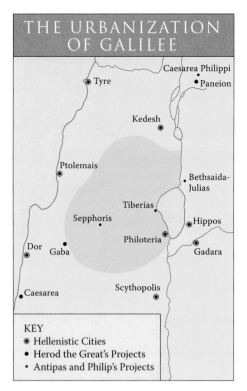

THE URBANIZATION OF GALILEE

Caesarea Philippi
Tyre
Paneion
Kedesh
Ptolemais
Bethsaida-Julias
Tiberias
Sepphoris
Hippos
Philoteria
Dor
Gaba
Gadara
Caesarea
Scythopolis

KEY
⊙ Hellenistic Cities
• Herod the Great's Projects
· Antipas and Philip's Projects

"Take no gold, or silver, or copper in your belts, no bag for your journey, or two tunics, or sandals, or a staff . . ."

MATTHEW 10:9–10

Jesus hailed from Nazareth in Lower Galilee, but most of the Gospels' stories about him center around the northwest shore of the Sea of Galilee, between Capernaum and Bethsaida, with most disciples coming from those two sites. His most prominent female disciple, Mary Magdalene, came from the town of Magdala, just a few miles south of Capernaum. Josephus calls Magdala by its Greek name, Taricheae, which means something like "Village of Dried Fish." Thus Jesus's ministry was situated near the water and in a border region, making it easy to quickly exit

". . . traveling with him and he has need of more four, deliver it to him.

Five artabs of groats.

[Regarding ten jars of foreign wine, which will have to be bought and given to him in Pelousion:] 'Leave the price blank'

Ten jars of home-grown [wine] from the Heliopolite nome to be presented to him there.

A half jar of honey 'at 3½ drachmas the chous' [about a gallon].

Oil, 'as much as sufficient'; one jar of sour wine 'costing 2 drachmas'; olives.

Pickled fish of all kinds and thrissa [a kind of fish] if there are any.

Pounded lentils."

Herod Antipas's territory, either by boat to the Decapolis or the adjacent domain of Herod Philip on the other side, or by foot along the Jordan River toward Upper Galilee and into the Huleh Valley, the district of Caesarea Philippi, areas with both Jewish settlements and Syro-Phoenician villages and towns.

THE ARCHAEOLOGY OF GALILEAN JUDAISM

Ironically, the initial excavations in Galilee during the early twentieth century, which sought to illuminate New Testament stories about Jesus, shed virtually no light on either Jesus or his world. Most every archaeologist who set out to uncover a New Testament site where Jesus had walked found only later Byzantine layers where Christian pilgrims had walked in the fourth, fifth, and sixth centuries CE. But that was all rather different from the first-century CE Jewish world of Jesus. It was not until the latter part of the twentieth century, when, paradoxically, most work in Galilee was directed by Jewish archaeologists and conducted at sites not mentioned in the New Testament, such as Gamla, Jotapata, and Sepphoris, that layers and artifacts were excavated from Jesus's first-century world, producing a serious archaeological contribution to understanding the world of the Gospels.

opposite page

Ruins of Gamla (Golan)

Zenon Papyrus (Egypt, 259 BCE)

this page

City Wall (Gamla)

Excavations at Scythopolis

Hippos of the Decapolis

The reliability of Josephus has often been questioned, but archaeological excavations at Gamla suggest that his account of the Roman siege there is relatively accurate. The wall was breached just about where Josephus claimed. Of course, other aspects of Josephus's narrative are still questionable, including his wildly exaggerated population figures and his theological claim that God was on Rome's side.

Officials traveled in style during a trip through Palestine in the third century BCE. The Ptolemaic official Zenon checked on commercial and agricultural accounts all around but not in Galilee, according to his itinerary, which included a visit to a palace belonging to Hellenized Jews at Iraq el-Emir. He traveled comfortably, as indicated by this papyrus from another trip, on which he expects to receive shipments of fine wine during his journey.

The cities of the Decapolis are frequently mentioned in the Gospels. These large pagan cities were right next to Galilee, including Hippos, just across the lake from Capernaum, and Scythopolis, south of Galilee near the Jordan River. The Gospels never say that Jesus and his disciples ever entered any of these Gentile cities; instead they went through the countryside controlled by them.

Those excavations make it clear that Galilee did not undergo the same kind of turmoil as Judea during the Maccabean Revolt. There were Hellenistic cities around Galilee but not inside Galilee; in fact, there is very little archaeological evidence at all from Galilee of the Hellenistic period, implying that it was sparsely inhabited before the arrival of the Hasmoneans in the late second century BCE. Other than a few small garrisons or way stations in places like Sepphoris, and scattered hamlets along the roads, not much was happening in Galilee, even after Alexander the Great, when surrounding Hellenistic cities like Kedesh, Ptolemais, Scythopolis, Gadara, and Gerasa were enjoying thriving economies and interregional trade. Confirmation for Galilee's third-century BCE insignificance is provided by the Zenon Papyri. This collection of over two thousand papyri dating between 261 and 240 BCE was discovered in Egypt. It preserves the records of a Ptolemaic official named Zenon, among them his itinerary through Palestine in 259 BCE, in which he disembarked at Straton's Tower, crossed the Jordan in the south, and then looped around Galilee, avoiding it entirely, presumably because it lacked profitable commercial and agricultural activity.

The picture in Galilee changes, however, toward the end of the Late Hellenistic period (167–50 BCE), with a dramatic increase in occupied sites. The architecture, pottery assemblages, and small finds in Galilee, however, are not like that of the neighboring areas, either the Iturean farmsteads to the northeast, the Syro-Phoenician towns and villages to the north and west, or the great Decapolis cities to the east and south. The Iturean settlements farther north were unwalled nucleated settlements of simple single-room buildings with open-air shrines made from erect stones. Their pottery was clumsily made in a distinctive brownish pink heavily tempered clay. Syro-Phoenician sites to the northwest and in the hinterland of port cities like Sidon, Tyre, and Ptolemais used pottery made with well-levigated clay in a pale buff color, spatter-painted wares, as well as *terra sigillata*, fine wares with a lustrous red slip that are generally absent in Galilee. They also used low-standing ceramic braziers for cooking, amphorae with stamped handles for transporting wine, and miniature ointment vials called *unguentaria*.

To the east and south of Galilee was the Decapolis — a loose confederation of Hellenistic cities that Rome had assembled to administer the area south

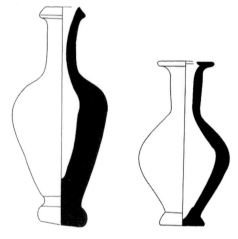

of Syria, which included Scythopolis (the only city west of the Jordan) and the large polis of Gadara and the smaller Hippos, both of which had harbor facilities on the Sea of Galilee. The Decapolis cities were built with the trappings of a Greco-Roman city, such as pagan temples, theaters, public baths, gates, and fountains, all set out on a rough grid and with due epigraphic or monumental honors to the Roman emperors. It is worth noting that whenever the Gospels mention Jesus journeying to the Decapolis, they describe him and his disciples only traveling "to the region" of the Decapolis, and never inside any city.

The material culture inside Galilee from the early first century BCE on, however, is very different from these

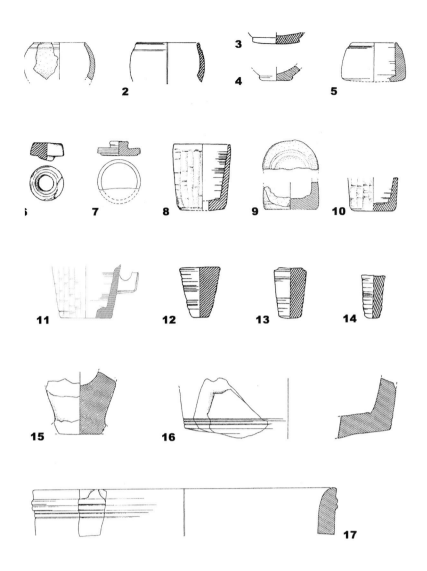

surrounding areas but remarkably similar to Judea and Jerusalem. The presence of many Hasmonean coins, especially those minted by Alexander Jannaeus, points to Galilee's close connection with Judea, whose inhabitants used these small bronze *prutot* for everyday purchases. The Galilean pottery is also similar to that in Judea; though made of local clay, Galilean cooking pots, jars, and jugs are shaped the same. And just like Judea, Galilee had very few imports in the Late Hellenistic period, pointing to

"For the Pharisees, and all the Jews, do not eat unless they thoroughly wash their hands, thus observing the tradition of the elders . . ."

MARK 7:3

opposite page

Ointment Vials (Israel, 1st c. BCE)

Glass Drawings (Tel Anafa, Israel)

this page

Stone Vessels Drawings

Stone Vessel Fragment (1st c. CE)

Ritual Bath (Jericho, 1st c. BCE)

Expensive perfumes and ointments were kept in small glass or ceramic vials, called unguentaria by archaeologists. While very common in the Gentile areas around Galilee, they are almost entirely absent from Galilee around the time of Jesus.

"And purity broke out in Israel" is how the Jewish Mishnah describes the interest in purity around the time of Jesus. Archaeologists have found fragments of stone vessels everywhere in Galilee, in almost every house excavated. Similarly, stepped, plastered pools for ritual bathing are found at most Jewish sites in Galilee and Judea, like this one excavated at Jericho.

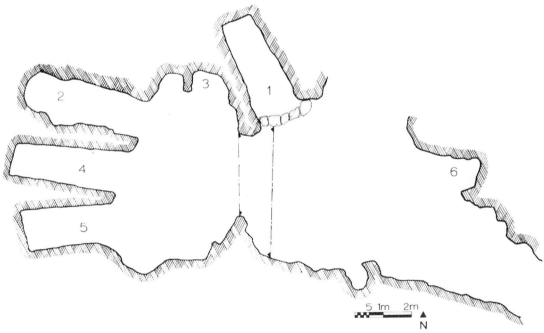

its conservatism and relative isolation. But most importantly, there are four features that recur in excavations at Galilean villages, towns, and cities from the first centuries BCE and CE that also occur in Judea and that are characteristic of Judaism: stone vessels, plastered and stepped pools for ritual bathing, the absence of pork in the diet, and burial in underground shaft tombs.

Stone vessels are made from soft, chalky limestone that is quarried near the surface across Galilee and fashioned into mugs, cups, jars, and lids. Most common are hand-carved mugs with distinctive chisel facets on the outside and one or two handles. These are often called "measuring cups" but in fact lack any uniformity and were probably not used for measurements. Somewhat rare are the enormously

large jars manufactured on large lathes powered by two men. Stone vessels are ubiquitous in Early Roman strata at Galilean sites, and more telling, they have been documented in every house from carefully excavated sites. Rabbinic texts connect them with Jewish concerns for ritual purity, describing them as impervious to impurity. Even lids made of stone kept a ceramic vessel's contents ritually clean. The New Tes-

state, one washes in appropriate water and waits an allotted period of time. Whether the mugs, cups, and jars were used for hand-washing, storing liquids, or drinking is uncertain, and whether the *mikvaoth* represent priestly purity concerns, Pharisee-inspired purity practices, or more widespread purity concerns is difficult to determine from archaeology alone. In fact, stone vessels and *mikvaoth* illustrate a limitation of archaeology: their use and meaning cannot be determined by material analysis alone. At the very least, though, they

> "Now the woman was a Gentile, of Syrophoenician origin. She begged [Jesus] to cast the demon out of her daughter."
>
> MARK 7:26

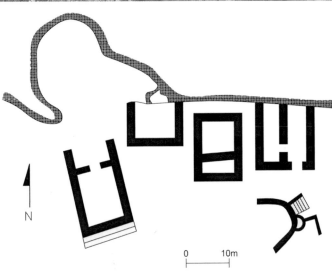

tament seems to connect them to the Pharisees, but Pharisees were not the only ones who used them, judging by how widespread they are in the archaeological record.

Also tied to ritual purity are the plastered stepped pools that have been uncovered in Roman strata in Galilee, the Golan, and Judea (in Hebrew, *mikveh*, plural *mikvaoth*). There are many around the Temple in Jerusalem and at Qumran, locations with pronounced purity concerns. In Galilee, smaller pools are found inside the private houses of the wealthy at cities like Sepphoris, where over thirty have been excavated. In rural areas and villages, they are often larger and perhaps public, like the one found at Gamla near an olive press and synagogue. Jewish scriptures prescribe ritual bathing in "living water," meaning a natural body of water, and rainwater collected in a carved-out and plastered pool seems to do the trick. We should stress that in Judaism, impurity is not equivalent to sin or a moral lapse. From the literary sources, we know that contact with a corpse, blood, or semen — which we might think of as either death-generating or life-giving materials — made people impure. They then could not approach priests or the Temple. To return to a pure

opposite page
Rolling Stone at Tomb (Nazareth)
Tomb Complex (Merion, Israel)
this page
Cave of Pan (Caesarea Philippi)
Plan of Temples (Caesarea Philippi)
Niche for Statue (2nd C. CE)

This tomb in Nazareth dates to the time of Jesus and is exactly as one imagines the Gospels's accounts of the rolling stone at Jesus's burial. Jews typically laid out the dead in underground tombs designed for secondary burial, in which bones were gathered together a year later and placed in a pit or ossuary.

Pagans lived all around Galilee, whether in the Decapolis cities to the southeast or in Syro-Phoenician cities northwest. Jesus's travels on the periphery of Galilee, such as through Caesarea Philippi, brought him into occasional contact with non-Jews, according to the Gospels.

indicate a Jewish population, a point confirmed by their absence in neighboring areas, such as the Gentile Decapolis or Samaria or towns along the coast. We must presume that Jesus's debates with the Pharisees over purity were not a matter that only interested the Pharisees; purity concerns were common to all Jews in Galilee.

Galilee's Jewishness is also indicated by its faunal remains and burial practices. The many animal bones discarded as kitchen scraps or leftovers at Roman-period sites in Galilee show a clear avoidance of pork. Like Judeans, Galileans ate primarily sheep or goat, some fish, and rarely wild deer or gazelle, while their neighbors, like all Mediterranean peoples, preferred pork or wild boar. Galilean and Judean Jews also shared the practice of secondary burial in underground shaft tombs, as distinct from Roman cremation or Greek burial, in which the corpse is not redeposited. Jews in the late Second Temple period built room-sized underground chambers that had been cut out of the bedrock, with a small opening that was tightly covered to keep out scavenging animals. They laid the dead either in a shaft (in Hebrew, *kokh*) extending fingerlike from the wall or on an arch-covered ledge along a wall (in Greek, *arcosolium*). About a year later, after the flesh had decomposed, the family returned to the chamber either by opening a rectangular stone door or by rolling back a round stone, then gathered the bones together and deposited them in a pit, cut inside the chamber, with the bones of previous generations.

The pervasiveness of these patterns in both Galilee and Judea shows that the Galileans were Jews. Because these practices all take place within the private realm — that is to say, in spheres of life that individuals controlled and that were not at the mercy of decisions by the ruling elites, as were inscriptions or public buildings — we can be more secure in this conclusion. When we consider the oft-repeated biblical phrase "Galilee of the Gentiles," we should not envision that Jesus's Galilee was inhabited by many Gentiles. Rather, Galilee was inhabited by Jews but encircled by Gentiles. Some interaction between Jews and Gentiles would be expected, but that typically involved the crossing of boundaries and not a cosmopolitan coexistence within a site.

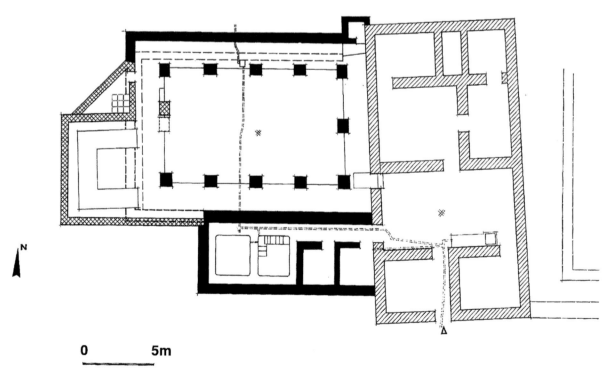

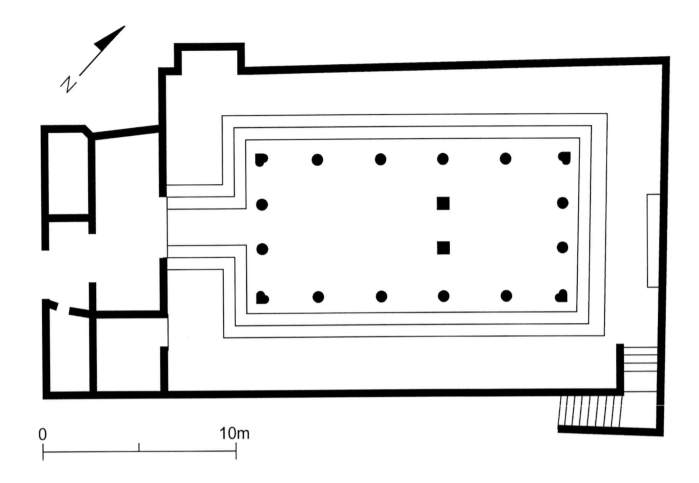

0   10m

SYNAGOGUES AT THE TIME OF JESUS?

Religious architecture also gives some indication of the Jewish identity of the Galileans. The absence of pagan temples in first-century CE Galilee is negative evidence for its Jewishness, especially in light of their prevalence all around Galilee, such as the temple to Augustus and Roma at Caesarea Maritima, the temple to Augustus at Sebaste, the Augusteum at Caesarea Philippi, the possibly imperial temple at Omrit, and the Temple of Dionysos in Scythopolis. Particularly noteworthy is the destruction of the pagan cult center at Mizpe Yammim in Upper Galilee in the Late Hellenistic period, presumably by the Hasmoneans, at the time Jews were settling the area.

Unfortunately, there is very little archaeological evidence in Galilee for Jewish synagogues from the time of Jesus, which is somewhat surprising given their ubiquity in the Gospels, like the synagogue at Capernaum where Jesus healed or the one at Nazareth where he taught. Not a single first-century CE synagogue has been discovered inside Galilee. Some have argued, unconvincingly, that a first-century CE wall underneath Capernaum's fifth-century CE synagogue belonged to the one mentioned in the Gospels, but this short row of foundation stones could be from a house or synagogue. Though numerous Galilean synagogues from the third through sixth centuries CE have been excavated, there are only five across all of Palestine that date to the first century CE, and none lies inside Galilee. The best-preserved synagogue was uncovered in nearby Gamla, which was destroyed by Roman legions in the first Jewish War. Two other first-century CE synagogues also date to that war; at Masada and the Herodium, rooms from earlier Herodian structures that were renovated by the Jewish zealots to serve as synagogues. Two other early synagogues were discovered in the 1990s, one at Qiryat Sefer to the west of Jerusalem and the other at Jericho, next to and perhaps even part of a Hasmonean palace complex.

None of these synagogues offer much information about religious aspects of first-century Judaism. There are no mosaics to interpret, no inscriptions to assess, and no clear symbolism from which to infer meaning. They were simple buildings with a room that served as a meeting hall, and were made of local stone using local building traditions. Next to the Gamla synagogue an inkwell was found, which may suggest some scribal activity at a school for studying the law, but we cannot be sure. The only architectural aspect they share are tiered benches along their walls, which suggests a community dynamic that was less hierarchical and more egalitarian than either the Jewish Temple in Jerusalem or pagan temples elsewhere. The structure at Gamla could seat around 150 on the benches, and another 100 or so could stand or sit in the center. The structures at Qiryat

opposite page

Capernaum Synagogue (5th C. CE)
Jericho Synagogue Plan (1st C. CE)

this page

Gamla Synagogue Plan (1st C. CE)

Synagogues from the time of Jesus are rare in the archaeological record. One of the best examples comes from Gamla in the Golan. Another likely synagogue, part of a Hasmonean palace, was found at Jericho. It might have been used for both religious and secular gatherings. But the synagogue at Capernaum dates to the fifth century CE and long after Jesus; the dark basalt foundation under it is not much earlier, though it is possible that a first-century CE synagogue lies underneath the present structure.

> "Look, those who put on fine clothing and live in luxury are in royal palaces."
>
> LUKE 7:25

Sefer and Jericho held half that many. We don't really know how cramped these synagogues would have felt, but we can be certain they would have been dark inside, since most such buildings lacked large windows like buildings today and the main source of light would have been many oil lamps.

The architecture of the first-century CE synagogue is so mundane and indistinct that archaeologists might have trouble distinguishing a synagogue from a building or house with a large room. It bears stressing that the Greek word *synagogue* at this time refers more to the gathering than the structure, and synagogues could have met also in a town square or a courtyard. In any case, first-century Jewish religion was dominated by the Temple in Jerusalem and not the synagogue.

ANTIPAS'S URBANIZATION AND PEASANT LIFE

Galilee changed when Herod Antipas took over after his father's death in 4 BCE. It had been a marginal part of Herod's kingdom, inhabited by Jews who themselves or their parents or grandparents had come from Judea. They lived in small hamlets like Nazareth with populations of around one hundred to four hundred, villages like Capernaum with populations around a thousand, or larger towns like Jotapata and Bethsaida with populations of two thousand to three thousand. They were overwhelmingly preoccupied with agriculture and, if they lived on the lake, fishing. But Herod Antipas rebuilt Sepphoris in 4 BCE and founded Tiberias in 19 CE, the first cities to be built inside Galilee. We cannot equate urban with pagan, city with Hellenization, however. Antipas's city-building did not infuse Galilee with Gentiles or pagans, nor did it excessively Hellenize or Romanize the Jewish inhabitants. Antipas was cautious, like his father had been in Jerusalem, of appearing too Hellenistic or too Roman, even as he adopted some of their architectural styles and materials. He named one city after the emperor Tiberius, but Antipas's coins were aniconic — they bore no portrait heads — and his cities contained no sculptures, no pagan temples, and no public baths or gymnasia, which had caused so many problems in Jerusalem over a century earlier. There was a theater and perhaps also a stadium at Tiberias for entertainment, but no signs of paganism have been found on or near them.

Those two cities nevertheless had an impact on Galilee, perhaps more socioeconomic than cultural or religious. The building of Sepphoris and Tiberias, coupled with moving rural and village Galileans to populate them, reconfigured the Galilean economy. Within a generation — the very generation of Jesus — there were suddenly

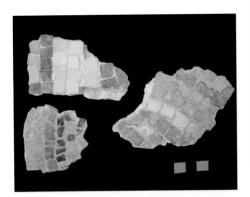

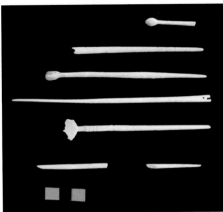

between eight thousand and twelve thousand people living in each city. Agrarian practices were intensified and economies of scale were created, and a more efficient means to collect taxes became necessary. Those economic developments might well account for the cycle of debt and foreclosure among the peasants and an increase in indentured servants, tenant farmers, and daily workers, not to mention the beggars and bandits that echo throughout Jesus's teaching in the Gospels.

At the same time, of course, more wealth was generated in Galilee than ever before, and the standard of living increased, mostly among the upper classes, as is apparent in the rise of luxury items concentrated mainly in the cities of Sepphoris and Tiberias, but which archaeologists have also found in large towns like Jotapata and Gamla. This wealth was acquired at the expense of the rural and village populations, whose standard of living and ability to acquire luxury goods could not keep pace with the cities. The new

wealth was unevenly distributed. The houses excavated on the western acropolis at Sepphoris, which clearly belonged to the Galilean urban elites, differ considerably from the houses excavated in villages like Capernaum.

At Sepphoris, for example, house walls were constructed with evenly shaped, regular-sized stone blocks called ashlars, and built upon solid bedrock and boulder foundations. They were two feet thick, built using the header-stretcher technique, which alternates between two rectangular ashlars positioned side by side with the longer side forming the wall's face (the stretcher), and a single ashlar placed with the shorter side forming the wall's face (the header). They could easily and probably did support a second story. Many rooms were covered with frescoes, though in *al secco* or dry fresco, a less complicated and cheaper technique that Romans would have scoffed at. The color scheme included the characteristic Pompeian red, and panels were painted with faux marble.

The ceilings were bordered with variously shaped moldings, and most floors were plastered, with a few covered in simple mosaics. Roofs were covered in terra-cotta tiles, which certainly made these houses distinct, even from great distances. Inside, there were some imports and luxury items, like *terra sigillata* pottery, molded glass, imported lamps, and a few ivory pins for hair and makeup applicators. In spite of having adopted so many Roman styles, the inhabitants of these wealthy houses refrained from displaying images, observed purity concerns — as the many stone vessels and *mikvaoth* indicate — and did not import wine from pagan areas.

opposite page

Coins of Antipas (28/29 CE)

Palace Floor (Tiberias, 1st C. CE)

Marble Fragments (Tiberias, 1st C. CE)

Fresco Fragment (Tiberias, 1st C. CE)

this page

Mosaic Fragments (Sepphoris)

Applicators and Hairpins (Sepphoris)

Fresco Fragments (Sepphoris)

Excavated Room (Sepphoris)

Herod's palace in Tiberias may have been found. This first-century CE room is one of a kind in Galilee, with a floor made of beautiful multicolored marble pieces imported from all over the Mediterranean, and walls covered in richly colored frescoes.

The wealthy of Sepphoris may not have had the extensive wealth of Herod Antipas, but they were not far behind. From this single room, whose walls were built by professional stonemasons, came frescoes, mosaic stones, bone or ivory hair needles, and makeup applicators.

These wealthy Galilean houses were not on a par with what has been excavated in the Italian cities of Pompeii and Herculaneum, but they were very different from those found in the towns, villages, and hamlets of Galilee. Walls there were mostly made of unhewn fieldstones, and the rounded basalt stones of the lake region made collapsing walls a regular occurrence. Smaller stones, mud, and clay were packed into the interstices between larger stones, and walls were not covered with white plaster or colored frescoes but simply smeared on the outside with mud or even dung and straw to add insulation. No tiles are found in first-century CE Galilean villages, so roofs must have been made with timber and reeds, with thick layers of clayish mud packed on top; occasional cylindrical roof-rollers made of a heavy stone have been found.

A boat discovered in the Sea of Galilee in 1986 sheds additional light on the socioeconomic status of Galileans in villages.

The construction and maintenance of this common fishing boat, found covered in mud when the sea level dropped during a drought, tell the remarkable story of the life of a fisherman on the Sea of Galilee. The dilapidated eight-by-twenty-six-foot boat had been stripped of its reusable parts sometime in the first century CE and then pushed offshore to sink. The hull had been kept together by a clever craftsman who lacked adequate materials. Originally, the boat was made from timbers salvaged from other boats and from inferior local woods like pine, jujube, and willow, which warped in water. The for-

"Then he stood over her and rebuked the fever, and it left her."

LUKE 4:39

ablanathanablanamacharamaracharamara[ch]

blanathanablanamacharamaracharama[ra]

l[a]nathanablanamacharamaracharamar

anathanablanamacharamaracharama

nathanablanamacharamaracharam

athanablanamacharamarachara

thanablanamacharamarachar

anablanamacharamaracha

nablanamacharamarach

ablanamacharamara

blanamacharamar

lanamacharama

anamacharam

namachara

amachar

macha

ach

a

". . . unwearied Kok Kouk Koul, keep Tais, whom Tar bore, from every chill, tertian or quartan or daily or occurring on alternate days or night fever [. . . because I am the father . . . Ko]k, Kouk, Koul."

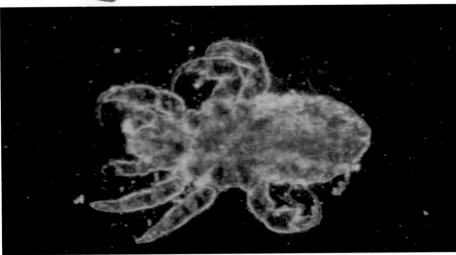

ered in a family tomb at the Upper Galilean site of Meiron, dating from the first century BCE to the fourth century CE. Of those, nearly half died before reaching eighteen, and of that half, 70 percent died before the age of five. In spite of living relatively close to the Sea of Galilee and its fishing industry, many of these teenagers, children, and infants suffered iron deficiencies. The adults' dental remains show a high rate of periodontal disease, and ground-down or missing molars suggest that bread and grain was their primary diet. They must have eaten very little meat. Most of the adults were short — the average man was 5'5" and the average woman 4'10" — and most had signs of arthritis in the hips, lower back, or shoulders, along with a high rate of fractured bones. All this indicates a life of hard work. The people of Galilee were, without being flippant about it, shorter with more crooked backs and atrophied limbs, more limps but fewer teeth, and many were anemic, susceptible to disease, slower to heal, and quicker to die.

The ancients coped with disease and death in various ways. The wealthy had the services of "doctors," who sold a variety of herbal, pharmaceutical, and what we would consider magical cures. Outright spells that got to the root of what the ancients thought was a spiri-

opposite page

"Jesus" Boat (Ginnosar, 1st C. CE)

Magical Papyrus (Egypt, 3rd C. CE)

this page

Gold Bridge (Italy, 4th C. BCE)

Louse (Israel, 1st C. CE)

The so-called Jesus Boat was discovered in the Sea of Galilee and caused quite a stir because it could seat twelve and an oarsman; comparisons to Jesus and the apostles were quick to follow. But the dilapidated boat is more important because it shows how hard Galilean fishermen had to work to keep their vessels afloat: plagued with inferior wood and inadequate materials, they reused scraps and nails from previous boats.

Ancient medicine and magic were probably indistinguishable to most people in antiquity. Lice, like this one found on a comb at the site of Qumran, presented a particularly nasty problem, as they spread diseases in antiquity. Although the very wealthy could afford some medical help, such as this set of fake teeth shaped into a golden bridge, the less fortunate had to rely on cures we consider magical, like this papyrus to cure a fever, which dates from the third century CE. The patient would repeatedly recite the magical word, dropping the first and last letter in each subsequent reading. This formed an inverted triangle that could also be read down one side and up the other.

ward keel was a piece of Lebanese cedar that had been used on an earlier boat whose joints were still visible. At some point the boat was beyond saving, and the owners stripped it of sail, anchor, and any reusable parts, such as nails and cedar wood, and pushed it out to sink. Fishermen worked hard to keep their vessels afloat; the need to patch, peg, and glue together boats made of inferior wood made constant repairs a way of life. Coupled with what archaeology tells us about the houses at places like Capernaum, it is clear that Antipas's urbanization did not elevate the standard of living for most Galileans. Thus, even though the Gospels say James and John's father hired servants in Capernaum to help with the catch (Mark 1:20), we should not imagine them as wealthy. He probably owned a modest house, a boat, and some nets, and occasionally hired a few day laborers who were worse off. But in general fishermen were a motley crew.

Life and health was, in Galilee and the whole ancient world, much more fragile than it is today. From skeletal remains and tomb inscriptions we know that the average life expectancy was somewhere in the twenties — the low twenties for women, who suffered the perils of childbirth. About every fourth birth resulted in a death, either of the mother or the child. Many diseases were common in the ancient world, including parasitic infections. Combs excavated in the dry climate at Masada and Qumran had an inordinate number of lice and lice eggs on them. Common infectious diseases included malaria, tuberculosis, and venereal and nonvenereal syphilis. The skin disease psoriasis was common, which also inflamed joints with arthritis and is probably the leprosy frequently mentioned in the New Testament (and not what modern medicine calls leprosy, or Hansen's Disease). In one case, the bones of nearly two hundred individuals were discov-

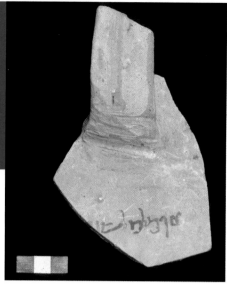

> "Jesus said to her, 'Mary!' She turned toward him and cried out in Aramaic, 'Rabbouni!' (which means Teacher)."
>
> JOHN 20:16

tual affliction were also common, and numerous papyri of the kind have been found in Egypt. Amulets could also be bought to ward off potential harm, and many crudely engraved cheap gems found by archaeologists served magical purposes. There was a fine line, perhaps even indistinguishable, between medicine and magic, science and the supernatural in the ancient world, and I suspect that in spite of Jewish monotheism, many Galileans turned to magic as a coping mechanism.

WHAT LANGUAGE DID JESUS SPEAK?

Though there is no evidence suggesting that Antipas introduced pagan or offensive Hellenistic practices into Galilee, the Greek language did make inroads there during his rule. The extent of Greek in Galilee during the first century has always been an important issue for students of Jesus and the Gospels, and the archaeological evidence presents a clear picture. But archaeologists do not simply tally the percentages of Greek, Aramaic, and Hebrew found on Galilean inscriptions and derive a linguistic profile. Instead, archaeologists look at each inscription's intended audience and date it using the stratigraphic context. The few inscriptions from Galilee and their relative infrequency point to Galilee's provincial character and show that Greek was just beginning to be used in Galilee at Jesus's time, alongside the more widespread Aramaic.

One inscription that illustrates the profile of Galilee is written on the handle of a jar used for storing olive oil, wine, or grain. Found at Sepphoris, the jar dates to the Late Hellenistic period and is inscribed with seven Hebrew/Aramaic letters in the standard Jewish square script used from the late second to early first century BCE.

Although the inscription is in the Aramaic language, commonly spoken since the Persian period by Jews — the first five letters spell out *epimelesh*, a transliteration of a Greek loanword, *epimeletes*, meaning "manager," "overseer," or what is used in inscriptions elsewhere for "office of the treasurer" or "tax collector." Thus this official of the Jewish community spoke Aramaic, wrote with the same letters used for sacred Hebrew biblical texts, but used a Greek term for his title, one that was also used in the Seleucid and Ptolemaic administrations. It points to an indigenous Jewish population that was beginning to borrow Greek terms for administrative purposes.

Three lead weights used for measuring in the agora, or market, of the Galilean cities show that Greek served as the official language, as do all the coins minted in the cities of Tiberias and Sepphoris. Two of the weights date to the first century CE and are likely from Tiberias, one of which names Agrippa II by the Greek title *agoranomos*, or "official of the market." The latest weight, from second-century Sepphoris, demonstrates the complex mix of cultures in Galilee. The inspectors have the Jewish names Simon son of Aionos and Justus (whose father's name is illegible), their title and the whole inscription is in Greek, but the weight is written in Greek as *hemi-litron* (a half-liter), which is derived from the Latin *libra*. These officials certainly still understood Aramaic, but the language of commerce and the ruling elite in Galilee was Greek.

In the first and second centuries CE, the few public inscriptions in Galilee were in Greek, but many burial inscriptions were bilingual — in Greek and either Aramaic or Hebrew. Greek had made considerable inroads into Sepphoris by the first century and continuing into the second century CE, to the point of not only being the administrative language but perhaps even, alongside Aramaic, the second language of a bilingual urban population. The burial site at Beth Shearim skews the statistics toward Greek, since many diaspora families brought the remains of their dead for interment there. But the abundance of Greek inscriptions from diaspora Jews should not be interpreted as taking away from Aramaic as the primary language of most first-century CE Galileans.

The evidence makes it unlikely that anyone other than the Galilean urban elites spoke Greek as their primary language in the early first century CE. Peasants in the surrounding areas, and certainly in the border villages or larger towns, would have heard Greek either from Gentiles or from the more Hellenized and perhaps Greek-speaking Jewish urbanites. It would not have been unheard of at places like Capernaum or especially Bethsaida, given the interaction with Gentiles on the lake, and anyone involved in administration, taxation, or scribal activities would have been bilingual, perhaps with Greek even as their primary language. But there were no indigenous Greek speakers in Galilee during Jesus's youth; the urban Jews in Sepphoris and later Tiberias

ny who puts on a mask. Though it is not unreasonable to think that Antipas built a theater at Sepphoris — he apparently built one at Tiberias — it is unlikely that someone from a small village and from the artisan class would have attended and heard Greek-style plays there. For one, Jesus, like most rural Galileans, would not feel welcome there, and second, most entertainment in provincial theaters was less cultured and tended toward farces, mimes, pantomimes, spectacles, jugglers, and the display of

opposite page

Ostracon (Sepphoris, 1st c. BCE)
Lead Weight (Sepphoris, 2nd c. CE)

this page

Theater at Sepphoris (1st c. CE)
Roman Milestone (Capernaum, 2nd c. CE)
Roman Bathhouse (Capernaum, 2nd c. CE)

Greek in Galilee was just beginning to be used at the time of Jesus, as these inscriptions from Sepphoris indicate. This ostracon from Sepphoris in the Hellenistic period contains in Aramaic lettering a Greek loanword for a civic official. The lead weight is from the second century CE and is in Greek, but the officials' names are clearly Jewish.

The theater at Sepphoris has been a matter of great debate among archaeologists. The excavators are divided about whether it dates to the time of Jesus or later in the century. One wonders whether a Jewish carpenter from Nazareth would have felt at ease in such a theater, regardless of its date.

The later Romanization of Galilee is clear in the archaeological record. In the early second century CE, Rome intensively urbanized Galilee and stationed Roman troops there to ensure its Jewish population would not revolt again. Among the evidence from this time is a mile marker from a Roman-built road and a bathhouse, which served the troops stationed in Capernaum.

were at the vanguard in adopting Greek. Peasants in places like Nazareth may only have picked up a rudimentary grasp of key Greek phrases.

THE CHANGING GALILEE AFTER JESUS

The linguistic profile of Galilean inscriptions shows a trajectory of increasing Greek beginning with Herod Antipas and growing steadily until it provoked a Jewish reaction in favor of the more traditional Hebrew and Aramaic in the Byzantine period (fourth to seventh centuries CE). Epigraphic remains from the second through third centuries CE are mostly in Greek, which coincides with the intensifica-tion of Roman urbanization in Galilee and Palestine as a whole. After two wars with Rome in 66–70 and 132–35 CE, Rome urbanized the area as a means of pacification. Archaeologists are wary, then, of anachronistically using evidence from the later second, third, or fourth century CE to characterize Jesus's first-century CE Galilee.

The debate over the theater excavated at Sepphoris illustrates this problem. The proximity of Sepphoris's theater to Nazareth has led to speculation that Jesus might have visited it and that his teachings might have been influenced by Greek plays. After all, the term Jesus applies to his opponents is *hypocrite,* the Greek word for a stage actor, a pho-

exotic animals. But more important, the ceramic evidence underneath the theater's cavities is dated by most archaeologists to the latter half of the first century. Stratigraphically, the theater probably dates to after Jesus's life.

Similarly, a villa with Dionysiac themes was excavated at Sepphoris in the 1980s and caused a stir among New Testament scholars, who saw in this evidence for a more pagan and Gentile city in Galilee at the time of Jesus. But that mosaic, depicting a drinking bout between Dionysos and Heracles, and the house in which it was found date to the third century CE, a full two centuries after Jesus and a time when the Roman emperors invested heavily in the cults of Dionysos and Heracles. The house represents either a third-century CE Sepphorean's attempt to find favor with the emperor or the work of an appointed administrator who governed Galilee. Many Jews were probably invited to and even felt welcome at this person's dinner parties, but this mosaic cannot be used as evidence for a syncretistic and pagan Sepphoris at the time of Jesus.

Similarly at Capernaum, there are artifacts and architecture characteristic of Galilee in the period after Rome intensified its urbanization policies across what became the province of Syria Palestina. But this Middle or Late Roman evidence cannot be used to characterize the Early Roman Galilee of Jesus. Two examples: A Roman milestone from the time of Emperor Hadrian (117–38 CE) has often been used to suggest that ancient Capernaum was located on an important highway, the Via Maris, and therefore was a busy caravan stop on the freeway of international commerce. But the archaeology of roads conclusively shows that sturdy Roman roads of the legionary kind were not built in Galilee until the second century CE. Of the more than 120 inscribed Roman mile markers found in Israel, the earliest dates to 69 CE and names the emperor Vespasian, but almost all others are from the emperors Trajan (98–117 CE) and Hadrian (117–38 CE); the latter emperor traveled widely in the East and funded extensive road-construction and city-beautification projects. In Galilee, much of the roadwork was completed by the Seventh Legion, nicknamed *Ferrata* (the Iron Legion), which fought in the Bar-Kokhba Revolt in 132–35 CE and later were stationed at Legio near ancient Megiddo. But none of them were in Galilee when Jesus was, nor had they built those roads in his time.

The second example at Capernaum is a Roman bathhouse that was excavated on the Greek Orthodox side of the site. This small, four-chambered bathhouse looks like those on the Roman frontier along the Rhine in Germany, the Danube in Romania, and the Euphrates in Syria. It is tempting to associate the Capernaum bathhouse with the centurion mentioned in the Gospels (Matthew 8:1–10; Luke 7:1–10; and John 4:46–54). But based on ceramic finds underneath it and its architectural typology, it was built in the second century CE, probably, if not exclusively, for Roman legionnaires headquartered at Legio. It bears stressing that there were no Romans permanently stationed in Galilee during the rule of Antipas and the life of Jesus, and that the word the Gospels use for the official, usually translated "centurion," was a common Greek administrative title and not exclusive to the Roman legions.

Finally, there is ample evidence for a highly syncretistic, Hellenistic- and Roman-influenced artistic tradition at some Galilean synagogues, but it dates to long after Jesus. Among that evidence are the mosaic floors from inside the synagogues at Beth Alpha. The surprisingly well-preserved mosaic is stylistically inferior to contemporaneous civic mosaics at nearby Scythopolis or Sepphoris, but its folk-art, even crude, style uses Jewish symbols, including the ark

of the Torah surrounded by menorahs. It also breaks with Jewish tradition by depicting a zodiac that personifies the four seasons on four sides with the sun god Helios in the center. Underneath, the hand of God is anthropomorphically pictured stretching down from heaven, in violation of the Second Commandment. A similar zodiac was excavated at Hammath-Tiberias in the 1920s, and in the early 2000s at Sepphoris. But none of that is of much value for assessing Judaism in Galilee at the time of Jesus, which from all archaeological indications was aniconic.

In this sense, a thorough knowledge of Galilean archaeology provides a negative contribution to the study of the

New Testament. By paying close attention to the chronological distinctions between the centuries, based primarily on a careful stratigraphic analysis dated with ceramic typologies, many claims based on finds and discoveries from later periods can be put to rest. Jesus did not live in a Gentile Galilee. Jesus did not speak Greek. Jesus did not live on an international highway. Jesus's Galilee was not as urbanized as Asia Minor or Greece, Egypt, and Syria.

But the larger, positive contribution of Galilean archaeology to the study of the Gospels is based on the material from Jesus's lifetime. That contribution lies primarily in identifying Galilee as overwhelming Jewish, inhabited by Jews

who adhered to some extent to purity laws, as shown by their use of stone vessels and *mikvaoth,* and who remained traditionalists in avoiding animal or human representations. This means that they were very similar to their fellow Jews in the south, around Jerusalem, but very different from their immediate neighbors on all sides. They never fully participated in the commercial activities that began under the Seleucids and Ptolemies two centuries before Jesus, and they seemed cool to many of the pagan and Hellenistic influences that were sweeping the Levant in the first century BCE. But they were not completely isolated or aloof from the larger world, and especially not at the time of Jesus. Herod Antipas had just begun a carefully planned and cautious integration of Galilee into the larger Roman world, using the cities of Sepphoris and Tiberias as his vehicles and naming the latter city after the Roman emperor, a trick he and his brother Philip learned from their father. Though he did not cloak Galilee with the cultural and religious aspects of Greco-Roman culture, he did drape his cities in a Roman urban architectural veneer and decked the homes of his ruling elites in the decorative parlance of the day. And that process both strained the economy in rural areas and accentuated the differences between rich and poor. Jesus's concern for the poor and for social justice beats like a drum throughout the Gospels; be it the opening blessing on the poor in the Sermon on the Mount or the feeding of the thousands in John, his kingdom of God was quite different from the kingdom that Antipas was building. Archaeology makes clear the tension between Antipas's kingdom-building and Jesus's kingdom-preaching.

opposite page

Synagogue Mosaic (Beth Alpha, 6th c. CE)

this page

Zodiac Mosaic (Hammath-Tiberias, 5th c. CE)

Spectacular synagogue mosaics, like these from Beth Alpha and Hammath-Tiberias, have been found in Galilee. Each contained a zodiac, and the mosaic at Hammath-Tiberias, which later had a wall built over it, featured the pagan god Helios in the center. At Beth Alpha, the hand of God is depicted stopping Abraham from sacrificing Isaac. Such art is unimaginable in the first-century world of Jesus, when the evidence for Judaism is aniconic — it uses no images, and certainly no images for God.

CAPERNAUM: JESUS'S BASE OF OPERATIONS

Capernaum is the site most frequently associated with Jesus in the Gospels. Edward Robinson identified Tell Hum as Capernaum in 1838, and in 1866 the British lieutenant Charles W. Wilson discovered the ruins of the limestone synagogue, whose white stones contrasted starkly with the surrounding gray-black basalt. The Franciscan Custodian of the Holy Land purchased much of the site from local bedouins in 1894, and the remainder was later sold to the Greek Orthodox patriarch of Jerusalem. Initial excavations at the site focused on two structures. The synagogue was first excavated by the Germans Heinrich Kohl and Carl Watzinger in 1905, and again in the 1920s by Father Orfali, who also exposed the supposed House of Saint Peter. The latter was in the form of a fifth-century CE octagonal church, which early pilgrims report being shown.

In 1968 Father Virgilio Corbo, assisted by Father Stanislao Loffreda, began a more careful stratigraphic excavation of these two buildings, which showed that the synagogue dates to the fifth century CE, though some earlier wall underneath might be from the first-century CE synagogue "of Jesus." In the case of the church, the excavators distinguished three phases: a first-century BCE house from when Capernaum was first settled, a fourth-century CE *domus-ekklesia,* a "house church," and finally in the fifth century CE, a church built in concentric octagons centered over one room left from the earliest house. Graffiti in several languages, including what might be Christian phrases (including *amen, Maria,* and *Petros*), were found in a room dating to as early as the second century, which has led the Franciscans to conclude that it commemorated in some way Jesus's visit there, Peter's living there, or an early Christian community worshipping there.

But all the fuss over whether or not the church or synagogue marks the right spot limits the contribution that

archaeology could otherwise make. It smacks of old-style biblical archaeology, which focused on *where* Jesus walked instead looking at *how* Jesus walked by studying his message within his world as reconstructed by archaeology. And for this purpose, the more enduring contribution has been the careful work over the past few decades of Father Loffredda, who has not only described the first-century layers of the synagogue and *insula sacra,* but has

CAPERNAUM IN THE NEW TESTAMENT

Only Jerusalem is mentioned more frequently than Capernaum in the New Testament. Although the Gospels at times call it a polis (Matthew 9:1; Mark 1:33; Luke 4:31), that has more to do with their loose use of the term than its actual size or status. At other times, it is described as a fishing village (Matthew 4:12–22), said to have a small toll house (Mark 2:14) and a small Herodian garrison with an official (the so-called centurion, Matthew 8:5–13; Luke 7:1–10; John 4:46–54). It appears to be the hub of Jesus's ministry, and Jesus is described as being "at home" there in Mark 2:1. Matthew says he settled down there in 4:13, and calls it "his own city" (Matthew 9:1).

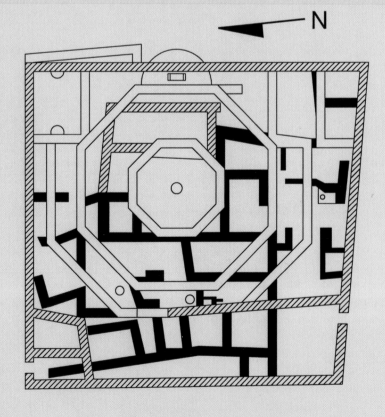

N

0   5m

provided rich characterizations of the Early Roman strata of the surrounding houses. This meticulous work has shown that Capernaum was a simple peasant and fisherman's village, inhabited by Jews who used stone vessels and locally produced pottery, with few imports or signs of wealth like fresco, plaster, or roof tiles.

Excavations by Vassilios Tzaferis during the late 1970s and 1980s on the Greek Orthodox side of Capernaum have been instructive in another way. Other than a small Roman bathhouse from the second century CE and some fishponds along the lake, most of the ruins on the eastern side of the site were from later Byzantine and Arab periods, with no Roman remains underneath. Capernaum clearly grew and expanded eastward in later centuries, and these ruins cannot be used to calculate the size of Capernaum at Jesus's time, as is often done. Thus first-century Capernaum could not have had much more than one thousand inhabitants.

The excavations at Sepphoris are central and hotly disputed in historical Jesus research. The site was initially excavated in a single 1931 season by Leroy Waterman of the University of Michigan. Waterman uncovered the theater, which he dated to the second century CE, and what he thought was an early Christian basilica, which has since been identified as an urban villa. At that time the New Testament scholar S. Jackson Case wrote an article called "Jesus and Sepphoris," which speculated on Hellenistic influences on Jesus's life based on reflections while visiting the excavations. But both the excavations and the article were quickly forgotten until fifty years later, when four different teams resumed work at the site in the mid-1980s. James F. Strange laid out squares on the lower market and acropolis, including probes in the theater; a joint project of Eric and Carol

SEPPHORIS IN THE NEW TESTAMENT

The New Testament never mentions Sepphoris, an omission scholars hotly debate. It was the largest city in Galilee, for a time its capital, but at only four miles from Nazareth, its absence is striking. Jesus must have visited the city at least on occasion for market days, and some have wondered if as a craftsman (the word usually translated as "carpenter"; *tekton* more broadly refers to people who work with their hands, including stone masons), he and his father might have worked on its construction. But he probably avoided Sepphoris during his ministry because of Antipas's presence — he did, after all, behead John the Baptist. Perhaps Sepphoris's citizens were too affluent or too Hellenized for Jesus's interests, or perhaps he went to the city but his activities are simply not mentioned in the Gospels.

Meyers and Ehud Netzer uncovered the Dionysos Mosaic and examined parts of the theater. Later, the Meyers concentrated on the domestic quarters on the acropolis's western slope, where so many *mikvaoth* were found, and Zeev Weiss of Hebrew University moved all across the lower city's market and also uncovered a fifth-century CE synagogue. Tzvika Tzuk, on behalf of Israel's National Parks Authority, cleared the extensive water reservoir outside the city.

Together, these excavations brought attention to the impact of Antipas's urbanization on Galilee and Jesus's ministry. The excavations show that the one-time Hasmonean administrative settlement, with a fortress and modest population, was significantly expanded and renovated under Antipas, and a rough grid pattern established with a *cardo* and *decumanus* running through the lower city. Although Josephus says that the Roman general Varus destroyed the city in 4 BCE after a tax revolt broke out, no evidence for a widespread conflagration at that time has been found. About two generations later, when the archaeological record shows massive destruction layers by

the Romans at the nearby sites of Jotapata and Gamla, there is no hint of disturbances at Sepphoris, which expanded and grew well into the second century. In fact, the earlier fortress was dismantled and filled in right before the revolt, very likely as a gesture to Rome. Another nod to Rome can be seen on coins minted with the legend "City of Peace." Much of the urban architecture and most of the site's renowned mosaics date to the Middle and Late Roman periods, when Roman urbanization flourished across the Levant. This was the period when Sepphoris figured prominently in the rabbinic literature (second only to Jerusalem), and Judah "the Prince" is said to have codified the Mishnah there. An earthquake in 363 CE destroyed much of the city, which then waned in importance. Even though Christian pilgrims occasionally visited the site and were shown the alleged birthplace of Saint Anne, the mother of Mary, by the Byzantime period Sepphoris was overtaken in importance by Nazareth.

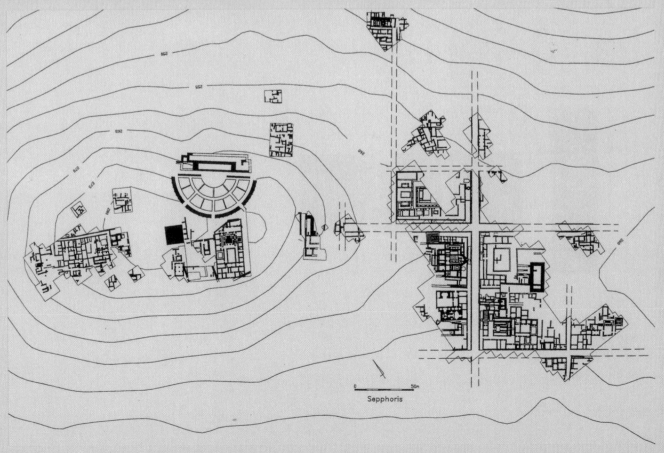

Sepphoris

5

THE ARCHAEOLOGY OF JERUSALEM AND JESUS'S PASSION

Jesus may have grown up and spent his ministry in Galilee, but a full third of the New Testament Gospels are devoted to his final visit to Jerusalem, where he was arrested, tried, and crucified. The story of his death, burial, and resurrection is at the heart of Christianity, and according to the Gospels, it took place in the geographical center of Judaism, in Jerusalem. Archaeological excavations over the past century, conducted with voracious intensity after the 1967 War, have provided such a wealth of information that one could hardly think of describing the city at the time of Jesus without a thorough knowledge of the newly discovered artifacts and architecture.

According to the Hebrew Bible, King David made Jerusalem his capital in the tenth century BCE, and his son Solomon built the First Temple there. That Temple was destroyed by the Babylonians in the sixth century BCE and rebuilt, on a more modest scale, by returning Jewish exiles; this is today referred to as the Second Temple. The Seleucid king Antiochus Epiphanes defiled it in 163 BCE, in an act the book of Daniel calls "the abomination of desolation" (11:31; 12:11), and the Jewish Maccabees had to have it cleansed. They also expanded and renovated it, efforts dwarfed by Herod the Great's

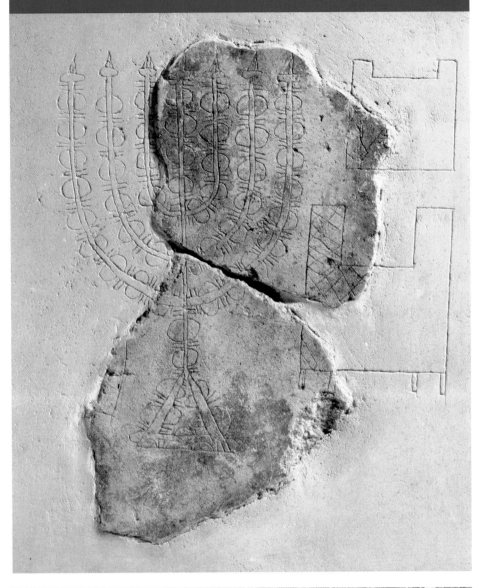

rebuilding of the Temple Mount right before Jesus's birth. He kept intact the inner workings of the Jewish priesthood, but encased their rituals and sacrifices in an imposing structure, so that later Jewish sages would say "whoever has not seen Herod's building has never seen a beautiful structure."

Herod somehow managed what previous rulers had not — to pull together Hellenistic and Roman components into a holistic architectural style without undermining Jewish sensibilities. His son and successor in Jerusalem, Archelaus, was less successful, as were the incompetent Roman governors who took over after Archelaus's exile in 6 CE, among them the Gospels' notorious Pontius Pilate. They exacerbated the underlying tensions between Jewish monotheism and Roman paganism, the Jewish sense of justice and the Roman sense of empire. Hostilities eventually broke out in a full-scale rebellion in 66 CE, which ended with the burning of the city and the enslavement of its inhabitants in 70 CE. Herod's Temple was destroyed.

But Herod the Great did more than renovate and expand the Temple Mount — he transformed the entire city. The first Romans who accompanied Pompey to Jerusalem in 63 BCE must have thought it an esoteric, conservative, and xenophobic Eastern city.

opposite page

Stone Jar (1st C. CE)

Silver Shekel with Temple (132–35 CE)

Inscription from Temple (1st C. CE)

this page

Menorah from Upper City (1st C. CE)

Temple Mount from Southeast

The sanctity of Jerusalem permeated all aspects of life in the city at the time of Jesus. Common in Jerusalem's wealthy homes were large stone vessels connected to Jewish purity laws. This coin from the second Jewish Revolt in 132–35 CE may preserve a historical memory of the Temple's appearance, and the menorah etched into the plaster of a first-century Jerusalem house may depict the candelabra that stood in the sanctuary.

Herod the Great's Temple Mount still dominates the Old City of Jerusalem, with the Islamic Dome of the Rock standing approximately on the site of the ancient Jewish sanctuary. Extensive excavations around the Temple Mount, seen here from the Mount of Olives, have found a piece of the rubble cast by Roman soldiers from the pinnacle of the Temple that contains the Hebrew inscription "For the place of trumpeting."

When Jesus arrived before the Temple in the thirties, parts of it were still under construction. But after Herod's project was complete, nearly a century after he began it, the city was world-class and the Temple awe-inspiring. The Roman general Titus wept when he ordered it destroyed in 70 CE. This chapter focuses on the excavations around the Temple Mount — places Jesus certainly visited — and also on excavations in the Upper City, inside houses Jesus probably never saw but which reveal the strategies of Jerusalem's elite as they eased into the Greco-Roman cultural orbit while trying to preserve their Jewish identity and traditions. Instead of looking at the traditional Christian holy sites in Jerusalem, like the location of Jesus's trial, the so-called Via Dolorosa, or the Holy Sepulcher, this chapter focuses on an archaeologically generated picture of the city as a whole, in order to imagine how Galilean fishermen and peasants might have perceived the bustling city, its wealthy inhabitants, and the Temple's priestly ceremonies.

JERUSALEM'S LANDSCAPE AND CITYSCAPE

If Galilee was geographically marginal, much the same could be said about Jerusalem. It was in the central hill country, surrounded by the barren Judean Wilderness. To reach Jerusalem from the eastern oasis of Jericho or the ancient King's Highway, one made an arduous ascent from 800 feet below sea level to Jerusalem's altitude of 2,500 feet. From any Mediterranean harbor, there was a more sinuous road with a gradual ascent, which steepened as it passed through deep ravines right before the city. Jerusalem was well off the major commercial routes of antiquity, somewhat difficult to access, lacking in large tracts of arable land, and without an adequate water supply. But Jerusalem had the Temple. That was the only place Jews could sacrifice to the one God, and that was the place where Jews believed that heaven and earth met.

Jerusalem's natural setting, however, did offer one advantage. Its various geological formations of limestone supplied an assortment of materials suitable for construction. Architects and craftsmen could quarry several kinds of limestone: *nari,* which was somewhat soft and to which plaster stuck like glue; *meleke,* which was hard but could be chipped with a chisel and took decorations well; and *mizzi yahudi,* which was very hard and was used for keystones, lintels, and thresholds. Deposits of soft limestone, which geologists consider chalk, provided the white material used for stone vessels, ossuaries, and tabletops. Roman cities after Augustus used brick and cement for their structures' cores, which were covered with brilliant marble and travertine veneers. But there was not enough wood in Judea to fire so many bricks, and transporting marble was

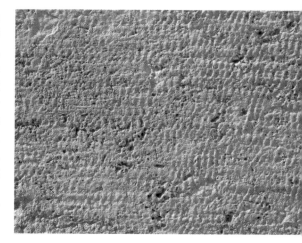

very expensive. Nevertheless, Jerusalem's geology cloaked the city in a unique color; local Jerusalem stone imparted a warm, inviting yellow hue that turned to soft orange at sunrise and sunset. Few cities had such a distinctive and appealing tone.

At Jesus's time, Jerusalem was spread over two hills, the western Upper City on the present-day Mount Zion, and the eastern Temple Mount on Mount Moriah. Between them was the Tyropoeon Valley, Greek for "Valley of the Cheesemakers." That is where the Lower City began, stretching from the Temple southward along the Ophel Ridge to the Gihon Spring. While the Lower City was packed with Jerusalem's lower classes, the Upper City was home to the wealthy, who had begun to move there in Hasmonean times. Herod the Great built his palace, which Roman procurators later used on their visits, in the Upper City. Jerusalem was constrained topographically to the south by the deep Hinnom Valley and to the east by Kidron Valley and the steep incline up to the Mount of Olives, where Jesus is said to have predicted the destruction of the Temple. These slopes were riddled with tomb complexes in and

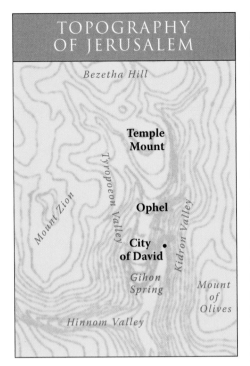

TOPOGRAPHY OF JERUSALEM

Bezetha Hill

Temple Mount

Tyropoeon Valley

Mount Zion

Ophel

City of David

Kidron Valley

Gihon Spring

Mount of Olives

Hinnom Valley

around gardens, orchards, and fields, whose open areas served as campgrounds for the many pilgrims that crowded Jerusalem at major festivals.

Jerusalem was compact at the time of Jesus. Herod had employed many people on the city's construction projects, and its grandeur attracted pilgrims from afar. The city was cramped inside the walls built by the Hasmoneans, so Herod expanded it northward into what was called the New City, building the Second Wall. The Third Wall, built even farther north by Herod Agrippa between 37 and 44 CE, testifies to Jerusalem's continued economic and demographic boom. Archaeologists have vigorously debated the precise location of these two walls; their courses are still uncertain because of the fragmentary nature of the archaeological evidence and the ambiguity of the literary evidence. The matter is of some importance to those interested in Golgotha, the site of Jesus's crucifixion, which presumably was outside the city wall at that time. The location of the First, Second, and Third Walls to the east and north of the Temple, and the date of their construction, to a great degree frame the question of whether or not the Church of the Holy Sepulcher is in the "right" place. A more important historical conclusion about these walls, however, wherever they are located, is that Jerusalem was bustling and expanding when Jesus set foot in the city.

Several probes by archaeologists suggest that the area between the Second and Third Walls was sparsely inhabited. Inside where most scholars think the Second Wall was located, Jerusalem covered an area of about 250 acres. The Temple Mount and surrounding public areas took up nearly a fifth of the city; the Lower City covered about sixty acres, as did the area enclosed by the Second Wall; the Upper City, Herod's palace, and his citadel comprised about eighty acres. We can assume that the Lower City was more densely inhabited — perhaps as many as two hundred people per acre — and that the wealthier areas would have been more spacious, with around one hundred people per acre. Thus the population inside the walls of Jerusalem at Jesus's time would have been around 32,000. This seems small by today's standards, and even in antiquity, it would not have been on a par with great Eastern cities like Alexandria, Antioch, and Ephesus, or even the nearby cities of Caesarea and Scythopolis. But Jerusalem's population had been on an upswing since Hasmonean independence, and its growth accelerated under Herod the Great, reaching its zenith at perhaps 50,000 when war broke out with Rome in 66 CE. Jerusalem was flourishing in the thirties.

The growing population, coupled with the pilgrims, who multiplied it by five- or tenfold on major festivals, made water a crucial commodity. Jerusalem had only one significant source, the old Gihon Spring on the southernmost edge of the Ophel, from which the eighth-century BCE King Hezekiah had cut a tunnel into the City of David. But that was not enough for late Second Temple Jerusalem, so the Hasmoneans began a two-pronged approach: a series of pools and reservoirs to store rainwater and aqueducts to bring freshwater from springs to the south.

Many wealthy inhabitants carved out cisterns in the bedrock under their homes, and several large reservoirs were scattered across the city to take care of public needs. Eight large pools have been identified from the Second Temple period, and two of them are likely those mentioned in the Gospel of John. The Pool of Bethesda (John 5:1–9) was discovered by explorers in the nineteenth century, and the Siloam Pool (John 9:7–11) was discovered in 2002 south of the Temple Mount. Located on the grounds of the Church of Saint Anne north of the Temple Mount, Bethesda's enormous two-chambered pool was cleared and excavated in stages over the last two centuries. The work gives an appreciation for the size of such pools and the extent of public planning behind the water system. There were two pools separated by a partition, hewn into bedrock and built up with ashlars, which together measured ninety-five meters in length, fifty to sixty meters in width, and fifteen meters in depth — about the dimensions of four Olympic-sized swimming pools, though much deeper.

The second prong of the water supply was an aqueduct system that collected spring water some fifteen miles south of Jerusalem. From three large pools, today called Solomon's Pools, a meandering low-level aqueduct and a more direct high-level aqueduct carried water to the city. The Hasmoneans

opposite page

Herodian Masonry
Inscribed Temple Stone
Jerusalem from Southeast

this page

Reconstructed Roller

The Bible's Mount Zion is another name for Jerusalem, located in the Judean Hills. The area right around the city served as the quarry, especially the area north of the Old City that supplied the stones for Herod the Great's enlargement of the Temple Mount.

Herod's distinct architectural style included stones with a trimmed three- to six-inch margin along the sides and a raised boss in the center, seen here with a later Hebrew inscription. Much of the stone was quarried uphill from the construction, and wheels allowed workers to roll stones into place with considerable ease.

built the earlier low-level aqueduct; Herod the Great constructed the later high-level aqueduct. Extensive repairs by the Roman Tenth Legion, who occupied the city in the second century CE, left scattered tiles with their insignia at various points along the high-level aqueduct, but it is doubtful they were its original architects. More recent examinations along several stretches of high-level aqueduct date it to the Herodian period, and it is similar in construction technique to two known Herodian aqueducts, one at Caesarea Maritima and the other an extension leading to Solomon's Pools. This Herodian aqueduct shows sophisticated engineering and careful planning; it drops at a steady but slight decline of thirty meters over fifteen miles. It is carved mostly alongside ridges but occasionally tunneled underground or carried over arches, and is coated with waterproofed cement and plaster. Herodian in date, it is very Roman in style.

The aqueduct was, of course, the characteristic feature of Roman engineering, and ample flowing water was the hallmark of a Roman-styled city. Herod's aqueduct not only met the daily needs of the growing population but it also reshaped the city along Roman lines by sprinkling it with fountains, pools, and an underground sewage system. All that water served as air-conditioning in the hot summers and sanitized the city throughout the year. But Herod kept Jerusalem distinct from other Greco-Roman cities in its use of water: he built no public bathhouses for leisure bathing, so typical of Roman life. He had the technology but consciously avoided bathhouses as too problematic for a conservative Jewish population, whether because of nudity, purity, or associations with paganism. Instead, scattered all around the city were ritual baths, which define Jerusalem as Jewish to its very core.

EVIDENCE FOR PILGRIMAGE TO THE HOLY CITY

Jerusalem is archaeologically different from other Mediterranean cities because of the number of stepped, plastered pools, or *mikvaoth,* dating to the late Second Temple period. Over 150 have been excavated in Jerusalem. Many are in private homes of the Upper and Lower Cities, while others are larger public pools, designed to serve Jewish pilgrims on their visits to the Temple. Several have been discovered outside Jerusalem, perhaps used by agricultural workers who made oil or wine of suitable purity for the Jerusalem priesthood. A number of larger stepped pools next to the main road leading to the city perhaps served pilgrims on their way to festivals, as did the pools immediately in front of the Temple Mount's southern entrances. Over ten have been excavated between the Temple's Hulda Gate and Robinson's Arch, and there is possible evidence for a few on the Temple Mount itself.

The two pools mentioned in the New Testament — Bethesda and Siloam — might also have served as ritual baths for pilgrims flocking to Jerusalem on high holy days, as described in Jesus's triumphal entry into the city. Discovered in 2002 along the ancient street leading up to the Tem-

> "Now in Jerusalem by the Sheep Gate there is a pool, called in Hebrew Beth-zatha, which has five porticoes."
>
> JOHN 5:2

ple by a French archaeologist. The Theodotus Inscription is the only archaeological evidence for a synagogue in Second Temple Jerusalem. Written in a steady Greek hand typical of the early first century CE, the inscription testifies to a synagogue that stood in the shadow of the Temple. It also offers a glimpse into the synagogue's purpose: reading and studying the Torah, as well as providing hostel and bathing facilities for diaspora Jews. The benefactor was Theodotus son of Vettenus, whose Greek name means "given by God," and whose father, Vettenus, was named after a neighborhood in Rome. He must have been a descendant of an enslaved and later freed Roman Jew. Theodotus's synagogue offered pilgrims, probably family members or

opposite page

Drain at Siloam Pool

Clay Pipes for Aqueduct

this page

Underground Sewer

Water Channel at Siloam Pool

Pool of Bethesda

Quenching Jerusalem's thirst for water was no mean feat, but before Jesus's lifetime Herod had made sure there was abundant water flowing though a ten-mile aqueduct that supplied the city of thirty-something thousand. There was enough water for underground sewage and a drainage system that included decorative holes.

Archaeologists discovered this biblical pool in the nineteenth century on the property of the Church of Saint Anne, but only recently did further studies and probes reveal a sluice that pushed water from one pool to another. That created occasional bubbling, which the Gospel of John says was attributed to an angel and welcomed for its healing properties.

ple, the trapezoidal Siloam Pool was seventy meters long and between forty and sixty meters wide. It was built with customary Herodian masonry and had a series of alternating steps and landings on each of the three excavated sides. These were designed so that bathers could descend to the water level, then stand and immerse. A channel funneled water directly from the nearby spring, which made it "living water" and therefore suitable for ritual bathing. At Bethesda, just north of the Temple, an upper pool served as a reservoir, and a southern, lower pool, used for washing, had a similar series

of steps and landings. The partition between them was six meters thick, and a horizontal underwater tunnel was controlled from above with a sluice, which could be opened so that the pressure from the fuller reservoir pushed water into the pool used for bathing. That, by the way, must have produced something like a bubbling described as "the stirring of water" in John 5:7, which was believed to have healing powers.

Another archaeological find links pilgrimage to ritual bathing. One of Jerusalem's most significant epigraphic discoveries was made in 1913 at the bottom of a cistern south of the Tem-

> "... and many went up from the country to Jerusalem before the Passover to purify themselves."
>
> JOHN 11:55

friends from Rome, accommodation and a place for ritual bathing as they visited the Temple. Unfortunately, we cannot know whether the inscription was placed outside or inside the synagogue, and whether it implies a high level of Greek in Jerusalem or among those visiting Jerusalem, or is reflective of a group of Hellenistic Jews living in the city and speaking Greek, as we see in the early chapters of the book of Acts.

Burial inscriptions provide a better look into Jerusalem's linguistic profile. Over two hundred ossuaries have inscriptions; over 60 percent are written in Aramaic/Hebrew script, 30 percent in Greek, and less than 10 percent are in Greek and Aramaic/Hebrew. Greek had made significant inroads in Jerusalem, and much of its increase can be attributed to diaspora Jews. Many Jews who once lived outside Jerusalem were interred in tombs around Jerusalem. Some had returned to live in Jerusalem, others had come to die in the holy city, and still others had their remains interred there. The most famous was Helena of Adiabene, a first-century convert to Judaism who built an extensive tomb complex just north of Jerusalem. Other ossuaries from Jerusalem list homes as far away as Bernice and Ptolemais in North Africa, Italian Capua, Egyptian Alexan-

"Theodotus, the son of Vettenus, priest and head of the synagogue [Greek *archisynagoguos*], son of the head of the synagogue and grandson of the head of the synagogue, built this synagogue for the reading of the law and the study of the commandments, and a guesthouse and rooms and water installations for hosting those in need from abroad. It was founded by his fathers, the elders, and Simonides."

Ancient Coinage at the Temple

1 Tyrian tetradrachma	= 4 denarii
	= 1 shekel
½ shekel	= 2 denarii
	= 392 *prutot*
	(singular *prutah*)
1 denarius	= 196 *prutot*

(The daily wage for a skilled worker was 1 denarius.)

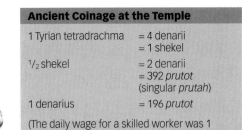

dria, Bithynia by the Black Sea, and Syria; without noting a specific place, two are in Latin and one in Palmyrene.

We do not know how often Jews made the pilgrimage to Jerusalem — it depended on wealth and distance. But all Jewish males over age twenty were expected to send an annual Temple tax to Jerusalem. This obligation became customary during the Hasmonean period and was set at a half-shekel for the maintenance of the Temple. Ironically, it was expected to be paid with a Tyrian shekel, on whose obverse was the pagan god Melkart/Heracles and on whose reverse was a Greek inscription calling Tyre the holy city. A large coin hoard found in 1960 at Isfiya on the coastal Carmel Ridge indicates that the tax was widely paid. Of 4,560 coins, 3,400 were Tyrian full-shekels, 1,000 Tyrian half-shekels, and only 160 were Roman denarii. This must have represented the Temple tax collected from Jews either along the coast or abroad: a one-shekel silver coin covered two people, but if someone

opposite page

Ritual Bath with Divider

Ritual Bath at Temple

Excavations at Siloam Pool

Theodotus Inscription (1st c. CE)

this page

Nicanor's Ossuary (1st c. CE)

Hoard of Tyrian Half-Shekels

Pure water was in demand to make the pilgrims ritually clean before they entered the Temple. For this reason, many ritual baths (in Hebrew *mikvaoth*) were placed around the Temple for use by both priests and pilgrims. The Siloam Pool, mentioned in John 9 and recently discovered, may have been used for ritual bathing. Pilgrims came from as far away as Rome and stayed in hostels attached to synagogues, according to the Theodotus Inscription.

The Temple tax was paid on an annual basis by all adult male Jews. Ironically, the preferred currency was from the pagan city of Tyre, due to its high silver content, but it depicted the god Melkart/Heracles on one side.

paid the half-shekel for himself, he was required to add on an exchange fee of 8 percent; that fee for 1,000 half-shekels would be exactly those remaining 160 Roman denarii. The hoard represents the tax for 7,800 male Jews, which was either embezzled, lost, or somehow forgotten. More precious than the silver coins themselves is the credence their discovery lends to the seriousness with which the Temple tax was treated around the time of Jesus.

THE TEMPLE AT THE TIME OF JESUS

The centerpiece of Herodian Jerusalem was the Temple Mount, a project more ambitious, complicated, and vast than any before and probably since in the land of Israel. Once completed, it became the largest sacred complex in the Roman Empire. Archaeological excavations and discoveries around the Temple Mount have shed considerable light on its overall design, construction details, and architectural techniques, all of which reveal key aspects of Herod's architectural program, which also reverberates in his other projects, like Caesarea or Masada. Architectural experts debate the extent to which Herodian architecture was Roman, Hellenistic, or indigenous, a question made more complicated by the fact that Greek culture at that time spread across the East through Roman influence, and even Greek cities were imitating Roman architectural components that had been inspired by the Greeks themselves. The world was becoming more cosmopolitan, and Herod was a leading architectural voice in fusing various strands into the Roman-inspired urban aesthetic that was emerging across the empire. In addition to projects in his kingdom, Herod also sponsored projects in places like Phoenician Tyre, Sidon, and Beirut; Syrian Antioch and Damascus; and Greek Rhodes, Delos, and Athens, where behind the Acropolis's Parthenon an inscription reads: "The People to King Herod, friend of Romans, because of his good works and good will toward the city."

Several themes in Herodian architecture communicate, at times subtly and at times forcefully, the character of Jerusalem's urban landscape. Herod's

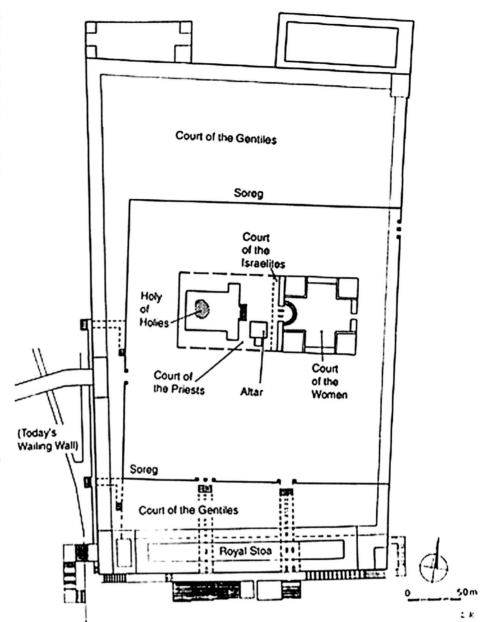

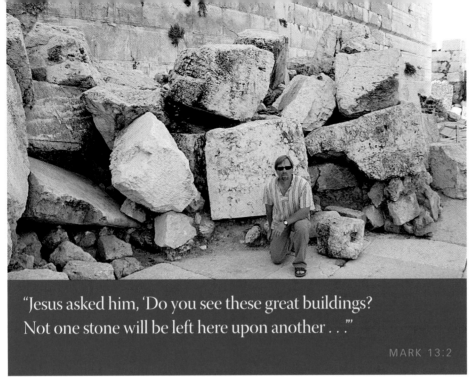

"Jesus asked him, 'Do you see these great buildings? Not one stone will be left here upon another . . .'"

MARK 13:2

"No foreigner is to enter within the balustrade and enclosure around the sanctuary. Whoever is caught will have himself to blame for his subsequent death."

Temple adopted characteristics of Augustan and Roman architecture: structures imposed onto the topography dominate the cityscape, facades accentuate grandeur and wealth, and social hierarchies are reinforced through entrances and spatial relations. These architectural messages contrast with

Jesus's message of the kingdom of God: Herod's domination versus Jesus's servitude, facades versus sincerity, hierarchy versus equality. Perhaps unintentionally but nonetheless emphatically, Jesus's teachings undermined the Roman-Herodian architectural program. Though Herod's Temple Mount was designed to impress these three themes on locals and visitors, the initial impulse for rebuilding was practical. The Hasmonean Temple Mount was too small to accommodate the increased visitors as Judea and Galilee's Jewish populations grew and safe travel under the *Pax Romana* brought more pilgrims.

Herod's primary task, then, was to expand the Temple Mount. He could not alter in any way the sanctuary

proper, which housed the divine — that had to remain in conformity with biblical prescriptions. But he could do as he pleased with the remaining sacred area, the area that in Greek is called the *temenos* and that delineated the sacred precinct from its profane surroundings. Herod forcefully imposed his will onto the cityscape by doubling the Hasmonean platform, which consumed nearly a fourth of the city. The new platform was slightly trapezoidal and covered roughly

opposite page

Plan of Temple Area

Southeast Corner of Temple

this page

Rubble from Temple

Temple Inscription (1st C. CE)

Reconstructed Decoration

Decoration from Inside Gate

Discovery of Decorated Fragment

"Not one stone upon another" is what Jesus predicted, according to the Gospels. Indeed the Romans destroyed the Temple in 70 CE, casting down many — but not all — stones from the upper courses of the Temple. Archaeologists have excavated piles of rubble on top of the streets around the southwest corner of the Temple Mount.

Paul was arrested for trespassing after being charged with bringing an uncircumcised Gentile into the inner portion of the Temple. According to Acts 21:24–26, he escorted the Gentile convert Trophimus into this area, which was punishable by death, according to this fragmentary inscription. It once was placed on what in Hebrew is called the *soreg*, which delineated the area into which only Jews could enter. Archaeologists also found a complete inscription that preserves the entire text.

1,000 feet east to west and 1,600 feet north to south. To accomplish this in Jerusalem's hilly terrain, Herod filled in the Betheza Valley to the north and built retaining walls over one hundred feet high on the southern and western sides into the Tyropoeon Valley. He needed absolutely secure foundations with solid construction and massive stones, so his architects dug down some sixty feet to bedrock. Labor was saved by quarrying nearby and uphill, and massive stones were hauled downhill on rollers pulled by oxen or inside specially constructed wooden wheels. The bottom courses were made of colossal stones, only portions of which can be seen inside underground tunnels along the Temple Mount. One stone, in the so-called master course, was forty feet long, ten feet high, and is estimated at fourteen feet wide; it weighs more than five tons and, by way of comparison, would dwarf the monoliths at Britain's Stonehenge.

The walls on each side, especially the southwestern corner, created an enormous facade, which dominated the urban landscape. There was nothing that compared either in Herod's kingdom or in Augustus's empire. Even the civic center in Ephesus, built by the emperor Domitian, is tiny by comparison. It's perhaps appropriate to think of Herod's Temple Mount as akin to an artificial

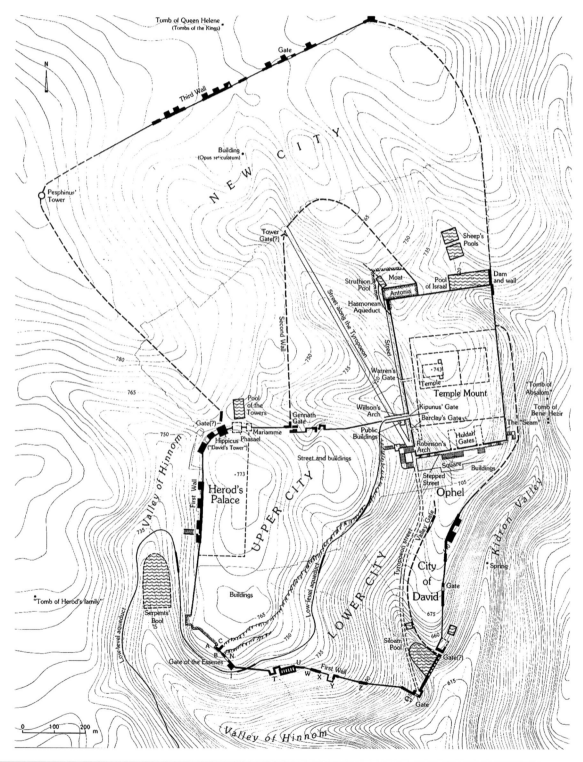

"This temple has been under construction for forty-six years, and will you raise it up in three days?"

JOHN 2:20

acropolis, which rises above the surrounding land and dominates the city in every way. Most visitors approached the Temple from the south or west, the sides with the highest facades. The main street ran along the western side of the Temple and right under Robinson's Arch; pedestrians would have had dizzying views either looking up at the pinnacle from the street or looking down onto the paved street from the Temple. Each course was set in by about an inch to create a slightly pyramidal effect, optically exaggerating the Temple Mount's height. It also had a unique aesthetic, with individual stones standing out with the typical Herodian boss-and-margin style, in which a smooth-cut frame of a few inches surrounded a central panel with a roughly cut texture.

None of the Temple Mount's upper courses — around the Royal Basilica or the Stoa on the southern edge — still stand, but they can be reconstructed from the debris and rubble cast down by the Romans in 70 CE. The excavations that began in 1968 at the bottom of the wall showed that the upper courses were decorated with pilasters — rectangular half-pillars embedded in the wall and topped with capitals. At the top was a rounded parapet, as can be seen from a fragmentary inscription in angular Hebrew letters, "For the place of trumpeting for/to. . . ." Perhaps from this parapet on a corner tower, heralds announced the Sabbath and other festivals with a trumpet blast.

As with all Roman architectural projects, the Herodian Temple Mount reinforced the social hierarchy by differentiating space, entrances, exits, and vistas. But more striking was its distinction between humanity and divinity. The sheer size of the Mount emphasized one's own minute scale in comparison to the divine. The ritual baths all around the Temple encouraged visitors to symbolically acknowledge, in a public and social manner, the purity and holiness of the Temple. The steps that led from the baths to the entrances alternated between short and long landings, forcing visitors to look down while ascending, thus compelling the masses to assume a reverent posture. Those traveling through the Double Portal of the Hulda Gates, which led from the bottom of the

Temple Mount through an internal staircase underneath the Royal Stoa up to an opening on the plaza, would have been struck by the sudden transition from a dark and ornately decorated passageway to the brilliant sun-drenched plaza. The move from darkness to light capped an already dramatic approach to the divine.

But there were also social divisions at work in the Temple Mount. Access to the sanctuary was increasingly restricted by a series of concentric barriers. The Court of the Gentiles, which comprised two-thirds of the Temple Mount, was open to all respectful visitors, after which a low balustrade, probably a stone barrier only a few feet high, marked off the area that Jews alone could enter. Two inscriptions, one complete and the other fragmentary, have been found that warn, in Greek, Gentiles to proceed no further. Beyond that barrier we have no archaeological evidence, since the Islamic Dome of the Rock blocks any excavation. But we know from literary sources that the next area was called the Court of Women; after that came the Court of the Israelites, then the Court of the Priests, and finally the sanctuary itself, inside which was the Holy of Holies, which was accessible only by the high priest on the Day of Atonement.

Two other structures shed light on Jesus's visit to the Temple: the Royal Stoa and the Antonia Fortress. The Royal Stoa was an enormous basilica along the southern edge of the Temple Mount that opened like a portico onto the plaza. Its roof was supported by four rows of columns, the final southern row incorporated as pilasters into the wall of the Temple Mount. The central columns were almost two meters in diameter and nearly ten meters high; spaced almost five meters apart, they made the basilica the largest roofed building in the land. This was where public and commercial activity took place, just like in pagan temples. Court cases were heard, scribes notarized financial transactions, and goods relating to sacrifices were sold, including sacrificial animals. Here, too, currency could be exchanged into Tyrian shekels for the Temple tax. This is probably where Jesus stirred up a riot when he "overturned the tables of the money-changers and the seats of those

who sold doves" (Matthew 21:12). Some have suggested that this disturbance took place below Robinson's Arch, where numerous shops have been found, but this is less likely, since Robinson's Arch was the last area to be constructed and was covered in scaffolding at the time of Jesus. Coins under the foundation date to decades after Jesus, and the pavement itself

opposite page

Plan of first-century CE Jerusalem.

this page

Lithostrotos **Pavement (2nd C. CE)**

Ecce Homo **Arch (2nd C. CE)**

A Dominican father and archaeologist showed that the *Lithostrotos* (the name given in John 19:13 for the pavement where Jesus was tried) and the *Ecce Homo* Arch (after Pilate's Latin exclamation "Behold the man" in John 19:5) date to a century after Jesus. Popular with modern tourists because they mark the beginning of the Via Dolorosa, they actually date to the rule of Hadrian (117–38 CE) and not the time of Pilate (26–36 CE).

shows few signs of wear. It was probably not accessible until shortly before the Romans destroyed it in 70 CE.

Only scant remains have been found of the Antonia Fortress, named after Mark Antony, which hovered over the Temple from the northwest. Although modern tourists are regularly shown the *Lithostrotos,* the stone pavement where Jesus was tried (according to John 19:13), and the *Ecce Homo* Arch (named after Pilate's Latin exclamation "Behold the man" in John 19:5), both date to the second century CE. Hence the current pilgrims' path along the Via Dolorosa to the Holy Sepulcher is probably inaccurate. The pavement is clearly a second-century CE construction, since it covers in part a first-century pool (called the Strouthion), and the arch was built later as a triumphal monument on the eastern forum of the city when it was renamed Aelia Capitolina by the Romans. These two features did not exist at the time of Jesus but were built after the emperor Hadrian (117–38 CE) destroyed and rebuilt the city.

Jesus may have been tried not at the Antonia but at Pilate's residence in the Upper City, in what was once Herod's palace. Nevertheless, the Antonia Fortress is important for understanding power dynamics in first-century Jerusalem, since it stood on the bedrock's highest point and provided a lookout over the Temple. The sanctuary is the Mount's center from an aerial perspective, but from a topographical perspective, the Antonia hovered over the mass of pilgrims and helped Roman soldiers keep an eye on the priests and crowds. In the architectural hierarchy of the Temple Mount, Rome was on top.

THE PRIESTLY ARISTOCRACY IN THE UPPER CITY

The Upper City was inextricably linked to the Temple — architecturally by a causeway to what archaeologists call Wilson's Arch, and socio-politically by the many priestly families who ran the Temple and lived in the Upper City. Extensive excavations reveal both the inhabitants' wealth and their adherence to Jewish tradition. Textual evidence suggests many high-priestly families

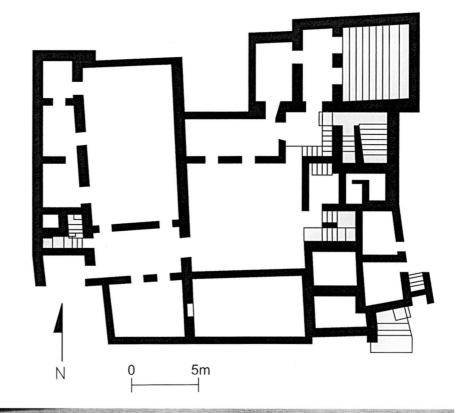

N   0   5m

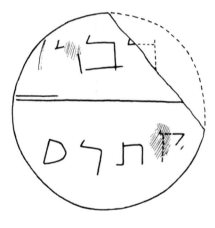

opposite page

Palatial Mansion (1st c. CE)

Geometric Mosaic (1st c. CE)

this page

Fresco from Upper City (1st c. CE)

Pottery from Upper City (1st c. CE)

Stone Vessels from Upper City (1st c. CE)

Burnt House (70 CE)

***Bar Kathros* Inscription (1st c. CE)**

Jerusalem's upper crust and high-priestly families lived in the Upper City, across the Tyropoeon Valley from the Temple. Archaeologists have uncovered the fine life that these inhabitants enjoyed, living in houses with elegant mosaics and frescoes and using stylish imported pottery and their imitations.

Households full of stoneware were also uncovered by excavations in the Upper City. Homes there were decked out in the best Roman style but remained thoroughly Jewish, observing the commandment against imagery and keeping purity with stone objects, including cups, mugs, jars, trays, and even tables. One inscription on a stone weight ties the inhabitants to Bar Kathros, a high-priestly family.

who belonged to the Sadducean party lived there, and one archaeological artifact attests as much: a stone weight found in what archaeologists call the Burnt House, inscribed in Aramaic with *Bar Kathros* ("son of Kathros"), a family name of high priests mentioned in ancient literary texts.

The Upper City's homes are the most affluent of Roman Palestine, exceeding by far those found in Sepphoris and rivaling those at Pompeii. One house covered six thousand square feet, about five times the size of houses at Sepphoris. Constructed as multi- and split-levels on hilly terrain around a central courtyard, the walls were solidly constructed by professionals and not simply built by the owner, as was the case in rural areas. Several rooms had mosaic-covered floors with large plain white tessarae stones, but a few had red-and-black geometric designs. One room boasted a floor in *opus sectile*, a Roman luxury style in which highly polished marble fragments were set puzzlelike into geometric patterns. Most walls were covered with elegant and colorful frescoes in what art historians call the Second Pompeiian style, which again shows an appetite for Roman tastes. They were executed in true fresco technique — painted while still wet, which is technically more demanding than the *al secco* or dry method. Decorations included garland strands, pomegranates, and apples, as well as imitated marble panels and geometric designs in red, ochre, or green; on occasion fluted ionic columns were painted onto the walls. In contrast to the rest of the Mediterranean world, the mosaics and frescoes from the Upper City show traditional Jewish conservatism in avoiding mythological, human, or even animal figures — with the one rather mundane exception of a small painted bird found on a fresco fragment on Mount Zion.

Pottery from the Upper City included many functional pots, jars, and jugs but also a surprising percentage of imported and local fine wares. These include *terra sigillata* wares, the classic red burnished bowls and plates with a lustrous slip and their maker's seal imprinted on the bottom. Most of these were the Eastern kind, which were imported from Syria, but some Western wares from Italy were also found. A rare molded Megarian bowl with large floral decorations was also discovered. Many thin, delicate, shallow bowls were excavated, which had been produced in or near Jerusalem. Their ringed floral patterns in red, brown, and black paint imitated the exquisite Nabatean bowls commonly found east of the Jordan, which underscores the inhabitants' desire for elegant and distinct dining wares. Alongside more simple blown glass wares, like vials for ointment and perfume, archaeologists uncovered a spectacular and rare glass jug made by a well-known glassmaker from Sidon.

All these artifacts show how the inhabitants selectively adopted or imitated Roman styles. But other artifacts underscore the Upper City's Jewishness. As in Galilee, the ubiquitous stone vessels and *mikvaoth* testify to purity concerns and lifestyle choices that distinguished Jews from their neighbors. Excavations after 1968 unearthed scores of stone vessels in each house, and recently production sites for these vessels were discovered on Mount Scopus and at Hizma just outside Jerusalem. Each Upper City house had several *mikvaoth*, and the Palatial Mansion had five. Whether multiple *mikvaoth* imply a division based on gender, separate facilities for servants, or perhaps some kind of seasonal rotation is unknown. Their frequency in the Upper City is probably due to the inhabitants' priestly lineages and the high priesthood's punctilious purity observances before officiating in the Temple. These stepped pools are distinct from other kinds of water installations found nearby, such as reservoirs for storing water, what look like bathtubs, and basins for washing feet. In addition, one finds in Upper City houses many round hypocaust tiles that were stacked as pillars to support a paved floor in a small room heated from below and used for saunalike steam baths. Such hot-bath rooms, *caldaria* in Latin, are found wherever Roman culture spread, always as part of large public baths. Archaeologists have uncovered similar baths at Herod the Great's palaces in Jericho and Masada.

Given the conspicuous absence of public bathhouses in Jerusalem, the *mikvaoth* and *caldaria* in the homes of the Upper City show a fine balance between accommodation to Romanization and adherence to Jewish traditions. The priestly elite built hot baths *inside* their homes and avoided the problems of public bathing: nudity, the mixing of sexes, and purity contamination through water. They enjoyed their steam baths but also set aside rainwater in *mikvaoth* to bathe ritually. They kept purity with the best-made and largest stone vessels ever found. In that sense, they shared Jewish purity concerns with their fellow Galileans, Jerusalem's lower classes, and pilgrims, but they did so in a much more elegant style.

CRUCIFIXION AND JEWISH BURIAL PRACTICES

Roman procurators and Jewish high priests collaborated in keeping Jerusalem's potentially unruly crowds under control, especially at Passover. Roman authorities commonly used crucifixion to instill fear in the masses. Although crucifixion was frequently imposed on noncitizens all across the Roman Empire, it has left slim archaeological evidence, as most victims were simply left on the cross to rot away. Nevertheless, archaeologists have identified one victim of Roman crucifixion, found in 1968 in an ossuary north of Jerusalem at Givat Hamivtar. The right heel bone of a man, estimated by physical anthropologists to have been 5'5" tall and in his mid-twenties, had been pierced by a six-inch nail. The man's legs had been made to straddle the beam and his ankles were nailed to it, with thin olivewood boards serving as washers to prevent him from pulling his leg off the end of the nail. After the crucifixion, a nail that had been hammered into a knot in the beam could not be removed, so his ankle was simply chopped off, along with a chunk of the beam, and then ankle, nail, and washer were gathered with the rest of the body and the bones were deposited in an ossuary with the man's name, Yehochanan, etched on the side. Careful analysis identified no trauma to his hand, wrist, or arm bones, sug-

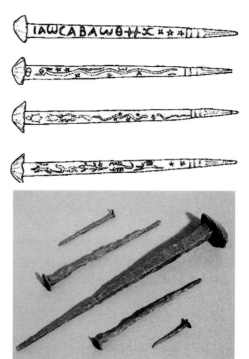

"So Joseph took the body and wrapped it in a clean linen cloth and laid it in his own new tomb, which he had hewn in the rock."

MATTHEW 27:59–60

Jesus's cross would have looked like is highly speculative, since Christians did not use the cross as a symbol until after the fourth century CE, when crucifixion ceased as a form of punishment.

Though there is little archaeological evidence regarding crucifixion, there is a lot for Jewish burial practices at the time of Jesus. Excavations of tombs around the ancient city show that Jewish burial practices were similar to that described in the Gospels, which the authors of the Gospels presume but rarely explain. First-century Jewish death rituals were based on the ancient Semitic tradition of secondary burial, in which the body was first laid out for about a year to decompose; in the secondary phase, the bones were gathered up and redeposited, which explains the Hebrew Bible's desire "to be gathered to my people" (Genesis 49:29). By the time of Jesus, the deceased were laid out in underground chambers either inside deep fingerlike

opposite page

Nails as Amulets (4th C. CE)
Roman Nails (Scotland, 1st C. CE)

this page

Crucified Ankle (Jerusalem, 1st C. CE)
Palatine Hill Graffiti (Rome, 2nd C. CE)
Rolling Stone (1st C. CE)
Rolling Stone, Side View
Shelf Inside Tomb

The agony of crucifixion is clear when one looks at the kind of nails the Romans used. The only crucified victim ever found had the nail slammed through his ankle as he straddled the beam, and not through the front of his feet as most icons depict. The nail was over six inches long and became thicker toward the head, as did all these Roman nails found at a legionary fort in Scotland.

Little definitive evidence exists for the details of crucifixion. All Christian depictions date to after the practice was outlawed. In the only early depiction, from the Palatine Hill in Rome, a pagan mocks a Christian named Alexamenos for worshipping an ass crucified on an upper T-shaped and not a lower t-shaped cross. The Gospels understandably offer virtually no details about the technical aspects of crucifixion.

The Gospels' description of Jesus's burial conforms remarkably well to the archaeological evidence. Although most underground burial chambers were closed with square or rectangular doors, several round stones that roll into place have been found, including this one from Herod's family tomb. Bodies were laid out on an *arcosolium* shelf, such as this one from the so-called Tombs of the Kings.

gesting that his arms were tied to the cross with ropes and not nailed through the hands, as the Gospels say was done with Jesus. There was, of course, no standard method of crucifixion. As the Roman philosopher Seneca, an eyewitness to Nero's brutality, says, "I see crosses not just of one kind but made in many different ways" (*Ad Marciam* 20). Determining what

shafts called *kokhim*, which extended some six feet from the chamber into the walls, or on shelves (called *arcosolia*) cut nichelike into the chamber. Corpses were tied together with a few strips of cloth, to keep the jaw shut and the arms and legs together as the body was, in what must have been an awkward moment, dragged through the chamber's small opening. In the first century CE, bones were often collected into ossuaries, whose lids and sides were sometimes decorated or had the names of the interred etched on their sides.

Why did ossuaries begin to be used in Jerusalem right before the time of Jesus? Some say they reflect the belief in bodily resurrection held by many Jews, most notably the Pharisees, in the late Second Temple period. Others say that depositing individual skeletons in discreet containers reflects a heightened sense of individuality, in line with the Hellenist spirit of the time. But it is hard to fit the archaeological evidence with those theological explanations.

Only a few ossuaries contained a single individual. The vast majority held several skeletons, and the names etched on their sides indicate that family burials were the norm, with endearing terms like the Aramaic *Abba* ("Daddy") or *Emma* ("Mommy"), along with "son of," "wife of," or "father of." These identifications helped survivors at a later time put a child, spouse, or parent with the desired loved ones. Though charnel pits with anonymous multiple interments of entire extended families were abandoned in the late Second Temple period, the numerous family members inside single ossuaries suggests that individuality was not the ideal. Each person, even in death, was bound to his or her family. Thus the Gospels' claim that Jesus was placed inside a "new tomb" (Matthew 27:60) or a tomb "where no one had ever been laid" (Luke 23:53) may sound attractive to modern ears, but to ancient Jewish ears it must have sounded like a lonely, isolated, and tragic end to Jesus's life.

Connecting ossuaries to belief in resurrection is likewise problematic. Caiaphas's ossuary shows just how hard it is to infer beliefs from practices. He was the ruling high priest from 18 to 37 CE, but he and all the first-century CE high-priestly families were Sadducees, who, unlike the Pharisees, did not believe in the resurrection of the dead (Mark 12:23–33; Acts 23:7–8). Another ossuary of a Sadducean family member has the Aramaic inscription "Yehochana daughter of Yehochanan, son of Thophlos, the high priest." The name *Thophlos* is probably an abbreviation of *Theophilos*, Greek for "lover of God," and was the name of the son of Annus, the high priest from 37–41 CE. Other common high-priestly family names on ossuaries include Boethos, Ananias, and Ananus, but it is unlikely that these Sadducees collected and preserved the bones of their loved ones in anticipation of the resurrection; more likely, they simply adopted the burial practice common among urban Jews of some means in Jerusalem.

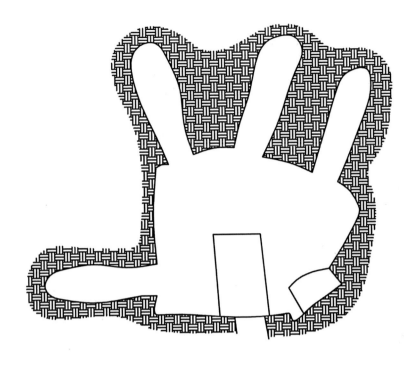

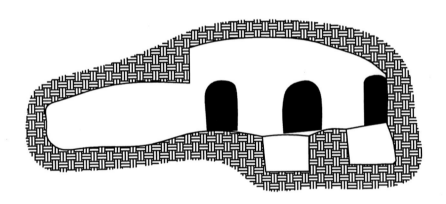

elite, who constructed highly visible monuments along the western slope of the Kidron Valley. These incorporated architectural styles common in Hellenistic tombs, like columns or architraves on their facades, or the round conical top of Absalom's tomb or the pyramid atop Zechariah's tomb, or ornaments in the form of scrolls and vines that derive from Italian artistic traditions. The Jewish elites borrowed elements from abroad, as they put their tombs on display and competed with each other for prestige and honor. But none could rival that of King Herod, who built a monument that he called the Herodium some eight miles south of Jerusalem. It was a complex that was part mausoleum, part fortress, and part pleasure palace. Herod shaped it as a large artificial mound in the Judean Wilderness and even leveled a hill east of the site to ensure it would be visible from Jerusalem and to make it look higher than it really was. Long after his death, it was a landmark visible from Jerusalem, a burial worthy of a king — and completely different from what Jesus received.

The Romans had executed Jesus as a criminal on a cross because they saw him as a threat. The broader archaeological context of Jerusalem makes clear what he was threatening. The high-priestly families lived luxuriously in the Upper City and benefited financially from the Temple. Indeed, the city as a whole was expanding and flourishing after Herod the Great. To enter that context and threaten the Temple in any way, as Jesus did, would be to threaten the tenuous collaboration between Roman rule and the Jewish high priesthood. It would bring to the surface

Caiaphas's ornately decorated ossuary reminds us that monuments for the dead are also ciphers for the present social life, and tombs indicate the deceased's position in the social hierarchy. This ossuary is one of the most beautiful ever found, and indicates what he or his family thought about his status relative to others in Jerusalem. Not everyone could afford an ossuary, and not every family had a plot for a burial chamber. Simpler graves farther outside Jerusalem — like those at Beit Safafa, which were accidentally discovered during road construction — would have otherwise escaped notice, since they were not marked by a tombstone or even a pile of stones. The rectangular vertical shafts went five to seven feet down and had a horizontal shaft at the bottom where bodies were laid. A limestone slab sealed the opening where the vertical and horizontal shafts met, and rocks and dirt filled in the vertical shaft. Most tombs contained one body; one contained a plain ossuary. Of the identifiable bones from forty-seven persons, forty-two were from adults and five were from children between five and eighteen years old. Given the reality of much higher rates of infant and child mortality, the chilling conclusion is that most of the young were disposed of hastily. Burials found outside Jerusalem for the very poor were shallow, foot-deep depressions cut into bedrock and then covered with stone slabs. Interred alongside the deceased were a few Hasmonean coins and a small glass vial or two.

Those simplest burials, inconspicuous and farther from the city, were very different from the tombs of the

opposite page

Caiaphas Ossuary (1st C. CE)

this page

Plan of Caiaphas Tomb

The ossuary of Caiaphas, high priest when Jesus was crucified, was found in 1990 inside a tomb with four *kokhim* shafts extending fingerlike from a central chamber. In one shaft was this ornately decorated ossuary with a faded orange wash barely visible on some areas. His name had been crudely etched by family members on one side, perhaps with one of the two nails found nearby. Inside, among other bones, were those of a sixty-some-year-old man believed to have been Caiaphas.

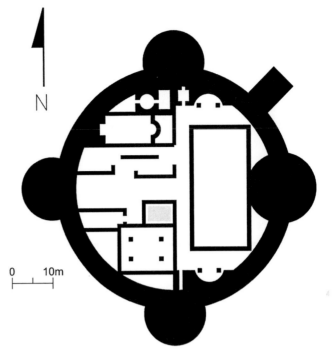

century-long tensions between Hellenistic and Roman acculturation and Jewish tradition. Jesus was crucified and given a Jewish burial, but no one would consider it an ideal burial. He was buried alone in a newly cut tomb without family or friends. He was not given a burial befitting a king like Herod the Great had at the Herodium. For that he would have to wait another four centuries, until Helena, the mother of Constantine the Great, built the Church of the Holy Sepulcher.

opposite page
Herod Family Tomb
Mount of Olives
this page
Absalom's Tomb
Herodium Plan
Herodium

The burials of the rich can be found all around the Old City of Jerusalem. The tomb believed to belong to Herod's family was found just north of the city walls. Its enormous rolling stone is still functional. Many elaborate monuments, in Hellenistic and Roman styles, line the Mount of Olives east of the city, like Absalom's tomb here.

Tombs mark social status, and no one was more important than Herod the Great. His burial complex, called the Herodium, southeast of Jerusalem included a massive artificial mound, visible all across the landscape and from Jerusalem. Like most rulers of the ancient world, he spent enormous energy on his own tomb, most likely with an eye to communicating his status to his subjects while still alive, rather than out of concern about his fate in the afterlife.

Jerusalem's stratigraphy is complex and confusing. The perennial destruction of the city and its constant reshaping, even in modern times, has left few open spaces for excavation in a three-dimensional puzzle of floors, walls, and building materials cobbled together from all possible periods. The city was completely destroyed on three occasions: by the Babylonians in the sixth century BCE and twice by the Romans, first in 70 CE and again in 135 CE. The two Roman conflagrations were so thorough and massive that they sealed much of the Second Temple underneath the new pagan city, called Aelia Capitolina, from which Jews were barred. Later Jerusalem would become the crown jewel of the Christian Holy Land, and so pagan temples were torn down and replaced with Christian churches; not long after that, Jerusalem became the third holiest city in Islam, and the Dome of the Rock was set smack in the middle of a heavily repaired Herodian Temple Mount. Jerusalem would endure devastating Crusader wars, the poverty of Ottoman rule, British colonial rule, a war of independence that divided the city, and the ravages of the 1967 Six-Day War. Because of that complex history, there has never been a comprehensive plan to excavate the city; instead, a who's-who of archaeologists have set spade to ground over the past two centuries somewhere in or around the city of Jerusalem for a season, a decade, or a lifetime. Students are left with the difficult task of finding those different publications and putting together some synthesis of the jumble of excavations.

The American Edward Robinson explored around Jerusalem in 1838, identifying the arch from the Temple Mount's western wall that still bears his name. The first excavations were by the Frenchman Louis Félicien de Saulcy (1807–1880) and the British Charles Warren (1840–1927) in the 1860s. The former excavated rather unsuccessfully the Tombs of the Kings, which he erroneously thought was the burial place of the Davidic dynasty but in fact belong to the first-century Jewish convert Queen Helena. Warren surveyed and mapped the Temple Mount on behalf of the Palestine Exploration Fund. His adventures included being stoned by locals as he scaled the walls of the Haram al-Sharif, being buried alive when an underground tunnel caved in on him, and nearly drowning in sewage when the walls of a pit collapsed.

Most of the early excavations were directed by archaeologists from the colonial powers of the Middle East, either British, French, American, or German. Kathleen Kenyon (1906–1978) of the British Palestine Explora-

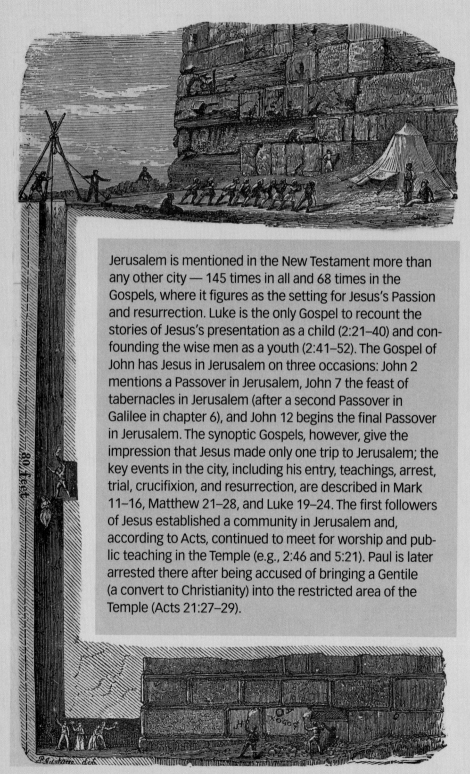

Jerusalem is mentioned in the New Testament more than any other city — 145 times in all and 68 times in the Gospels, where it figures as the setting for Jesus's Passion and resurrection. Luke is the only Gospel to recount the stories of Jesus's presentation as a child (2:21–40) and confounding the wise men as a youth (2:41–52). The Gospel of John has Jesus in Jerusalem on three occasions: John 2 mentions a Passover in Jerusalem, John 7 the feast of tabernacles in Jerusalem (after a second Passover in Galilee in chapter 6), and John 12 begins the final Passover in Jerusalem. The synoptic Gospels, however, give the impression that Jesus made only one trip to Jerusalem; the key events in the city, including his entry, teachings, arrest, trial, crucifixion, and resurrection, are described in Mark 11–16, Matthew 21–28, and Luke 19–24. The first followers of Jesus established a community in Jerusalem and, according to Acts, continued to meet for worship and public teaching in the Temple (e.g., 2:46 and 5:21). Paul is later arrested there after being accused of bringing a Gentile (a convert to Christianity) into the restricted area of the Temple (Acts 21:27–29).

tion Fund excavated between 1961 and 1967 south of the Temple Mount. She was the first to meticulously excavate in squares and carefully record stratigraphy; her work set the benchmark for future excavations.

At the end of the Six-Day War in 1967, Israeli archaeologists began archaeological excavations on an unprecedented scale. Benjamin Mazar worked just south of the Temple Mount, and Nahman Avigad excavated in the Upper City, in what is now known as the Old City's Jewish Quarter. Together, these two projects generated unprecedented materials from Herodian Jerusalem up to the city's destruction in 70 CE — the very city as Jesus knew it. The most dramatic discovery was the Burnt House, in which was found the weight belonging to the high priestly family Kathros. Romans pillaging the house in 70 CE had left it a mess, and the terror of that final moment was frozen in time: a woman's forearm clutched at the stairs as she tried to escape, and a spear leaning against a wall had either been forgotten by a Roman soldier or left unused by a Jewish defender. In 1994, Ronni Reich began excavations south and southwest of the Temple Mount.

Major Excavations with Key Herodian Finds

Excavators	Dates of Excavation	Discoveries/Areas
E. Robinson	1838	Robinson's Arch
C. Wilson	1867–68	Wilson's Arch on Temple Mount
C. W. Warren	1867–70	Warren's Shaft, Siloam Tunnel, Strouthion Pool, shafts to bedrock around Temple Mount
L. F. de Saulcy	1863	Tombs of the Kings
C. Clermont–Ganneau	1869–71, 1873–74	Absalom's Tomb, Antonia Region, *Ecce Homo* Arch, Soreg Inscription
K. Mauss	1863–76, 1888–1900	Pool of Bethesda, Church of Saint Anne
C. Schick	1886–1901	Herod's family tomb, Gihon Spring
L. H. Vincent	1910–13	Portions of Third Wall
R. Weill	1913–14 1923–24	South of Temple Mount, Theodotus Inscription
E. L. Sukenik	1925–46	Portions of Third Wall, Nicanor's Tomb on Mount Scopus, tombs
R. W. Hamilton	1931, 1937–38	Street and channel in Tyropoeon Valley, Damascus Gate, Second Wall
N. Avigad	1945–47	Tombs, incl. Bene Hezir
P. Bagatti & G. Milik	1953–55	Tombs of Dominus Flevit on Mount of Olives
K. M. Kenyon	1961–67	Destruction of Temple by Romans, Mount Zion
J. Hennessy	1964–66	Damascus Gate, Third Wall
B. Mazar	1968–78	South and southwest of the Herodian Temple Mount
N. Avigad	1969–82	Upper City, residences including the Palatial Mansion
M. Broshi	1971–77	Homes in the Armenian Garden and Mount Zion
P. Benoit	1972	Probes around the *Lithostrotos*
Y. Shiloh	1978–85	City of David excavations, mostly earlier periods, but ample Hellenistic and Herodian finds in fills
R. Reich	1994–present	The Herodian Street, shops, and pier of Robinson's Arch, debris from Royal Stoa, Warren's shaft and water-system, Siloam Pool

6

PAUL AND THE CITIES OF THE ROMAN EMPIRE

As background for Jesus and the Gospels, we examined the archaeology of a very small region, Galilee, and then the excavations in a single city, Jerusalem. To understand Paul, who figures prominently in the book of Acts and wrote the bulk of the New Testament's letters, we have to cover the eastern half of the Mediterranean. His travels took him from Jerusalem through modern-day Syria, Turkey, Greece, and ultimately Italy to Rome itself. That is a vast geographical area, with hundreds of archaeological excavations and countless archaeological finds in the form of architecture, shipwrecks, mosaics, inscriptions, pottery, frescoes, and coins. But the task is made easier by Paul's own itinerary, which concentrated on provincial capitals like Pisidian Antioch, Thessalonica, Corinth, and Ephesus. So we focus in this chapter on the urban context of Paul's ministry and what life was like in the cities of the Roman Empire. We will pay special attention to what archaeology reveals about how diaspora Jews lived in these pagan cities. As in previous chapters, we will not restrict ourselves to those places mentioned in Acts or Paul's letters, but will pursue the archaeologist to whatever excavations best illustrate urban life in the Roman Empire. Thematically, this chapter moves from the archaeology of public spaces, like the forum and its many temples, to semipublic religious meeting places, including Jewish synagogues, to domestic neighborhoods and private houses, and even an intimate look inside the ancient bedroom, all with the goal of generating an archaeological context for Paul's life. At the end of the chapter, we will look at travel on land and sea, and consider what shipwrecks say about the danger of Paul's many travels.

According to Acts, Paul traveled on three long missionary journeys through Turkey and Greece, and then, after a two-year imprisonment in Caesarea Maritima, was taken in chains on a fourth trip, when he sailed, shipwrecked, and sailed on to house arrest in Rome and an appeal to Caesar himself. Acts describes the typical pattern of his ministry as entering a city, preaching in the synagogue, where he is always rejected and often accused before Roman authorities, and then establishing small communities of mixed Gentiles and Jews. His message, as preserved in his letters, is that Jesus was the Christ, the anointed one and Son of God who was resurrected from the dead. But his resurrection was only the first of many, since Jesus would soon return, bringing a general resurrection that would transform the entire world. The most controversial part of his vision was that Gentiles could join Jews in the church — which he called in Greek *ekklesia* — without undergoing the Jewish rites of circumcision or adhering to Jewish dietary and purity laws. Moral behavior alone would show that one was "in Christ."

Archaeology can't confirm the truth of Paul's message. The many archaeological discoveries relating to people, places, or titles mentioned in Acts do lend credence to its historicity at one level; many of the specific details in Acts are factual. Archaeology rules out a fantastic fabrication that is completely disconnected from the first-century CE Roman world, but it cannot confirm or deny the point of the speeches in Acts, the reality of its miracles, or even the itinerary of the apostle. Archaeology can, however, provide a rich and full description of Acts and Paul's urban context, which

> "Bring me a denarius . . . whose head is this, and whose title?"
>
> MARK 12:15–16

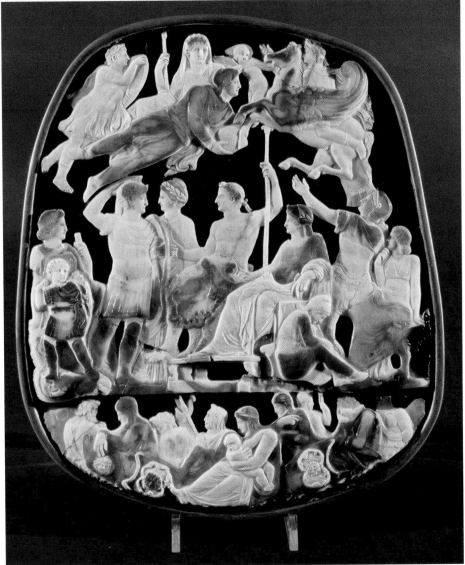

revolutionizes our understanding of their radicalness. And Roman imperial art, images, inscriptions, and temples explain why Roman religious tolerance reached its limits with Paul and the first Christians.

opposite page

Augustus's Star Coin (12 BCE)
Octavian's *Imperator* Coin (31–29 BCE)
Octavian's *Victoria* Coin (31–29 BCE)

this page

Antonius's Ascension (2nd C. CE)
Cameo of Tiberius (1st C. CE)

The real son of God, according to almost every coin minted in the Roman Empire, was the Roman emperor. Julius Caesar was divinized by the Senate upon his death, and his son Octavian, later named Augustus, proclaimed that a comet over Rome was Julius Caesar taking his place among the gods, and featured that star prominently on his coins. Augustus then called himself the *son of god,* a title abbreviated in Latin as DI FI, which each subsequent emperor adopted but Christians rejected.

The widespread belief in the resurrection is illustrated on this ten-by-twelve-inch cameo, which depicts the apotheosis of the imperial family and not the resurrection of Jesus. The *Grande Camée de France* in Paris has in its middle panel the enthroned Tiberius in near duplication of Jupiter; the top register shows a member of the Julio-Claudian dynasty ascending to heaven. The second-century relief in the Vatican shows the later emperor Antonius Pius and his wife Faustina ascending to heaven.

THE OTHER SON OF GOD

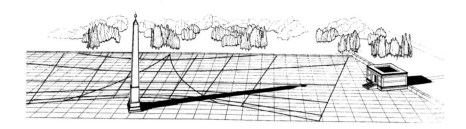

The idea that a divine savior had risen to take his place in heaven would seem familiar to every first-century Mediterranean. But they would be puzzled that it was a Jewish carpenter crucified under Pilate in Jerusalem. Most everyone had heard — and certainly seen in sculptural images, decorative iconography, and numismatic symbols — that the Roman emperors since Augustus were divine men who ascended after death to take their place among the gods in heaven.

We have already seen that coins had declared Alexander the Great and Antiochus Epiphanes divine in their own lifetimes. But those coins were no match for the immense visual display that deified the Roman emperors. After Julius Caesar's assassination in 44 BCE, his eighteen-year-old adopted son, Octavian, celebrated games honoring the slain Caesar with impeccable timing, because right then a comet appeared in the sky. Octavian promoted it as the apotheosis of Julius Caesar, now divine and ascending to take his

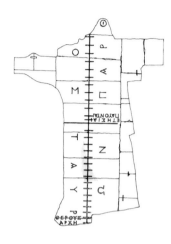

heavenly place with the gods. Archaeologists find that star on engraved gemstones, clay seal impressions, and cheap glass beads, but it is displayed most prominently on coins minted by Octavian. His subsequent coins draw the logical conclusion that, if Julius Caesar is divine, then his son is "son of a divine one" or "son of god." The Latin title is variously abbreviated from DIVI FILIUS as DIVI FI, DIVI F, or DI FI. Coins were the mass media of antiquity, and the message of his and subsequent caesars' divinity was read and understood by all across the Roman-controlled world — including Galilee, to judge by Jesus, who challenged that divinity at its very foundations when he said, "Give to Caesar what is

Caesar's and to God what is God's" (Matthew 22:15–22; Mark 12:13–17; and Luke 20:20–26).

After Octavian put an end to civil wars, the Senate gave him the name Augustus, which in Latin means "the

"... when they say, 'There is peace and security,' then sudden destruction will come upon them."

1 THESSALONIANS 5:3

tinuing to his successor, Tiberius (14–37 CE), who ruled when Jesus was executed, through Caligula (37–41 CE) and Claudius (41–54 CE), under whom Paul actively ministered; and Nero (54–68 CE), under whom Paul was probably executed in Rome. They would all be "sons of god," and took the titular name Augustus. In Greek they and their immediate families were called the *Sebastoi,* or "the revered ones." The archaeological and epigraphic evidence shows that the caesars were honored and worshipped in various ways in each city. The phenomenon was not unified under a set of Latin doctrines or regulated by a Rome-based priestly hierarchy, even though the emperor was also the *pontifex maximus,* the high priest and supreme bridge-builder between heaven and earth. Instead, the diverse archaeological evidence suggests that local initiatives variously honored the Julio-Claudian emperors based on local political conditions and local religious traditions, as cities and provinces competed with lavish and creative tributes to the emperor.

These varied imperial cults were the most recognizable feature in the hundreds of cities that dotted the Mediterranean, and Paul would have to contend with these in each city he entered. Thousands of inscriptions show that it was the ideological and theological glue that held the cities of the Roman Empire together, seducing the urban poor with festivals and banquets

revered one," "the increaser," or "the majestic one." He was also called "Lord and Savior," since after defeating his rival Antony in 31 BCE, he ended the social chaos and economic hardships caused all across the Mediterranean by civil war. Those titles were completely credible to the empire's population, who under Augustus enjoyed the benefits of Roman peace. At Myra in Turkey an inscription calls him "the God Augustus, Son of God, Caesar, Autocrat of land and sea, the Benefactor and Savior of the whole cosmos." Another from Halicarnassus on Turkey's western coast calls him "Father of his own Fatherland, Divine Rome, Zeus Paternal,

and Savior of the whole human race." And in Narbonne in France, the inhabitants committed in inscription to bind "themselves to the worship of his divinity in perpetuity" by celebrating rites there on Augustus's birthday. His birthday was given cosmic significance, and astrological phenomena were used to bolster his status in numismatic, epigraphic, and iconographic emblems all over the empire.

PAGAN WORSHIP IN PUBLIC SPACES

Augustus was not only divine, but his extraordinary authority extended that divinity throughout the dynasty, con-

whose sacrificial meat and complementary drinks in the name of the emperor were hard to resist. Freed slaves and artisans received philanthropic benefits like free gladiatorial games, chariot races, or spectacles in the name of the emperor. And the ambitious elites acquired positions of power within their communities as they assumed priestly offices in the imperial cult.

Artifacts, from small coins to large temples to entire cities, give an absolutely clear archaeological picture of Caesar's centrality to the empire's inhabitants. For example, at Pisidian Antioch, where, according to Acts, Paul stopped on his first missionary journey (Acts 13:13–52), archaeologists have uncovered the civic center that dominated the urban landscape and whose design, detail, and setting mimicked Rome's Augustan Forum with a long plaza surrounded by a two-storied colonnade and portico. Its eastern apse-like end faced Rome, and not east as was customary. It was approached by ascending from the west on the plaza-like *Tiberia Plateia* ("the Tiberian Boulevard") through a monumental triple-arched gate, and those who entered could read a large inscription in bronze letters, since stripped but decipherable to epigraphers from the many peg holes that held the letters in place. It read: IMP. CAES[ARI DI]VI F. AUGUSTO. PONFI[F]ICI M[AXIM]O, "For the Imperator Caesar Augustus, son of god, *pontifix maximus.*" Around this gate, archaeologists have found fragments of the Latin *Acts of the Divine Augustus,* an autobiography that was widely distributed across the empire and served as the Augustan gospel.

At Thessalonica, which Paul visited on his second missionary journey, according to Acts, and to whose Christian community he wrote, two statues have been found from the time of Paul. One is of Augustus, entirely nude except for a robe wrapped around his waist and draped over his forearm. This pose, his near nudity, and his bare feet are unmistakable claims to divinity in the iconography of Greco-Roman statues. The second statue is identical from the neck down and is probably of Claudius, who ruled while Paul was in

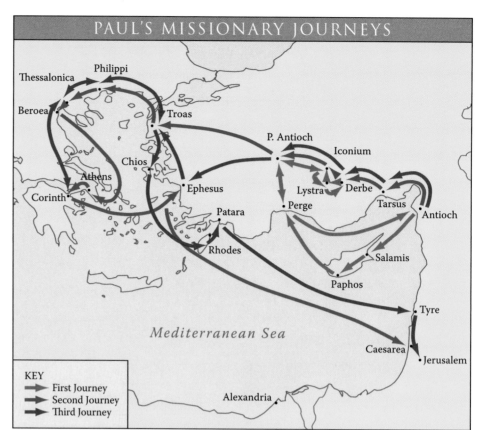

PAUL'S MISSIONARY JOURNEYS

KEY
→ First Journey
→ Second Journey
→ Third Journey

Mediterranean Sea

Thessalonica. Both were probably cult statues inside a temple, or stood in the forum around which Thessalonian civic leaders offered sacrifices. Thousands of similar statues across the empire made the caesars the most recognizable figures in the world. At Caesarea Maritima, where Paul was imprisoned for two years before being taken to stand trial in Rome, the Temple of Roma and Augustus dominated the city. According to Josephus, Augustus's statue in that temple was seated like Zeus. Two now-headless but seated statues have been found of later emperors, probably Trajan and Hadrian, which served as cult statues inside the temple. And as we saw in chapter 3, the inscription by Pontius Pilate excavated in the theater commemorated a *Tiberium,* a structure set aside for the imperial cult and the worship of the living divine Tiberius.

We can imagine, then, given the ubiquity of the imperial cult, why Paul and other early Christians who proclaimed that Jesus Christ was Lord and Savior, God and Son of God, would have been met with suspicion, ridicule, and persecution. Most everyone deemed the conquering caesars, who brought peace to the world and benefits to its cities, to be worthy of such praise; to give those titles to a crucified Jew from the provinces was preposterous. Religion and the gods permeated all aspects of public life, and it is hard to imagine how a Jew or a Christian could extricate him- or herself from their pervasiveness. Excavations in cities across the empire show how difficult it would have been to avoid paganism. The daily visits to the public baths took place in the shadow of the gods' statues, court proceedings began with an offering to a god and Caesar, and before embarking on a ship sacrifices were made to the gods.

We can imagine the consternation that paganism caused Paul's community when we look at the archaeology in and around Corinth. Archaeologists have uncovered in the city center stalls belonging to a *macellum,* or market, where meat from animals sacrificed to the gods in nearby temples was sold. Did a Christian or a Jew abstain from buying such meat? The common prescription for ailments of all kinds was a visit to the Asclepion, which included a temple to the healing god Asclepius and was run by priests, but which essentially was a spa where patients ate well, bathed, and then slept in a chamber and discussed their dreams with the priests. It was a sort of ancient dream-therapy and spa combined. Would a Christian or a Jew visit such ancient hospitals? Finally, the most

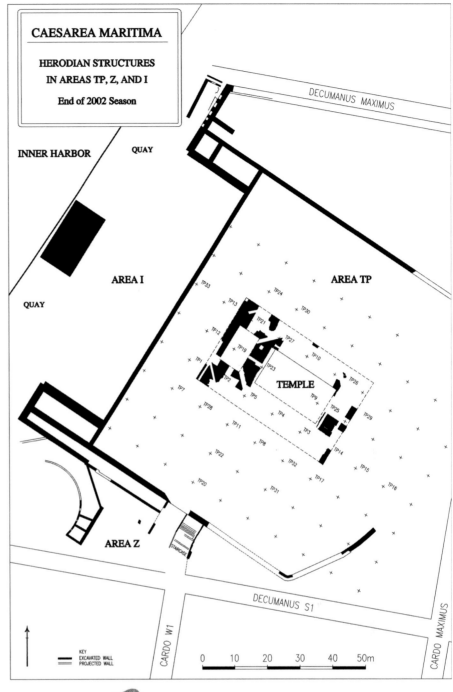

opposite page

Antioch Excavations (1924)
Augustus Statue (Thessalonica, 1st C. CE)

this page

Plan of Caesarea Temple
Claudius Statue (Thessalonica, 1st C. CE)

In every city Caesar was lord; excavations show that wherever Paul went, the imperial cult was already there. At Pisidian Antioch in Galatia, excavators in 1924 found a main street, called the *Tiberia Plateia* after the emperor Tiberius, which led to a temple dedicated to Augustus. At Thessalonica, to whose Christian community Paul wrote, two statues of the emperors Augustus and Claudius were found, both styled after a god. Even at Caesarea Maritima, where Paul was eventually imprisoned, archaeologists have found the outlines of a massive temple dedicated to the god Augustus and the goddess Roma.

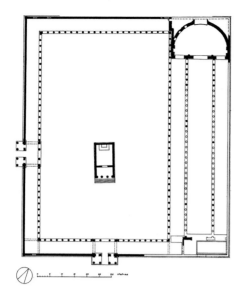

popular form of entertainment in Roman cities like Corinth at Paul's time were the various chariot, horse, and human races, as well as other athletic competitions that occurred at key festivals on a regular basis. Corinth's famous Isthmian Games were held every two years and were considered the most important competition, like the modern Olympics, World Cup, and Super Bowl wrapped into one. Sometime around the middle of the first century CE, the games moved to the nearby Temple of Poseidon in Isthmia, and additional games, called the Caesarean Games, were brought to Corinth on a four-year rotation. The excavations at Isthmia clearly show how interwoven temple and games were, as the entire festival served to worship the gods, whether Poseidon or Caesar. Many male contests were held in the nude, and these games were one of the few competitions to include women, who may have been scantily clad from a Jewish or Christian perspective. Nevertheless, Paul's letters show considerable familiarity with such athletic contests, and we can surmise that he was quite the sports fan. He uses expressions like "running my course in vain" (Galatians 2:2), "my contest" (Philippians 1:30), and pressing "on toward the goal to win the prize" (Philippians 3:14). And his first letter to the Corinthians includes an extended athletic metaphor that shows considerable acquaintance with such athletic competitions:

> Do you not know that in a race the runners all compete, but only one receives the prize? Run in such a way that you

> "...what pagans sacrifice, they sacrifice to demons and not to God."
>
> 1 CORINTHIANS 10:20

may win it. Athletes exercise self-control in all things; they do it to receive a perishable wreath, but we an imperishable one. So I do not run aimlessly, nor do I box as though beating the air; but I punish my body and enslave it, so that after proclaiming to others I myself should not be disqualified. (9:24–27)

The prominence of such athletic events is clear in the archaeological record at Corinth, Isthmia, and other cities, and shows that Paul was a man of his day. He was a sports fan. But what is puzzling is that such games were observed as an act of worship to pagan gods, if not the emperor himself, and were accompanied by sacrificial ceremonies and processional hymns at a temple or shine that was a central component of the athletic complex. Paul must have been an eager spectator but somehow avoided or thought he was avoiding participation in the games' religious ceremonies.

RELIGIOUS MEETINGS IN THE ROMAN WORLD

These inscriptions, statues, and temples remind us that in the Roman Empire, most religious activities were conducted outdoors and in public. The archaeology of Greek and Roman

temples shows that, unlike religion in the modern West, which tends to be monotheistic and primarily concerned with personal beliefs, paganism at the time of Paul was polytheistic and primarily concerned with civic cults. A great variety of gods and goddesses were appeased with gifts, vows, and, above all, animal sacrifices. Their temples stood next to or facing each other in the city's forum, and there is no hint of antagonism or competition among the deities. Local calendars regulated a series of scheduled festivals, which were often holidays for the whole city, so that people could gather, mingle, and eat the sacrifices in a kind of public barbeque.

From numerous depictions on altars and even cups, we know that the priests officiating at these ceremonies supervised the sacrifices in a civic performance with processions, pomp, and song. Those ceremonies not only bonded community and deity, they also brought community members together and articulated the social hierarchy. From the many inscriptions, we know that with rare exceptions, only male landowning aristocrats were eligible for the civic priesthood. They did not study for these priestly offices and needed no sense of calling; rather they purchased them outright or were elected to them based on their contributions to civic projects.

Roman authorities were generally tolerant of the worship of local gods and fully expected public sacrifices to indigenous or favored deities to continue alongside the imperial cult. But religious or other meetings that were not conducted in public were viewed with suspicion. One way to avoid that suspicion and still gather outside the public view was to include some visible gesture to the emperor. At Ephesus — where Paul spent perhaps several years, according to Acts, and from which he wrote to the Corinthian church — many associations that functioned like guilds and had a patron deity also included visible honors to

"When they heard this, they were enraged and shouted, 'Great is Artemis of the Ephesians!'"

ACTS 19:28

opposite page

Temple Plan (Cyrene, North Africa)
Fresco of Isis Temple (Pompeii, 1st c. CE)
Procession on Altar (Pompeii, 1st c. CE)

this page

Boscoreale Cup (1st c. CE)
Artemis Statue (Ephesus, 2nd c. CE)
Coin with Artemis (117 CE)
Ephesus Theater (1st c. CE)

Roman temples were hierarchical in their architecture, and worship took place in front of the temple. Many Eastern temples had an enclosed sacred area (*temenos*), exemplified by this imperial temple in North Africa, whose plan is similar to Herod's Temple in Jerusalem. People watched the priests in front of the temple proper, similar to the worship of the goddess Isis in this painted fresco from Pompeii. This cup from Boscoreale shows how priests and assistants stunned animals and then slit the throat to drain the blood. Blood, a few body parts, and often wine were burned on the altar.

Paul stirred up a riot at Ephesus in this theater, according to Acts 19. The silversmiths, an important guild that manufactured silver statues of the goddess Artemis, rioted after they heard Paul denounce man-made gods. The goddess was frequently depicted with many breasts on silver coins and in statues, such as this one excavated at the site of the temple called the Artemesion.

Caesar in their inscriptions. Nearly a quarter of the over one hundred Ephesian inscriptions for associations somehow also incorporate the worship of Caesar. One fragmentary inscription, of interest given Paul's trouble with them (Acts 19:23–41), records the silversmiths' devotion to the Ephesian goddess Artemis as well as the Roman emperor. Another inscription ties these same silversmiths to the official imperial cult statue in Asia Minor. The text reads, "The silversmiths of the greatest metropolis of Asia and three times temple-warden of the *Sebastoi* of the Ephesians." There were also lower-class associations, called the *Augustales,* who met for the express purpose of worshipping the emperors. Members pooled their resources and erected monuments to the *Augusti* or *Sebastoi,* as at the Corinthian forum, where a huge marble step has been found that once supported an enormous statue of Augustus.

EXCAVATING THE DIASPORA SYNAGOGUE

How did Jewish synagogues in the cities of the Roman Empire cope with the tensions inherent in meeting indoors rather than outside in public? How could diaspora Jews balance their absolute monotheism with the demands of the divine caesars? Most synagogues were not instantly recognizable as synagogues from the outside. With the exception of the strikingly large and well-decorated synagogue at Sardis, which dates to centuries after Paul and was converted from a bathhouse, synagogues were not located in the city's center. The late first-century CE synagogue at the Roman port of Ostia and the first-century BCE synagogue on the island of Delos were on the outskirts of town, and that at Priene was tucked away in a residential area. In fact, the synagogue at Ostia was probably formerly a private house, as was the third-century CE synagogue at Dura-Europos (in modern Syria), which was brilliantly frescoed on the inside but drab and indistinct outside. But the function of the synagogue buildings and their association with Jews must have been known by their neighbors, even though they were not in any way like a pagan temple, shrine, or cult center.

Several inscriptions indicate that Jewish communities in the diaspora integrated into civic life in a way that offered protection and diminished suspicion. For example, at Ostia, a late second-century inscription otherwise in Greek begins with the Latin phrase *Pro Saluti Aug[usti],* "for the well-being of the emperor," which would put their neighbors at ease: though not sacrificing *to* the emperor, the Ostian Jews prayed *for* the emperor. Similarly, at Bernice in North Africa, two inscriptions record resolutions honoring Roman officials. In one case, Decimus Valerius Dionysios is honored for plastering the synagogue's floors and painting its walls. In the other case, the inscription notes that Marcus Tittius "publicly and privately has been supportive, in his own goodness behaving in a worthy manner." In each case, resolutions were passed by unanimous vote ("all the stones cast were white") to crown the recipients "with an olive wreath" and to mention their names "at each assembly" and at the new moon. That presumably meant offering a prayer *for* these helpful Romans, but did not include offering a prayer or sacrifice *to* the emperor. A synagogue inscription uncovered in Phrygian Acmonia from the eighties or nineties CE even honors a pagan woman for constructing the synagogue. Julia Severa was from a leading aristocratic family; her husband served as the city's *decurion;* and her son later was a member of the Roman Senate. A coin's inscription reveals that she was also a rarity, a pagan priestess of the imperial cult. But that did not prevent her patronage and protection of the local Jewish community.

Some Jewish communities were able to gain the support of prominent pagans whose primary interest was to garner local political alliances or ele-

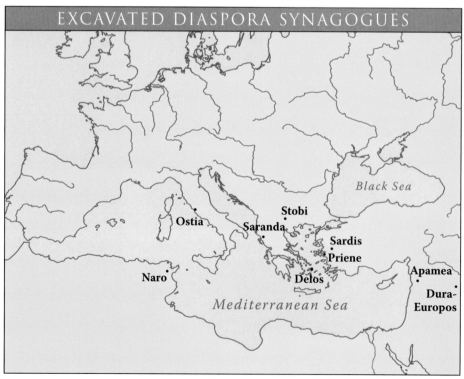

EXCAVATED DIASPORA SYNAGOGUES

"In Caesarea there was a man named Cornelius, . . . a devout man who feared God."

ACTS 10:1–2

vate their standing in the community. But other pagans were drawn to Jewish monotheism and the morality of Jewish law. Throughout the book of Acts, we read not only about Jews and Gentiles but also about a third group, an in-between group that is called either "God-fearers" or "God-worshippers" (Acts 10–18). They are clearly distinguished from Jews but are not pagans either, since they accept Judaism, believe in Jewish monotheism, and respect the moral law of the Hebrew scriptures. They do not, however, convert as proselytes or submit to its ritual law, especially circumcision. Male reluctance to consider circumcision must have prevented many from fully converting to Judaism. The clearest evidence for God-fearers comes from an inscription found at Aphrodisias in western Turkey. A marble column, dating to about a century after Acts was written, honors 126 individuals who organized and funded the synagogue's construction. Of those, nearly half are called "God-fearers." Nine of the God-fearers were also members of the governing city council.

A few God-fearers may have been Gentile slaves who were freed by their Jewish masters and for whom the synagogue took on some legal responsibilities. Inscriptions from the Bosporus on the Black Sea record that the synagogue was the setting, guarantor, and medium for freeing slaves. These recently freed slaves supported the synagogue in menial ways or by attendance. A similar process was customary at pagan temples — in the great Temple of Apollo at Delphi, about 1,300 such manumission inscriptions were found, including three Jewish ones. Slaves were even known to flee to the Ephesian Temple of Artemis, which granted asylum to those mistreated by their masters. Perhaps this is how the runaway slave Onesimus met Paul in Ephesus, when he fled from his owner Philemon in nearby Colossae. Both owner and slave were converted by Paul, and in his letter to Philemon, he urges him to treat the now-converted slave as a brother and no longer a slave, much like the way synagogues adopted former slaves.

PAUL'S HOUSE CHURCHES

The synagogue was not the setting for Paul's early Christian communities. He calls his communities *ekklesiai*, from the Greek word *ekklesia*, whose root meaning is "to be called out." That word had been used to designate the assembly of adult, landowning males in the classical Greek *polis*, but in the first century CE it referred to the theaterlike structure where the elected city council met. Paul means it in the sense of the assembled body of believers and not the structure. What the space used by those Christian assemblies looked like is unclear, since Paul never describes the physical setting in his letters. But archaeology can help set the parameters of the size and structures of those early churches.

According to Acts and Paul's own letters, Paul worked as a tentmaker to support his ministry, often laboring alongside Prisca and Aquila. They first met in Corinth, where the couple had moved after the emperor Claudius expelled the Jewish community from Rome. Paul stayed with them there for some time (Acts 18:2–3), then all three moved to Ephesus (Act 18:18–19), and later Prisca and Aquila moved back to Rome, because in his letter to the Romans, Paul greets them and "the church in their house" (Romans 16:5). What kind of houses are we to imagine in Rome, Ephesus, and Corinth? It's possible Paul, Prisca, and Aquila initially met at Corinth and Ephesus in the shop space where they worked. They may have been granted workspace through some family or business connection, living in an attached room nearby under some arrangement with

opposite page
Synagogue at Sardis (6th c. CE)

this page
God-Fearer Column (Aphrodisias, 2nd c. CE)
Close-up of Inscription

Few diaspora synagogues from around the time of Paul have been discovered. Only six survive from antiquity, though many more inscriptions have been found. These six synagogues do not seem to conform to one model, but use local materials and styles. The Sardis synagogue is unique in size and decoration because it was converted from an imperial bath in the Byzantine period. Most have a niche, presumably for scrolls, and some water installation near the entrance.

The God-fearer inscription from Aphrodisias is one of the most important discoveries for understanding diaspora Judaism. The six-foot-plus honorific column includes the names of Jews, proselytes, and God-worshippers (or God-fearers). The latter were attracted to Judaism and supported the synagogue but did not undergo complete conversion, which for men would include adult circumcision.

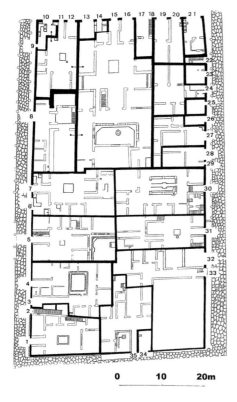

place to dine, meet, or receive guests. House size varied. Over half of the houses on Delos, for example, measured between 650 and 1,800 square feet. More affluent houses were 2,700 to 7,500 square feet. The owners of these larger houses added columns around the courtyard to create a peristyle (from the Greek *peristylos,* "surrounded by columns"); the columns supported a roof over a walkway reminiscent of a porticoed stoa. This area was covered with mosaics and frescoes, and served as a reception area for the owner's guests. The roofs over the surrounding rooms were tiled and sloped inward to guide rainwater into a pool in the middle of the atrium. If Paul's communities met in smaller houses without a peristyle, they may have crammed two dozen into one of the larger rooms, more if they spilled out into a small courtyard in warm weather.

Perhaps the most interesting aspect of domestic areas that archaeologists have uncovered is that houses did not cluster in "good" or "bad" neighborhoods like today. Larger, lavishly decorated houses mingled with smaller, less luxurious houses in what excavators call an *insula,* a block bounded on four sides by streets. The insulae were fronted with shops and workshops interspersed with entrances to interior rooms. The excavations at Pompeii and Herculaneum have shown that

the wealthy owner of the complex. If that were the case, their meetings would be limited to around a dozen people, based on the kinds of shops excavated across the Roman world. Prisca and Aquila would not have been wealthy, given their profession. The Roman upper crust despised manual labor and even skilled crafts, and given that real estate in cities usually stayed within families, it is unlikely that Prisca and Aquila's house church in Rome met in something like the grand

houses excavated at Pompeii, Herculaneum, or Ephesus.

Archaeological excavations at sites like Delos, Olympus, Dion, Priene, and Pergamum, along with the cities destroyed by Vesuvius, Pompeii and Herculaneum, tell us much about house and neighborhood patterns at the time of Paul. Most houses were elongated rectangles with a central courtyard onto which rooms opened from the front, side, and rear. One large room, often the triclinium or dining room, served as a

opposite page

Plan of House of the Bicentenary

Neighborhood at Pergamum

House of the Bicentenary (Herculaneum)

this page

Sculptural Workshop (Aphrodisias)

Oracle at Delphi (Greece)

Gallio Inscription (Delphi)

Bronze Citizenship Diploma (Egypt, 79 CE)

Neighborhoods in the Roman world were divided not by class, with good and bad neighborhoods, but into *insulae* — islands surrounded by streets, with their own internal hierarchies. At Pergamum in Asia Minor, one enormous peristyle house is surrounded by smaller peristyle houses, three courtyard houses, and around them a small apartment complex and many shops, workshops, or service rooms. At Herculaneum, the House of the Bicentenary shows how closely connected shops and houses were. The sculptor's shop at Aphrodisias might have been similar in shape and size to the kind of shop in which Paul, Prisca, and Aquila made tents and in which they met for worship.

Paul claimed Roman citizenship, which had once been a carefully guarded privilege. Citizenship was granted to non-Italians in the first century CE often after service in the legions — as was the case for Marcus Papirius, who served for twenty-five years in the Egyptian fleet and whose discharge was inscribed on a bronze plaque. We do not know how Paul obtained his citizenship, but it limited the severity of corporal punishment: he could not be crucified and had the right to appeal any conviction to Caesar.

A Pauline chronology may be possible because of this find at the Greek oracle site of Delphi. The inscription records a letter to the people at Delphi and notes that the Roman proconsul began his tenure in the summer of 51 CE. According to Acts, Paul had already been in Corinth for many months before he stood trial before Gallio, so most scholars place Paul's arrival in Corinth in 50 and his departure in 51.

"Paul said, 'But I was born a citizen.'"

ACTS 22:28

Chronology of Paul	
5–10 CE (?)	Birth
26–36 CE	Pilate rules Judea
30 CE (?)	Jesus's crucifixion
35–40	Paul's conversion and escape from the Arabian king Aretas in Damascus
40	Aretas IV dies
50–51	Paul in Corinth, where he writes Galatians and Thessalonians
51	Gallio arrives in Corinth
52–60	Paul in Ephesus, writes to the Corinthians
	Returns to Corinth, writes Romans
	Imprisoned in Caesarea Maritima, writes additional letters
62?	Killed in Rome by Nero during the great persecution

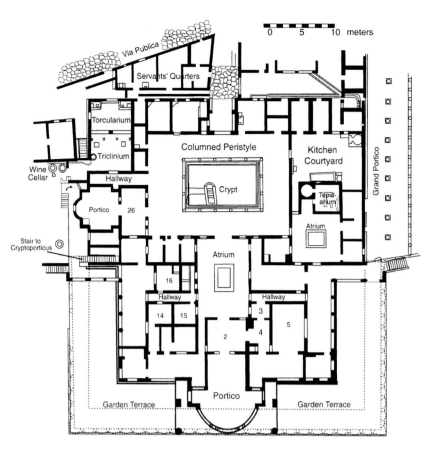

would work at rented shops that were not only next door to the wealthy patron's home but often connected to it via back doors.

Religion permeated the Roman house. Excavations and artifacts show that religion was intricately interwoven with domestic life. Even the humblest Mediterranean house had an area dedicated to one or more gods, often simply a wall painting or a niche into which toy-sized statues were placed, as have so often been found on the island of Delos. Moderate to larger homes set aside an area that was almost shrinelike, called a *lararium* in Latin, where the household gods, the *lares* or *penates*, were worshipped by the household under the priestlike supervision of the head of the household. This was usually located in the atrium or the kitchen, or in larger houses, near the

neighborhoods were shaped along patronal lines. A wealthy patron entered through a large, guarded but open entrance to his atrium, which was the largest and most elegant living space in the *insula*. It was living *al fresco,* outdoors in a garden-enhanced, fountainair-conditioned, partially covered environment. An intergenerational

family, along with a few slaves, might all live together in rooms around the atrium, and clustered around that home in descending size were smaller homes, a few also with atria, where married sons, manumitted slaves, and others under the master's patronage lived. Additional slaves, recently freed slaves, and itinerant artisans like Paul

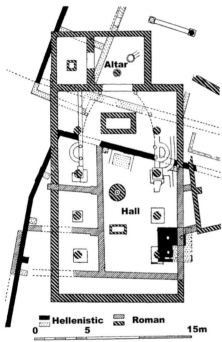

Hellenistic ▨ Roman
0   5   15m

triclinium where meals and feasts were served.

The very rich set aside more than some well-decorated wall-space for their family's religious devotion. At Cumae near modern Napoli, excava-

tors found what they first thought was a temple of the goddess Isis but later realized was a large shrine attached to a seaside mansion. In Dion at the foot of Greece's Mount Olympus, a magnificent villa set aside both a triclinium with Dionysiac themes and an internal basilica dedicated to Dionysos with a larger-than-life statue. The owner worshipped Dionysos in the basilicalike room, and in the triclinium enjoyed Dionysos's wine with his guests at spectacular dinners. The most impressive private room dedicated to religion, however, was excavated at Pompeii. The Villa of the Mysteries has frescoes on all sides that depict scenes relating to Dionysiac rituals, with many more women than men represented. Among them are a woman startled by Dionysos, a youth reading a scroll, a hidden object being revealed behind a sheet, a young girl being flagellated who may represent the initiate, dancing maenads, and a women with cupids grooming herself under the watchful eye of a matron. The function of that

opposite page

Household Shrine (Delos, 1st C. BCE)
Villa of the Mysteries (Pompeii, 1st C. CE)
Dionysiac Fresco (1st C. CE)
Terrace Houses at Ephesus (1st C. CE)

this page

Herodes Theater (Athens, 2nd C. CE)
***Iobacchoii* Inscription (Athens, 2nd C. CE)**
Plan of *Iobacchoii* Hall
Erastus Inscription (Corinth, 1st C. CE)

Religion was central to life in homes of the Greco-Roman period. Each house, no matter how poor, had a shrine called a *lararium* set aside for worship of the household gods. Many houses set aside entire rooms. What went on in Pompeii's Villa of the Mysteries, however, is uncertain; ecstatic initiation ceremonies into the Dionysiac mysteries may have been held there, judging by its spiritual and sensual frescoes. The terraced houses at Ephesus were likewise full of mythological and religious frescoes.

The semireligious drinking club dedicated to Dionysos met in this meeting hall in Athens. Judging by the inscription on a stele, they were fiercely competitive with other so-called Iobacchic groups. The stele boasts, "We are the greatest of the *Iobacchoii*" because they had the patronage of Herodes Atticus, the Roman émigré and richest Athenian of the day, who built the little theater under the Acropolis in the second century CE. The stele hails: "Long live the most excellent priest Herodes! Now you are fortunate; now we are first of all the *Baccheiai*!"

The Erastus of the New Testament may be preserved on this inscription from Corinth. The bronze from a pavement inscription has long since been removed, but the letters can still be read: ERASTVS. PRO. AED. S. P. STRAVIT ("Erastus, in return for his aedileship, laid this pavement at his own expense"). Paul's letter to the Romans mentions an Erastus who is called the Corinthian city treasurer in 16:23.

frescoed room is intensely debated; it may have been a place where initiates entered into the mysteries of Dionysos, a bridal preparatory room, the master bedroom, or a triclinium for family and guests. There are two other shrines in this villa: a stone altar and a set of painted images near the hearth of the Roman handicraft goddess Minerva and the fire god Volcanus. Even without understanding the details, this villa illustrates how religion was intimately woven into the architectural and decorative fabric of the Roman house.

The houses at Ephesus, where Paul wrote his letters to the Corinthians, also contain much religious imagery. Seven residential units from around Paul's time have been excavated on a terraced slope along the Curetes Street. Shops and taverns alternated with the houses' main entrances, and ancient pedestrians got a passing glimpse at the wealth and decorations inside. Visitors to those homes were dazzled by a rich array of marble and mosaic floors, walls painted with faux-marble in geometric and floral patterns, and a concoction of religious and mythological motifs, including scenes from Dionysos's wedding and from Apuleius's religio-erotic novel, *The Golden Ass,* which chronicles the tale of one believer's conversion and initiation into the worship of the Egyptian mother-goddess Isis.

If Paul's communities at Ephesus met not in one of those front shops but in one of the main rooms, like the triclinium, there would have been enough space for thirty or more, perhaps up to sixty, if they spilled out into the atrium. The few houses from the time of Paul that have been found at Corinth are about the same size. The first-century CE Anaploga Villa had a banquet room with a now badly damaged mosaic that measured about 375 square feet. That is enough for nine guests reclining on couches in the usual dinner setup, but if people crammed in a bit, with some sitting on the floor and others standing in the atrium, there could have been as many as fifty at an early Christian communal meal. Such a triclinium setting seems to be at the heart of one of Paul's many problems with the Corinthian community. He scorns the wealthy Christians who

came early, ate all the food, and guzzled the wine: "Each of you goes ahead with your own supper, and one goes hungry and another becomes drunk. What! Do you not have homes to eat and drink in? Or do you show contempt for the church of God and humiliate those who have nothing?" (1 Corinthians 11:21–22). That presupposes the standard hierarchical arrangement at Roman dinners in the triclinium.

Gathering in such an aristocratic house explains one of the more serious concerns expressed in the Corinthian letters. We must imagine that at some point the communities established by Paul were moving from a small shop-church and into a triclinium-church or atrium-church, so to speak: they moved from the periphery of the shop into the wealthy home next door. There it was natural for the household's patriarch to assume and even assert his authority over the meeting. The divisions that Paul struggled with at Corinth were probably not just theological, but social, as the patrons of house churches competed for members and prestige. For Paul, that kind of intracommunal competition undermined the very heart of Christianity: Jesus's message of egalitarianism.

There is a tantalizing clue in Corinth's archaeological record for that level of higher patronage. Just below the city's theater, a first-century CE paving stone records that a man named Erastus was given the important civic office of *aediles* in exchange for building the pavement. We would call that a bribe, but at the time this was an accepted and expected practice. In his letter to the Romans, Paul mentions an Erastus — probably the same man — "the city treasurer," who sends his greetings from Corinth to Rome (16:23). Paul, however, calls him an *oikonomos,* which is a full notch below the office of *aediles.* Does the inscription prove or disprove the New Testament? Maybe it is not the same person, or maybe Paul was unclear about those civic distinctions. Or maybe Erastus had risen in rank since Paul left Corinth for Ephesus. Either way, the pavement's inscription illuminates a problem faced by Corinthian and other

ARCHAEOLOGY OF THE ROMAN BEDROOM

Excavations inside Roman houses also shed light on another problem Paul had with the Corinthians and other Christians: their sexual relationships. While bits of evidence have been found throughout the Roman world regarding ancient sexuality, the excavations at Pompeii and Herculaneum have allowed more than a glimpse inside the bedroom and into what we might call the gutters of antiquity. The Mediterranean world was patriarchal, and women were wives, daughters, or sisters under male control if not possession. Images from Pompeii show that normative sexual behavior was scripted according to power relations based on gender, age, and status, with the landowning adult male at the top. As we saw in chapter 3, the phallus on border-statues or herms possessed protective powers. Most private houses in Pompeii displayed a phallus, either engraved or scratched near the entrance, to ward off evil spirits, protect from intrusion, and ensure fertility. It's not surprising, then, that normative sexual behavior in Paul's time was based on male control and power, mostly but not exclusively over women, and at times involves what looks more like subjugation and humiliation. This can be seen in images and inscriptions from bedrooms and brothels

churches. According to 1 Corinthians 1, there were a few well-to-do and politically connected Christians in Corinth, but most were of lower birth. When the churches began to meet in larger houses, such as the kind that Erastus owned, the highborn assumed leadership. Not only that: house churches began to compete over the size and importance of their meetings. The Erastus inscription raises the possibility that he was one of those patrons who so angered Paul in his letters to the Corinthians.

The power of the phallus protected temples and houses according to ancient belief. Its role as protector of the house is not clearly distinguished from its role in sensual pleasure, as the ambiguity of this inscription from Pompeii makes clear: *Hic habitat felicitas,* "Herein dwells happiness." Priapus was a mischievous woodland god whose statues in gardens or portraits in frescoes scared off thieves through the threat of rape. Similarly at Delos, whereas Apollo's sanctuary was guarded by a row of lion statues, Dionysos's temple was guarded by two enormous phalli, not only the symbol of uncontrollable pleasure and the sacred object of his mysteries, but also associated with protective powers.

Erotic or pornographic images from the Roman world point to male-dominated sexual norms, particularly for wealthy men, who could do almost anything to either sex, provided they were socially inferior. In this sense pedophilia was tolerated, if it was performed by an elite on a servant or slave.

> "Christ Jesus . . . emptied himself, taking the form of a slave . . . he humbled himself. . . ."
>
> PHILIPPIANS 2:5–8

alike. The essential attitude is captured in a graffito from the House of the Moralist in Pompeii, which warns: "Don't cast lustful glances, or make eyes at other men's wives." Women were under the control of men, and erotic scenes on disc-shaped oil lamps found across the Mediterranean portray sexual positions in which the man was considered by Romans to be active and the woman passive.

But sexual roles were not demarcated exclusively by gender. Class and status factored into the equation almost as much as gender. Wealthy men were free to penetrate almost anyone — a woman, boy, or lower-class man. This is how the widespread depictions of homosexuality in the Roman world must be understood, where rich men included in their household teenage boy-slaves, preferably curly-haired slaves imported from Asia Minor, who were particularly prized for sexual usage. They were pursued and penetrated like women, then discarded and replaced when they reached manhood and grew facial hair; they never penetrated their masters. That kind of exploitation might well explain some of the anger Paul expresses on the topic.

What is lacking in Roman erotic images are egalitarian positions, egalitarian escapades, and egalitarian relationships. Equality was not in any script, whether between man and woman, man and boy, or man and man. Jewish morality, of course, was emphatically different, not only with regard to public nudity. Simply put, in the Jewish ideal, sex was restricted to marriage between husband and wife and instead primarily for the purpose of procreation. Given these differences in moral standards, it's not at all surprising that right before Pompeii was engulfed in ashes, a Jew scribbled on the wall: "Sodom and Gomorrah!" Paul seems to have been equally offended by the sexual mores of the cities of the Roman Empire, but also seems amazingly liberal when he states that the wife does not control her own body but rather her husband does, adding that "likewise the husband does not have authority over his own body, but the wife does" (1 Corinthians 7:4).

Visual representations of patriarchal power and male domination of females also appear in imperial sculptural imagery. For example, the sculpture galleries of the *Sebasteion* at Aphrodisias contained at the top allegorical figures for time and place, night and day, and at the middle level nations that had been conquered by Rome. There were some fifty personifications of conquered nations in native dress, their names inscribed on the bases, including Jews, Egyptians, Cretans, and Cypriots. Those provinces were all personified as *women* conquered by Augustus and now submissive to the *pater patriae*, the father of the fatherland.

It was not uncommon to depict the provinces in imperial art as women; such depictions are found for example on the *Ara Pacis Augustae* and on coins minted after the first Jewish Revolt, which depict Judea as a captive woman. Two of the best-preserved sculptural panels from Aphrodisias are striking in their eroticism and violence. One shows the nude emperor Claudius standing over defeated Britannia, poised to pierce her with a spear. She is pinned to the ground by his knee, her tunic exposing her right breast; she grasps her garment with one hand and holds up the other hand in a futile attempt to protect herself. Claudius grabs her loosened hair, which symbolizes her uncontrollable barbarian or female qualities. The other panel depicts Nero's victory over Armenia. He stands — youthful, muscular, and nude — astride a slumped Armenia. He holds her up with a firm grasp, his sword ready in the other hand. She is completely naked except for the Roman iconographic symbols for Orientals: high boots and a Phrygian cap.

Each caesar is about to kill his conquest with a weapon, and those two women-peoples will then be raised up, as it were, to join the rest of the conquered personifications in the gallery. They are concubines of the imperial father and part of his harem, and they stand as trophies, quiet and submissive under Caesar's control in the gallery. Whether in the bedroom or on the battlefield, men rose in status by exerting power and subordinating others, especially women. The kind of lordship exemplified by the Roman emperors, but which other men were implicitly expected to exert over their females, is a far cry from Paul's description of Jesus's lordship, when he exhorted the Philippians to humble themselves like Christ and not seek leadership through domination.

THE DANGER OF TRAVEL AND PAUL'S SHIPWRECKS

Finally, let us examine the dangers Paul and other Christians faced as they spread their message. Even though Augustus had rid the seas of pirates and Roman legions had built a network of roads, travel in the ancient world was still perilous. Shipwrecks presented the greatest danger, but archaeological excavations in Roman cities remind us also of the more common dangers and moral temptations that accompanied any itinerary. Thieves and pickpockets preyed on travelers, and one papyrus letter discovered in Egypt records a husband's advice to his wife who is about to return to him: "When you come, bring your gold ornaments, but do not wear them on the boat." Theft in way stations or ports was common, so travelers welcomed referrals or recommendations to stay at a trusted person's home. Cities offered temptations in the form of brothels and prostitution, which were widespread in the Roman world. Excavators have uncovered a startling number of brothels in Pompeii, with sleazy graffiti and paintings, and at Ephesus, where Paul lived for some time, prostitutes were advertised on the main street. Archaeologists uncovered a crude picture of what was intended to be an alluring prostitute etched into a marble pavement stone with a foot to her left, meaning "this way" or "look to the left foot side." That kind of temptation was everywhere for Paul and his traveling companions.

But shipwrecks were the most serious hazard, judging from the many sunken hulls that litter the coastal waters of the Mediterranean. Winter weather made travel by ship possible only for part of the year. The safest months were between May and September, and courageous captains might venture out in April and October, but from November to March ships quartered in safe harbors. Overcast skies in the cooler months also curtailed shipping, as clouds and marine layers obscured the stars and sunsets that were used to navigate. Sailors would then have to sail their ships even closer to land and the dangerous reefs that provide abundant finds for underwater archaeologists.

Most Roman ships that have been discovered or are depicted in relief had a single sail and were therefore at the wind's mercy to a greater degree than modern sailboats. With decent winds they could travel seven miles per hour, and unlike travel on land they could maintain that rate day and night. At that pace, Paul could have embarked at Corinth's port at Cenchreae and disembarked at Ephesus in a week. And his letter to the Romans could have made it from Corinth to Rome in ten

days. But that was in ideal conditions. Most ships stopped at intervening harbors to unload and load cargo or passengers, which could easily double passage times. And if there was rough water or storms out of season, then the ship might wait it out in a harbor. Insufficient or unfavorable winds could force a ship to tack and double the distance traveled. It could have taken Paul three weeks to finally arrive at Ephesus from Corinth or a month for his letter to arrive in Rome. And that is if he was lucky enough to avoid disaster.

It is hard to tell what percentage of ships sank. Paul takes four long journeys across the eastern Mediterranean in the book of Acts and shipwrecks on one of them (Acts 27). He states in an earlier letter that he was shipwrecked three times (2 Corinthians 11:25). All over the Mediterranean, but especially along the coast of Turkey where Paul frequently traveled, archaeologists have discovered evidence of that danger. Hulls stacked atop one another at the bottom of the ocean testify to particularly dangerous spots. The contents of these vessels reveal much about international trade at the time, and show that each boat picked up all kinds of cargo at multiple ports as they circumnavigated the Mediterranean, usually in a clockwise direction from Rome through Greece to

Turkey, along the Levant to Egypt, and then across North Africa and back to Rome.

During the Roman period, ships were built differently than now; rather than the skeleton-first technique used today, in antiquity the outer shell of planks was fastened directly to the keel, and only after the shell was constructed was an internal skeleton added for support. The planks — often cypress wood, which was light and resistant to water — were held together with tenon-and-mortise joints: a thin tongue (tenon) protruding from one plank was slipped into a groove (mortise) in the adjacent plank, and a hole was drilled through that joint, which was then locked with a tightly fitting peg. The wood in some wrecks shows evidence of charring, which suggests

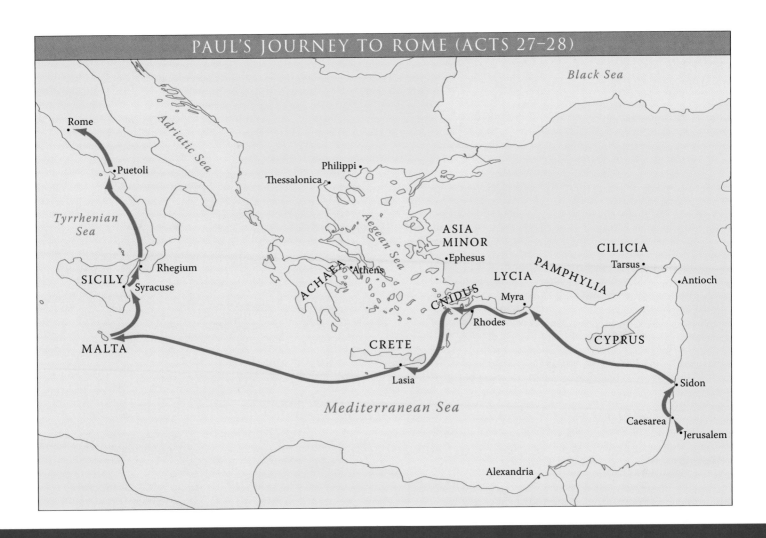

Black Sea

Adriatic Sea

Rome

Puetoli

Tyrrhenian
Sea

Philippi

Thessalonica

ASIA
MINOR

CILICIA

Tarsus

Rhegium

SICILY

Syracuse

ACHAEA

Athens

Aegean Sea

Ephesus

LYCIA

PAMPHYLIA

Antioch

Myra

CNIDUS

Rhodes

CYPRUS

MALTA

CRETE

Lasia

Sidon

Mediterranean Sea

Caesarea

Jerusalem

Alexandria

"Three times I was shipwrecked; for a night and a day I was adrift at sea;
on frequent journeys, in danger . . ."

2 CORINTHIANS 11:25

that it had been heated and then bent into shape in a fairly sophisticated operation. With good craftsmanship, a boat could bear considerable freight. One wreck, at Kizilburun near Ephesus, carried eight marble column drums with diameters over five feet and totaling thirty feet in length. Another shipwreck, off the Greek island of Cos, held over one thousand amphorae in its cargo bay. This ship hit a reef that extended some two hundred meters off the coast. Its cypress hull and white oak keel were held together with weak, widely spaced tenon-and-mortise joints, so that the sixty-five-foot-long ship was doomed to sink sooner or later. But even well-constructed boats, like the seventy-five-foot ship off the coast of Israel at Tantura Lagoon, could snap like matchsticks when they ran aground at high speed. It is no wonder, then, that the goddess Isis, patron deity of sailors and sailing, was so popular.

The archaeology of shipwrecks illustrates the dangers of sailing and makes evident Paul's commitment. He was intimately familiar with the perils of travel but nevertheless made numerous journeys across the eastern Mediterranean. He was a veteran traveler. But traveling was not the only danger to which Paul subjected himself. The very message of Paul, his gospel of Jesus as the Christ and Son of God, Lord and Savior, ran counter to Rome's gospel of the caesars as *divus filius*, son of god, lord and savior, which is so clear in the coins, statues, and structures of the Roman cities. Denying or undermining that Roman imperial theology in favor of a monotheistic Jewish theology was equally hazardous. Paul was not only willing to take the risk when he spread his message but he was also willing to work at a menial task, in the tiny shops that lined the streets of cities across the eastern

Mediterranean, to support his ministry. Knowing Paul's humble beginnings in those shops, so clear in the archaeological record, makes his gospel's eventual success even more remarkable.

opposite page

Sunken Columns (Kizilburun, Turkey)

Shipwrecks (Tantura Lagoon, Israel)

Isis Statue (Delos)

Via Egnatia (Philippi)

Shipwrecks are excavated by underwater archaeologists all over the Mediterranean. Their frequency testifies to the dangers of sea travel in the Roman world. Here, a heavy set of column drums helped the ship sink straight to the bottom off the coast of Turkey. Another ship's hull cracked when it tried to make it inside the Tantura Lagoon off the coast of Israel, presumably to avoid rough seas. Even the goddess Isis, to whom sailors prayed, could not offer protection.

Roman roads and pirateless seas made Paul's travels possible. The *Pax Romana* made travel more safe than ever before, and well-constructed Roman roads, like the Via Egnatia outside Philippi, which Paul must have traveled, made land travel quicker.

Ancient Corinth was ideally located by the isthmus, the four-mile strip that connects the Greek mainland to the Peloponnesus. In antiquity the city had two harbors, Lechaeum to the north for sailing to the Adriatic and Italy and Cenchreae to the east for sailing to the Aegean and Asia Minor (from which Paul wrote his letter to the Romans). A prominent Greek city of the classical period, it was razed by Roman legions in 146 BCE, refounded as a colony by Julius Caesar in 44 BCE, and has been excavated by the American School of Classical Studies since 1896. Those excavations have served as a training ground for America's classical archaeologists, and their history is a bellwether of the discipline's transformation over the past century.

In the early part of the twentieth century, the excavations focused on identifying elements of the ancient Greek polis, since in classical scholarship at the time, classical Greece and its sculptures were considered the cultural apex; Romans were viewed as mere copyists, and there was little interest in their later colony. Toward the middle of the twentieth century, however, there was an intense interest in the Roman city and its urban monuments. It was during this time that much of the Roman forum was uncovered, including temples and markets, and the theater and Asclepion. During this period numerous architectural features were revealed that could be connected to Acts's stories of Paul and his letters to the Corinthians. Excavators located the *bema*, or tribunal, from which the Roman prefect heard Paul's case (Acts 18); shops were found where meat sacrificed to idols was sold, a notorious problem for many Christians (1 Corinthians 10); terracotta body parts dedicated to Asclepeius have been excavated, which might have inspired Paul's church-body metaphor (1 Corinthians 12). A synagogue inscription was discovered, though it dates to long after that mentioned in Acts 18. And of course the famous Erastus inscription was uncovered, which was commissioned by the man mentioned in Romans 16:23. But the forum's excavations also illustrate the centrality of religion to all aspects of Roman urban life, with the imperial cult taking center stage. There were many temples. Highest on the western side was an imperial temple, perhaps to Octavia; beneath it was one to Venus, who was a Julian family favorite, and another to Apollo, who was Augustus's favorite; across the forum on the east was the Julian Basilica, where cases were heard under the eye of effigies of the current and previous emperors; and in the center of the forum, there was a statue of Augustus.

Since the 1970s, however, a methodological revolution in field archaeology has taken place at Corinth's excavations, showing a greater interest in the past's human rather than architectural side. The excavations are more tightly supervised, smaller artifacts have been recovered, recording is more fastidious, and post-dig scientific analysis is more rigorous. There has been a shift away from relying exclusively on coins and architectural typology to date buildings, toward use of ceramic shards in accompanying soil strata. Whereas interest in ceramics was once limited to fine wares, archaeologists now also examine coarse wares and what they reveal about everyday life. To the studies of potters as artists is added the analysis of pottery as an indicator of trading patterns, cooking habits, and diet. Squares are laid not just in the city center but on the periphery, and surveys of the surrounding rural areas examine Roman surveying techniques, land distribution and use, and general urban-rural relations in antiquity, findings that are also of considerable importance for those interested in Galilean urban-rural relations.

Under the current direction of G. D. R. Sanders, the excavations of ancient Corinth have set the benchmark for archaeological sophistication. Studies of the finds from ongoing excavations, as well as analysis of artifacts and architecture unearthed in the previous century, suggest that a complete reinterpretation of Corinth is at hand. For those of us interested in the New Testament, these future archaeological studies offer much promise for understanding Paul's Corinthian correspondence and his time in this city.

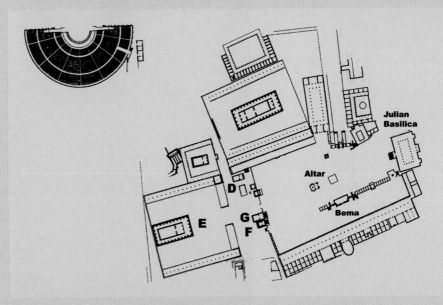

7

THE FIRST CHRISTIANS AND THE JEWISH WARS

The defining event in early Christian history was the first Jewish War with Rome, which ended with the destruction of the Temple in 70 CE. The defeat of the Jews in Judea forced Judaism to shift from a Temple-centered community to a book-centered religion, and also motivated Christians to distinguish themselves from Jews. Jesus lived in an entirely Jewish context in the thirties, though he occasionally operated on Galilee's periphery, where he encountered Gentiles. Paul took the bold step a few decades later of extending fellowship to the uncircumcised, though he seems to have operated on the assumption that those Gentiles were entering into messianic Judaism. But after the emperor Nero persecuted followers of Jesus in Rome in the sixties CE and the emperor Vespasian crushed the Jewish Revolt in Judea in 70 CE, each group began to define itself in

EGYPT AND THE FAYUM

Mediterranean Sea

Alexandria

Fayum
Lake Moeris • Memphis
• Crocodilopolis
Tebtunis

Oxyrhynchus

Nile River

Red Sea

Nag Hammadi •
• Thebes

EGYPTIAN PAPYRI AND NEW TESTAMENT LETTERS

In the previous chapter we looked at how the archaeology of the eastern cities of the Roman Empire helps us understand the meaning of Paul's letters. Now we turn to how the discovery of ancient letters has shed light on the style and form of the letters that make up much of the New Testament. Archaeologists working in Egypt's arid climate have discovered thousands of papyri from the Hellenistic and Roman periods, especially west of the Nile, in an area called the Fayum. Ptolemaic Greeks heavily colonized the area around Lake Moeris, south of the Nile Delta, in the Hellenistic period, and it remained an important part of the later Roman province of Egypt. That history, combined with its arid climate, helped preserve a treasure of ancient writings that provide a window onto the workings of the ancient world and at times give a glimpse of people's most intimate thoughts.

Papyrology, the study of these ancient documents, has immensely contributed to the study of the New Testament. Among the many papyri discovered in the past century is a thumbnail-sized fragment containing a few verses of the Gospel of John. Catalogued after its acquisition in 1920 as P 52, it dates to the first half of the second century CE, according to paleographers (scholars of ancient script styles). This represents the earliest copy of any New Testament text and is, in fact, the oldest Christian artifact of any kind. But

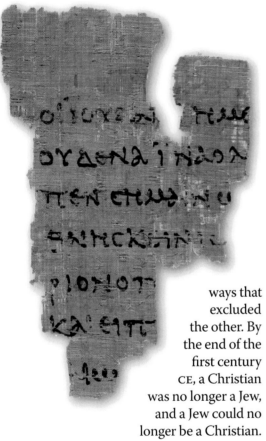

ways that excluded the other. By the end of the first century CE, a Christian was no longer a Jew, and a Jew could no longer be a Christian. Jewish-Christian tensions are not apparent in the archaeological record — it is hard to distinguish either group from their contemporaneous pagan context — but the Roman pressure that came down on both is obvious in archaeological strata from Judea to Rome. The violent Roman response to two Jewish revolts, in 66–70 CE and 132–35 CE, will be our concern later in this chapter. We begin, however, with the medium by which early Christians addressed so many of their communal problems: the ancient letter.

opposite page

Augustus with Cross (Ephesus)

Tax Receipt (Egypt, 3rd c. CE)

this page

Excavations at Oxyrhynchus (1903)

Fragment of John 18 (Egypt, ca. 125 CE)

Christ over Caesar is the message that a later Christian chiseled onto this statue of Augustus from Ephesus in Asia Minor. A cross was cut into its forehead, underlining the Christian Son of God's victory over the imperial son of god.

The treasure trove for ancient papyri is the Fayum region in Egypt, south of the Nile Delta. The combination of arid temperatures, ample papyrus plants growing nearby, and both Hellenistic and Roman occupation left thousands of papyri for archaeologists to uncover in the early part of the twentieth century. Most of them are mundane but invaluable for understanding the New Testament world, such as this third-century CE fishing contract, which shows remarkably high rates of taxation that must have haunted fishermen also on the Sea of Galilee.

The oldest Gospel fragment is this papyrus from Egypt labeled P 52 and now in the John Rylands Library in Manchester, Great Britain. Dating to around 125 CE, it contains a portion of John 18 on the front and back, showing that Christians at that time were using books rather than scrolls. It is the oldest identifiable Christian object uncovered by archaeologists.

letter-writers used common epistolary conventions of their day.

All letters had a simple three-part structure, with an opening, a body, and a closing. Greek letters from the Roman era that were found in Egypt opened with the standard formula, "From x to y, greetings." Paul's opening prescript is very similar, but he changes it slightly by substituting the Greek *charis,* "grace," for the similar Greek *chairein,* "greetings." And Paul adds the standard Jewish salutation, from the Hebrew *shalom,* "peace." Most formal letters would begin with a Roman tripartite name, made up of first name (*praenomen*), family name (*nomen*), and surname (*cognomen*); contractual letters often included the sender's hometown. But when the letter-writer was intimate with the recipients, the author would use only one name. It is telling that Paul, James, Peter, and Jude's New Testament letters begin with a single name, imparting a sense of intimacy even when they write to communities they have not yet visited, like Paul to Rome. It was also customary for ancient letter openings to offer a prayer or thanksgiving for the recipient. For example, we read the opening of a second-century CE papyrus: "Aphrodite to Arsinoes, greetings. I make supplication for you to the gods of this place every day, praying for your health." This is not unlike Paul's 1 Thessalonians, which begins, "We always give thanks to God for all of you and mention you in our prayers. . . ."

the numerous fragments from noncanonical gospels, like the three Greek fragments from the *Gospel of Thomas* that were found in Egypt, show that a multitude of gospels were in circulation by the late second century CE — before the New Testament was compiled. The papyri are important because they cast light on the world of the New Testament. We saw in a previous chapter that a nearly illiterate village secretary had to practice writing, which suggests how few people could write in antiquity. We saw a magical spell that was used to cure fever, which suggests how perilous health was in antiquity and how many people sought spiritual-magical aid for relief from a disease. And we saw a husband's letter to his wife warning her not to wear gold jewelry on the boat, which indicates the dangers that Paul and other Christians faced when traveling. Each papyrus adds an important dimension to the study of the New Testament, though none directly refers to the New Testament or to anyone in the New Testament.

But the most significant contribution of papyrology to the study of the New Testament is what it tells us about ancient letters and about letter-writing. Among the countless papyri from Roman Egypt are thousands of letters, some personal, others official, a few from the emperor himself. They provide a wealth of comparative material for examining the structure, vocabulary, style, and etiquette of New Testament epistles. They show clearly that Paul and the other New Testament

The closings of ancient letters were likewise formulaic and included multiple greetings to the recipient's relatives or mutual acquaintances. So we read, for example, in Damas's first-century CE letter, "Greet your mother and your father. I pray for your health." Soterichos's second-century CE letter ends, "Greet all your family for me; I pray for the health and prosperity of them and you and all your household." And Paul concludes 1 Thessalonians: "Greet all the brothers and sisters with a holy kiss . . . the grace of our Lord Jesus Christ be with you" (5:26–28). The church had become Paul's family, and his letters include greetings for *brothers* and *sisters*. Other acquaintances are often also greeted, and some letters from Egypt devote fifteen to twenty lines to third-party greetings, reminiscent of Paul's letter to the Romans, in which third-party greetings occupy almost the entire final chapter. Even the scribe adds a salutation: "I Tertius, the writer of this letter, greet you in the Lord" (Romans 16:22). Paul and most ancient authors used a professional scribe to write their letters. For Christian letters, they were probably, like Tertius, scribes who had become Christian and offered their services for

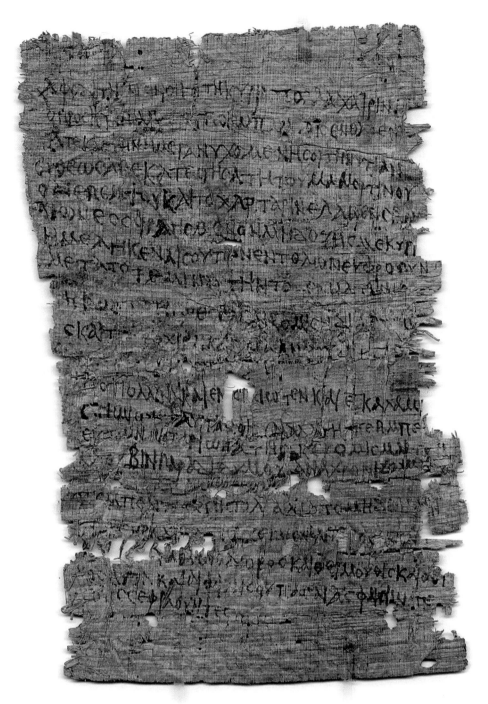

opposite page

Wet Nurse Contract (Egypt, 2nd c. CE)
Writing Tablet (Britain, ca. 100 CE)
Mummified Crocodile (Egypt, 2nd–3rd c. CE)

this page

Letter to Slave (Egypt, 1st c. CE)

Reading, **writing**, **and the rich** were tightly connected in antiquity, as illustrated in this second-century CE wet-nurse contract. Many wealthy women in the Roman era preferred to hire someone to breastfeed their newborns; this contract was written on the backside of a page ripped from Homer's *Iliad*. Only the wealthy and their trained scribes could read, afford books, and hire such servants.

Government-issued stationery was found near the River Walbrook in London, England. Dating to the first century CE, this wooden tablet once held a thin layer of wax filling in the recessed rectangle, onto which the text was inscribed with bronze pens. Burned into the tablet's upper left corner is PROC AVG DEDERVNT BRIT PROV, "The imperial procurators of the province of Britain issued this."

This mummified crocodile is an odd source of ancient papyri. In ancient Tebtunis, where the crocodile god was worshipped, numerous such beasts were covered in a papier-mâché-like wrapping, made up of discarded papyri documents relating to everyday life.

A Letter to a Slave

"Aphrodite to her mistress Arsinoes, many greetings. I make supplication for you to the gods of this place every day, praying for your health.

I restored at once to Mamertinus's wife what you sent, and Serenion took the papyrus sealed. Do not think, mistress, that I am negligent of your commands. Euphrosune, after she had cut the robe, inquired of Isidoros. Receive through Artes (?) the hold-all, four bags, four Puteolan articles, one . . . and five reeds of thread; it was arranged with you that these should be sent from her earnings. I have received the shirt from Didumos. We are late in sending you letters because we have no . . . Ambrosia, . . .,

Athenodoros, Thermouthis and her household salute you, and all your friends salute your friends."

Paul's Letter About a Slave and a Master

"Paul, a prisoner of Christ Jesus, and Timothy our brother, to Philemon our dear friend and fellow worker . . . Grace to you and peace . . . I always thank my God as I remember you in my prayer . . .

Therefore, although in Christ I could be bold and order you to do what you ought to do, yet I appeal to you on the basis of love. I then, as Paul — an old man and now also a prisoner of Christ Jesus — I appeal to you for my son Onesimus, who became my son while I was in chains. Formerly he was useless to you, but now he has become useful both to you and to me. . . . Perhaps the reason he was separated from you for a little while was that you might have him back for good — no longer as a slave, but better than a slave, as a dear brother. . . .

Epaphras, my fellow prisoner in Christ Jesus sends you greetings. And so do Mark, Aristarchus, Demas, and Luke, my fellow workers. The grace of the Lord Jesus Christ be with your spirit."

"... even now, therefore, I conjure the Alexandrians to behave gently and kindly toward the Jews who have inhabited the same city for many years, and not to dishonor any of their customs in their worship of their god, but to allow them to keep their own ways, as they did in the time of the god Augustus, as I too, having heard both sides, have confirmed. The Jews, on the other hand, I order not to aim at more than they have previously had . . . since they enjoy what is their own, and in a city that is not their own they possess an abundance of all good things. Nor are they to bring in or invite Jews coming from Syria or Egypt, or I shall be forced to conceive graver suspicions. If they disobey, I shall proceed against them in every way as fomenting a common plague for the world. If you both give up your present ways and are willing to live in gentleness and kindness with one another, I for my part will care for the city as much as I can, as one which had long been closely connected with us."

free. The extent to which a scribe helped shape the form and style of the letter, such as the opening and closing or even the common conventions in the body of the letter, is unclear. But it is clear that Paul's letters shared the vocabulary and conventions of contemporaneous letters discovered in the sands of Egypt.

One letter discovered in Egypt, similar in structure to Paul's, points to the tensions between Jews and Christians. Written on both sides of a papyrus discovered in 1912 at ancient Philadelpheia, it is a copy of the emperor Claudius's letter to the city of Alexandria in 41 CE attempting to quell tensions between the Egyptian city council and its Jewish population. Claudius's opening line reads like any New Testament or Greco-Roman letter, using the formulaic prescript "From x to y, greet-

ings." But the emperor's many names and titles are given in full: "Tiberius Claudius Caesar Augustus Germanicus the Emperor, *Pontifex Maximus*, holder of the Tibunician Power, consul designate, to the city of Alexandria, greetings." Like other ancient letters, which continued on a positive note with a blessing, prayer, or compliment, Claudius's imperial letter adds some courtesies and a few diplomatic niceties. Then, in the body of the letter, the emperor accepts the Alexandrians' erection of statues of himself as divine and addresses the issue raised by an Alexandrian delegation that met with him in Rome. The bulk of the letter concerns the recent Jew-Gentile violence in Alexandria, and Claudius is particularly forceful. The Alexandrian city council had blamed the Jews for the riots, but he

"Aquila, a native of Pontus, . . . had recently come from Italy with his wife Priscilla, because Claudius had ordered all Jews to leave Rome."

ACTS 18:2

As was customary, Claudius closes with personal greetings, thanking two members of the Greek Alexandrian delegation whom he calls friends. The original letter would have taken weeks to reach Alexandria from Rome by imperial courier (no fear of thieves, like those carrying Paul's letters had). Once in Alexandria, it would have been read aloud in the assembly, but it was also, according to the papyrus, posted by the Roman prefect across the region "so that each one of you may read it and wonder at the greatness of our god Caesar and be thankful for his goodwill toward the city." Thus imperial scribes copied and circulated the letter well beyond Alexandria, and one of those copies, complete with spelling mistakes and accidentally omitted words, wound up in Philadelpheia, where it was discovered two millennia later. New Testament letters underwent a similar process. They were read

sternly warns both sides that he's not interested in investigating the cause. Instead, he demands that hostilities cease, lest all involved see "what a benevolent ruler can be when he is turned to righteous indignation." He chides *both* sides, ordering the Greek civic leaders to respect and protect Jewish traditions and the Jews to limit their demands.

Claudius's imperial letter was discovered in 1912 and is now stored in the British Museum. It resembles Paul's New Testament letters, following a common style and structure. Claudius (41–54 CE) wrote the letter to put an end to Jewish-pagan ethnic strife in the Egyptian city of Alexandria; in it he also accepted the Alexandrians' wish to worship him as a god by erecting a statue, perhaps a bronze one like that discovered in 1907 in Suffolk, England.

The Augustan reorganization of Rome included the division of the city into wards, which are still apparent on this second-century CE stone plan. At the crossroads of each major intersection, Augustus had altars erected where local festivals in honor of the *Lares Augustales,* the Augustan guardian spirits, could take place.

Nero's decadence is clear from his lavish Golden House, the Domus Aurea, with this Octagonal Hall and arched room painted in the latter Pompeian style. Nero blamed Christians for a fire in Rome and then constructed his palace in a recently burned area. Nero's self-indulgence is apparent on his coins, with an early gold coin from 56–57 CE portraying a slender youth, and a coin from the end of his rule in 64–68 CE portraying an obese man.

in church assemblies, dictated, and copied, but by local rather than imperial scribes. They circulated from Christian community to community, but could never be posted or made public. It is ironic, then, given the inferior sponsorship of those early Christian letters in the New Testament, that they are so frequently preserved in papyri and parchment in antiquity, with hundreds of exemplars, while Claudius's letter lay in obscurity for centuries until its discovery in 1912.

Claudius strikes a reasonable tone in this letter and appears tolerant yet firm. Claudius likewise comes across as a judicious and reasonable ruler, to judge from his major construction projects. He avoided the spectacular but tended to Rome's infrastructure. Several inscriptions record his repair and construction of aqueducts, and his engineers dredged and built flood-control mechanisms on the Tiber River. He also founded the port at Ostia to facilitate the flow of goods to and from Rome along the Tiber River.

EXCAVATING NERO'S GOLDEN HOUSE

Architecture gives an indication of a ruler's self-perception and character, and in that regard, nothing could be more telling than the architecture of Claudius's successor, Nero (54–68 CE). He was overly ambitious, strove for the spectacular but often came up short, and was self-absorbed. Near Corinth he began an extraordinary project to carve a canal from the Gulf of Corinth to the Saronic Gulf, but like his reign it was never finished. Literary sources say he built an amphitheater and *macellum*, or meat-market, but little of either survives in the archaeological record. What made a lasting mark in the archaeological layers of Rome, however, is his so-called Golden House, the Domus Aurea, which reveals his self-absorption at the expense of the empire. Nero's Domus Aurea, now beneath the Arch of Titus in the center of Rome, was a megalomaniacal palace-garden-lake complex that sprawled across the heart of Rome. It was, undoubtedly, the most ostentatious Roman house ever built. Archaeologists recognize its architectural audacity

from bits and pieces discovered underground, especially underneath baths built later by Trajan.

Nero's self-centered house is completely different from Augustus's architectural program; Augustus first restored temples in Rome, then organized and enhanced the city, and finally contributed to cities across the Roman Empire. Augustus renovated Rome's dilapidated temples as a public display of piety, and built the Augustan Forum, the Temple of Mars Ultor, and the Altar of the Augustan Peace. Augustus also spread his wealth among the city's inhabitants; inscriptions tell of a grain dole for the poor, games for the masses, and aqueducts where the populace could bathe. Archaeologists have learned that Augustus reorganized the city around altars. He restructured Rome into 14 districts and 265 wards, then appointed freedman-magistrates and slave-ministers in each neighborhood, but he placed himself squarely in the middle of this reorganization by erecting an altar to the *lares augusti* at each ward's main intersection. Previously, small neighborhood shrines dedicated to the *lares compitales*, the "guardian spirits of the crossroads," had stood at intersections, but Augustus changed their dedication to the *lares augusti*, the Augustan guardian spirit of the empire. They became the focal point of religious devotion in the blocklike *insulae* where the lower classes lived. Local games, festivals, and sacrifices offered plenty of food and drink, with the largest celebration taking place on August 1, the beginning of the month named after Augustus. Inscriptions on these Augustan altars include the names of local freedmen, slaves, and even some women. Jews, given their long-standing tradition, would not be expected to participate in such events, but for recently converted Christians, dropping out of such festivals would have raised suspicions.

These Augustan altars are very different from Nero's single but massive Golden House. The energy and expense expended on that palace overshadowed anything Nero did for the empire. Rome was built on seven hills, and the Golden House spread across

three of them; though called a house, it was actually a compound of gardens and vineyards, pavilions and palaces, which covered over three hundred acres. While other Roman aristocrats built villas in rustic settings outside Rome, Nero brought the countryside to Rome with sprawling gardens and an artificial lake. Archaeologists have uncovered most of the Domus's Esquiline Wing, a suite of some 140 rooms cut along a terrace that overlooked the artificial lake, which Nero filled by redirecting the Aqua Claudia aqueduct. An enormous *nymphaeum*, or fountain-and-pool structure, was built next to the unfinished Temple of the Divine Claudius, a project that Nero suspended while building his own house. One of the Domus's rooms mimicked a grotto: it was completely dark and had artificial stalactites made of pumice descending from the vaulted ceiling. Decorated with a mosaic of Odysseus and the cave-dwelling Polyphemus, it was part Disney World, part kitsch-fantasy, part high-culture.

Archaeologists also have found an octagonal room that once dazzled and delighted visitors with multicolored marble, geometrical *opus sectile* floors, and blue, green, and translucent glass tessarae ceilings. The room was backlit from the surrounding rooms. Light and airy within, the weighty dome was invisibly supported by concrete struts along the radial walls of the adjacent rooms — an ingenious architectural trick. The Golden House was a pleasure palace that suited Nero's Greek and artistic inclination, and cost a fortune to build.

But the Golden House was haunted by the great Roman fire of 64 CE, which

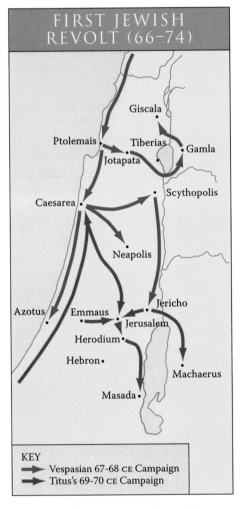

FIRST JEWISH REVOLT (66–74)

Giscala

Ptolemais Tiberias Gamla
Jotapata

Scythopolis

Caesarea

Neapolis

Azotus Emmaus Jericho
Jerusalem
Herodium
Hebron
Machaerus
Masada

KEY
➤ Vespasian 67-68 CE Campaign
➤ Titus's 69-70 CE Campaign

destroyed nearly four-fifths of the city. Nero constructed his parklike palace over the ruins of several lower-class neighborhoods that had burned to the ground while his adjacent property on the Palatine Hill remained untouched. Rumors spread that Nero had started it. Also untouched by the fire was Trastevere, where a high concentration of Christians lived. Nero spread

counter-rumors that Christians had started the fire, and the first persecution of Christians was on. During this time, according to tradition, both Paul and Peter were martyred, along with numerous nameless others who were used as torches to light Nero's gardens in the Golden House, according to one Roman historian. Jews at this time would want to clarify that they were not Christians, and that Christians were not really Jews.

ARCHAEOLOGY OF THE FIRST JEWISH WAR

Nero's self-indulgent rule brought to an end the Julio-Claudian dynasty; he was forced to commit suicide in 68 CE, and Rome was thrown into a year of uncertainty as three successive emperors were crowned and then killed in what looked like a resumption of the earlier civil wars. The Augustan promise imploded with Nero. His reign had repercussions across the empire, as he was inattentive to matters in faraway places like Judea, where trouble was brewing. Appointed governors followed Nero's lead and ruled not for Rome but for their own gain, according to historians like Josephus — a problem that contributed to the first Jewish War in 66–70 CE. That war left an indelible mark on the archaeological record of Galilee and Judea, as soon-to-be Emperor Vespasian led the Tenth Legion (*Fretensis*) and Fifth Legion (*Macedonica*) from the port of Ptolemais through Jotapata in Galilee

to Gamla in the Golan, and then moved south to encircle and destroy Jerusalem. We saw in chapter 4 the conflagration layers at Jotapata and Gamla, and in chapter 5 the severity of Jerusalem's destruction. We turn now to a site that has become emblematic for the Jewish struggle against Rome:

opposite page

Jewish Silver Shekel (66 CE)

"City of Peace" Coin (67/68 CE)

this page

Masada from South

Bust of Vespasian (Carthage, 70–80 CE)

"Holy Jerusalem" and "City of Peace" are two competing messages of Jewish coins from the first revolt. The first is a silver shekel minted by the Jewish rebels, and includes a cup on one side and pomegranate tree on the other; dated to Year One of the revolt, the inscription reads in part "Holy Jerusalem." The other coin was minted at Sepphoris, which did not participate in the revolt and signaled its pacifism by inscribing its coins with the Greek word *Eirenopolis*, "City of Peace."

The battle-hardened Vespasian has a characteristically strained expression in this marble statue found in North African Carthage. A veteran of numerous campaigns in Britain, Nero called on him to put down the Jewish Revolt, but Vespasian later succeeded him as emperor in 69 CE. Vespasian spared the life of the Jewish general Josephus, who later would write a history of the war that describes the Flavian dynasty in glowing messianic terms.

the one-time Herodian palace-fortress Masada, where a few Jewish resistors stubbornly held out for four years after the sack of Jerusalem in 70 CE.

In 69 CE, Vespasian departed Judea while still a general but arrived in Rome as its emperor. His son and successor, Titus, crushed the rebellion by burning Jerusalem and the Temple in 70 CE, and then spent another four years at Masada, west of the Dead Sea. Located on an imposing cliff with a shelflike top, archaeologists have excavated three distinct layers that help sketch the relationship between Judaism and Rome: first, the original Herodian fortress-palace, then the occupation by the Jewish rebels, and finally the Roman destruction and reoccupation. Masada's archaeology reflects the clash of ideals between the Jewish defenders and Herod the Great's original architecture. Just prior to the birth of Jesus, Herod had turned the rock of Masada into an impenetrable fortress with palaces that adopted Roman styles and showed Hellenistic cultural inclinations. Along its northern terraces were triclinia and baths covered in frescoes and mosaics in the finest Roman styles. He imported delicacies and fine wine from abroad; according to the inking on storage jars and stamped amphorae, he offered his guests preserved apples

from Italian Cumae, Pompeiian fish-sauce, fine wine from Italian Brundisium, and even finer wine from Campania, labeled "excellent Massic wine."

But when the Jewish zealots took over Masada nearly a century later, they completely transformed its palaces and structures. Instead of some families living in the elegant northern and western palaces, they converted these into administrative centers and defensive positions and made simpler buildings with crude partitions to create evenly sized living quarters across the top of the plateau. These must have looked like squatter camps, with walls of stones and mud and covered with canvas, wicker, or thatch roofs. They transformed Herod's elaborate storage facilities into a redistributive system that rationed goods with a system of ostraca (fragments of broken pots inscribed with Aramaic and Hebrew). Over seven hundred such ostraca were found, a few of which were labeled in the old Hebrew script. Most were found near storerooms and were tagged with a single letter or a name followed by a letter; since letters were also used as numerals, this was perhaps a rationing system used by the defenders. The names provide a remarkably personal link to the past;

they were all typically Jewish (and found in the New Testament), such as *Yehochanan* (John), *Yehudah* (Jude), *Ya'akov* (Jacob/James), and *Yeshua* (Jesus). Several storage jars were set aside for priests or marked as either appropriately pure or impure: "priest's tithe" or "suited for the purity of holy things" were written across the shoulders of several; others were marked "disqualified" or "these jars are disqualified."

Whereas Herod used water for pleasure bathing, the Jewish defenders constructed stepped pools to maintain purity with what little water was available in the dry climate. At both ends of Masada, *mikvaoth* had been dug into Herodian rooms and sealed with thick layers of dark plaster. Each installation had three pools. One probably served as a footbath, where those about to immerse could wash the dust off their feet and hence keep the pool hygienically cleaner. A pool with steps served for immersion, and a third pool functioned as a reservoir and was connected to the former by a pipe or channel. Several stone vessels found on Masada indicate the defenders' insistence on living a distinctly Jewish life and adhering to traditional purity concerns.

The defenders also built a synagogue in the western casemate wall. Walls were knocked out of the preexisting room, its pillars were rearranged, and tiered benches were built along the sides. The northwest corner was closed off for use as a storage area. Archaeologists think this may have been a *geniza* used to store sacred scrolls, as fragments of biblical texts were found in two pits dug under the floor of the

agogue, in contrast, encouraged egalitarianism by its arrangement and required those seated to look at one another. Much the same could be said for the use of water. During Herod's use of both sites, he enjoyed a magnificent Roman-style bath. At the Herodium, the changing room (*apodyterium*) was decorated with frescoes in the First Pompeian Style, as was its circular, dome-capped warm room (*tepidarium*), which pictured water birds. The hot room (*caldarium*) was heated by Roman-engineered hypocaust tiles

> "... baptism ... now saves you — not as a removal of dirt from the body, but as an appeal to God for a good conscience."
>
> 1 PETER 3:21.

opposite page

Rebels' Synagogue (Herodium)

Fortress at Herodium (Israel)

this page

Synagogue (Masada)

Herodian Bathhouse (Masada)

Zealot Ritual Bath (Masada)

Synagogue Plan (Masada)

Perched atop a massive artificial mound, the palace called the Herodium commands a view of the region southeast of Jerusalem. Herod built the mound, fortress, and palace complex below both for security and as his burial place. Archaeologists are still seeking to determine exactly where his body would have been buried. But like Masada, Jewish rebels took control of the site sometime during the first revolt and transformed the palace's dining hall into a synagogue.

Zealots transformed Roman structures into Jewish ones in Masada, which they occupied at the end of the first Jewish Revolt. Herod the Great had built palaces there in Roman style, but the Jewish defenders dismantled the Roman-style bathhouse and replaced it with Jewish ritual baths. They also converted a room in the casemate wall into a synagogue, one of the oldest ever discovered in Israel. In addition to the tiered seating, scraps of biblical texts found there helped identify the room's later use as a place of religious worship.

synagogue. A similar transformation took place at another Herodian palace-fortress, the Herodium, which, like Masada, was occupied by the rebels during the first Jewish Revolt. The Herodium was a two-part complex: a lower area held baths, pools, and palace rooms, while above was a massive artificial mound topped by a fortress. Inside the fortress, a fifteen-by-ten-meter triclinium had been rebuilt as a synagogue with tiered benches along three walls. The rebels also added a stepped pool for ritual bathing in front of the synagogue. The transformation of a triclinium into a synagogue reveals the ideological differences driving Roman and Jewish social life. A triclinium was hierarchical in its very design: three benches for the host and two key guests, with the remaining seats assigned by status. The Jewish syn-

under the floor and clay pipes in the walls. But the bathing complex was never used by the later Jewish occupants; instead they used a portion of their scant water resources for ritual bathing. Excavations at Masada and the Herodium vividly remind us of the struggles between imperial Romanization and traditional Jewish values. The war may have had all kinds of causes that can never be revealed by archaeological excavations, but the tensions between Roman culture and Jewish religion are clear in those places.

The excavations at Masada reveal the lengths to which Rome went to preserve the *Pax Romana*. Nothing signals Rome's desire to utterly crush all Jewish resistance like their siege works at Masada. Steep cliffs on all sides made Masada impenetrable, and a few men could hold off an entire army at the Snake Path winding up the eastern slope. Herod had built a system for collecting and storing rainwater and stocked the silos with abundant grain, and the defenders were ready for a protracted siege. Excavations around the cliffs show how methodical the Roman legions were in their siege, first building a six-foot-thick wall surrounding the entire site, with towers at intervals to allow sentries to spot the enemy. Escape was impossible. They constructed eight rectangular and square encampments, two of which were classic legionary camps — walled minifortresses with four entrances. But the most impressive ruin at the site is the Roman siege ramp constructed on the cliff's western side.

Titus directed the legions to construct a massive ramp on Masada's western side that was over 650 feet long, over 650 feet wide, and 250 feet at its highest point. Timber was brought from far away to assemble a scaffold that held rocks, stones, and packed earth and provided sufficient stability for a siege machine to be rolled to the top. The Jewish defenders made a futile attempt to reinforce the casemate where the ramp's battering ram met the wall, but grapefruit-sized catapult stones and arrowheads scattered around the area bear testimony to their demise at the hands of the Romans. In 74 CE all overt Jewish resistance ended.

The defeat of the Jews on the empire's eastern edge was big news across the empire. It was also well publicized by Rome. The Jewish Revolt was the first serious challenge to the *Pax Romana* in nearly a century, and the new emperor Vespasian and his general and son Titus made sure the victory was widely advertised. A triumphal procession in the city of Rome celebrated their victory, and various honors were offered them in cities across the empire. Coins were minted to commemorate the defeat of the Jews, which were inscribed in large Latin letters IUDAEA CAPTA, "Judea Captured." That phrase harkened back to Augustus's AEGUPTO CAPTA coins in 28 BCE, and linked Vespasian to the earlier Julio-Claudians. The IUDAEA CAPTA coins outnumbered any other commemorative issues and were minted for ten years, to 81 CE. Whether gold, silver, or bronze denominations, they had the head of Vespasian, his older son Titus, or his younger son Domitian on one side, and on the other most often a palm tree next to a seated female representation of Judea sulking with head held in hand. Although most had a female Judea, a few had a male captive or a raised trophy. Others had a legionnaire with his foot on an orb next to a seated and bound Judea. Those minted in Caesarea Maritima,

though a bit cruder than those minted elsewhere, were inscribed in Greek rather than Latin to make sure locals got the message.

After the destruction of the Jewish Temple, Vespasian instituted a tax on the Jews, so that instead of Jewish adult males paying a half-shekel to the Temple in Jerusalem, they paid it for the maintenance of the Temple to Capitoline Jupiter in Rome. A few papyri from Egypt suggest that even males under eighteen were liable for this tax.

With the booty from the Jewish War, Vespasian began and Titus completed the largest

the goddess Victory following his triumphal procession. Pictured between these two scenes, in the middle of the arch, is Titus being carried to heaven on the back of Jupiter's eagle. Like all the Julio-Claudian emperors since Augustus, all the Flavian caesars — Vespasian, Titus, and Domitian — would ascend to heaven and be seated among the gods.

Given the abundance of the IU-DAEA CAPTA coins, the new tax on Jews, and the Arch of Titus and the Coliseum, we can imagine that Jews

opposite page

Roman Camps around Masada

Roman Arrows (Masada)

***Iudaea Capta* Coin (71 CE)**

this page

Coliseum (Rome, 1st C. CE)

Arch of Titus (Rome, 1st C. CE)

Menorah on Arch of Titus

Rome signaled "no way out" to the Jewish defenders at Masada when they began construction of walls and forts all around the cliff. The rebels posed no serious strategic threat to Rome and could easily have been starved out or allowed to flee to neighboring lands. But Rome's policy was to make an example of all dissidents; there was no way to escape the wrath and control of Rome.

The Jews' defeat was highly publicized all over the empire, especially in Rome. The Flavian dynasty of Vespasian, Titus, and Domitian minted coins with the inscription IUDAEA CAPTA, "Judea captured" or "Judea defeated." The reverse of this coin from 71 CE features a grieving Jewish woman beside a palm tree; a Roman soldier's foot stands on an orb to indicate victory. With the proceeds of the war, Vespasian and Titus built the Coliseum in Rome and Domitian built the Arch of Titus, commemorating the divine Titus's ascension to heaven and his victory in the Jewish War.

amphitheater in the Roman Empire, the giant oval known as the Coliseum. An inscription on a marble lintel from inside the western entrance notes that it was dedicated by Titus in 80 CE. Vespasian's statement of the Coliseum's original purpose can still be reconstructed from the holes left by the pinholes from bronze letters since removed: "The emperor Caesar Vespasian Augustus had this new amphitheater erected with the spoils of war." The name for the Coliseum came, ironically, from the colossal statue of Nero that once stood near his Golden House and which the austere Flavians dismantled. With its marble, Vespasian constructed the new Temple of Pax and completed the Temple of the Divine Claudius, which Nero had left unfinished.

The best-known monument celebrating the Roman defeat of the Jews is the Arch of Titus. Erected right after Titus's death by his younger brother and successor, Domitian, it spans the old sacred way from the Forum to the Coliseum. Its inside southern curve contains a deep-cut frieze of the legions carrying off Jerusalem's golden treasures. Included in the booty is a menorah, probably based on eyewitness reports of those who saw the Temple's menorah carried off. The arch's inside northern curve depicts Titus driving a four-horse chariot, with the goddess Roma preceding and

throughout the diaspora were carefully watched. It is very likely that followers of Jesus at this time wanted to distance themselves from Jews, just as Jews distanced themselves from Christians in Nero's time. It is no surprise that in the latter part of the first century CE, the church and the synagogue split, and Christians and Jews separated, at the very time the Gospels were written.

ARCHAEOLOGY AND THE APOCALYPSE

After the first Jewish War, Christians were suspect not only because of their connection to Judaism but because they did not participate in the imperial cult. Archaeology sheds light on Christian opposition to the imperial cult as it is reflected in the most cryptic book of the New Testament, the Apocalypse of John, often called Revelation. Written in Asia Minor, probably during the reign of Domitian (81–96 CE), archaeological excavations and artifacts cannot confirm even one item or place in John's vision, but they do characterize the context in which the book was written and point to it being the most subversive, if not outright seditious, book of the New Testament.

Two coins from around the time Revelation was written shed light on the Christian defiance of the Roman imperial cult that can be found in Revelation. One coin depicts Domitia, the wife of Domitian, on one side, and on the other their son seated on a globe with his hands spread and raised upward. Seven stars encircle the cosmic youth and future emperor, accompanied by the inscription "The Divine Caesar Imperator Domitian." This cosmic vision is uncannily similar to that recounted in Revelation 1, where the narrator says he "saw one like a son of man, . . . who in his right hand held seven stars." The second coin depicts the goddess Roma sitting on seven hills next to a tiny she-wolf suckling Romulus and Remus, who represent the city of Rome. Minted in 71 CE, it is similar to the account in Revelation of a woman sitting on seven hills who is no goddess but a whore dressed in purple and whose golden cup is filled with "the impurities of her fornication" (17:4). The whore of Babylon is none other than the goddess Roma, the city of Rome, the Roman Empire. The Christian vision is a direct challenge to the iconography of the coins.

Most New Testament scholars think that Revelation was written in or near Ephesus, and archaeological excavations there have uncovered enormous construction projects during the reign of Domitian, who extensively altered the cityscape. In the upper area of Ephesus, he built the Temple of the Sebastoi on a massive artificial platform some three hundred feet long and two hundred feet wide, supported on its southern side by a three-story, colonnaded portico. It towered forty feet above the plaza below and was the most visible feature from the lower city and harbor. Its columns were shaped like deities, similar to the famous Athenian caryatids, to suggest that the Roman imperial temple was supported, physically and symbolically, by the gods themselves. Its style was closer to local Asian than Roman, suggesting that the Ephesian elites designed it for Domitian rather than him ordering it built to his own specifications. A head and other fragments of a nearly twenty-foot-tall marble statue, once thought to be of Domitian but probably of Titus, were discovered in 1930. Cuts around the shoulders suggest that it was made partly of wood and covered with clothing, and though the face and head were carefully executed on the front and sides, the back was only roughly finished. This was clearly a cult statue that

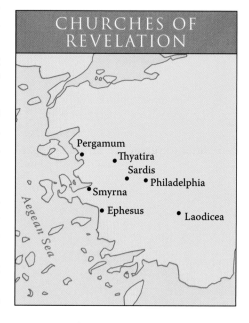

CHURCHES OF REVELATION

priests and worshippers saw only from the front, as they offered sacrifices. Today called the Temple of Domitian, ancient inscriptions identify it as the Temple of the Sebastoi; it was used to worship the earlier Flavians and later emperors, even after Domitian was assassinated and scratched off the roll of deities.

In addition to the temple, imperial baths were built at the time of Domitian near the harbor. According to an inscription for the Greek city of Issos honoring a victorious athlete, religious-athletic games were also held at Ephesus to honor Domitian. Ephesus became the leading city of the imperial cult in Asia Minor; according to coins and inscriptions dating to 89 or 90 CE, it was awarded the title *neokoros,* which made it the prestigious warden of the imperial temple for the entire province. Christians in the area were hardly enthusiastic. They had been persecuted by Nero after the great fire, and as is apparent in Revelation, they were still persecuted, even to the point of death.

An Egyptian papyrus suggests that Nero was the archetype of evil in the book of Revelation. The papyrus is a fragment of a copy of the book of Revelation and gives the number of the beast not as 666, as most manuscripts do, but as 616. It was common in the ancient world to use letters for numbers, and if *Caesar Nero* is put into Hebrew letters and added up as numbers, the total is 666. Nero, then, is probably the beast. But there are two ways to spell his name: either Nero or Neron. Since the numerical value of the Hebrew N is fifty, one may surmise that the scribe of one papyrus copy of Revelation knew that Nero was the beast, and when he checked the math using the alternative spelling, he changed it to 616. After Nero's suicide, several pretenders claimed to be him and sought, with the support of the Parthians, to retake the throne from the Flavian emperors. None was successful, but Christians feared Nero's return even more than Domitian's rule. Nero — either the actual emperor who ruled from 54–68 CE, or more likely the feared return of a Nero-like caesar during the reign of Domitian (81–96 CE) — was the incarnation of evil on earth. The book of Revelation, then, not unlike Paul's letters, pits the Christian Son of God against the Roman son of god, and hopes for the destruction of Rome and Roman rule to be replaced by the kingdom of God and the New Jerusalem descending from heaven.

THE BAR-KOKHBA REVOLT AND THE NEW JERUSALEM

But Christians were not the only ones anxious about Rome and hoping for a new Jerusalem. After the first revolt and the destruction of the Temple in 70 CE, many Jews in Judea still longed to throw off Rome's yoke and rebuild the Temple. In 132, Simeon Bar Kosiba, who was then called *Bar-Kokhba* (Aramaic for "Son of the Star"), proclaimed an independent Jewish kingdom and ruled it for three years, until Rome crushed the uprising in 135 CE. The emperor Hadrian had agitated the Jewish population when he began to rebuild Jerusalem with a temple dedicated to the Roman god Jupiter instead of to the one Jewish God. The foundation of the pagan temple is commemorated in coins minted in 132 CE,

> " … in the midst of the lampstands was one like a son of man … "
>
> REVELATION 1:13

opposite page

Domitian's Temple (Ephesus, 1st C. CE)
Imperial Inscription (Ephesus, 1st C. CE)
Coin with Roma (71 CE)

this page

Golden Lamp Stand (Ephesus, 1st C. CE)
Fragment of Revelation (Egypt, 3rd C. CE)
Relief with Lion (Ephesus, ca. 100 CE)

The imperial temple towered over Ephesus after much of the city was transformed during the emperor Domitian's rule (81–96 CE). Ephesus was not only an important early Christian center mentioned in the book of Revelation, it also become the center of Asia Minor's imperial cult. Although popular in Ephesus, Domitian was despised by the Roman Senate, and after his death they condemned his name and memory, ordering that his name be scratched off all inscriptions, like this one from Ephesus.

Apocalypse and archaeology might seem like an unlikely match. But archaeological artifacts help enlighten several aspects of the book of Revelation. This coin, for example, shows the goddess Roma sitting on Rome's seven hills — John's vision calls her a whore sitting on seven hills. This lamp stand found at Ephesus is likely the kind envisioned in Revelation. This local relief of a lion eating a victim reminds us of the severity of Roman persecution.

The number of the beast reveals his identity, and this papyrus fragment from Egypt helps solve the riddle. Caesar Nero could be spelled two different ways, and the numerical value of his name spelled one way in Hebrew letters is 666; spelled the other way, it is 616. This fragment of Revelation, along with several others, uses 616.

after which the Jewish population united under the leadership of Bar-Kokhba, who is described in messianic terms in some literary sources. His very name, Son of the Star, challenges the much older Augustan messianic claim signaled by the comet of Julius Caesar. Although literary sources provide only sparse information about the war, archaeologists across Israel have found considerable evidence of the war's devastating consequences in numerous caves and underground chambers, in both Galilee and Judea, that were built in the decades leading up to the war. This uprising had been better planned and anticipated than the first, which was largely spontaneous.

In the end, however, the revolt was crushed. Archaeologists found scattered hideouts of the Jewish rebels in the difficult terrain of the eastern Judean Wilderness beginning in the 1960s. Everything necessary for a protracted holdout was found in these caves, including stoves, pots, baskets, textiles, and shoes. In one cave, skeletal remains of several people were found. As the remains lacked any signs of violence, they probably starved to death as they hid in the cave. In another cave, archaeologists found beautiful bronze dishes with pagan imagery, which had probably been stolen from the Romans. In a recently discovered cave, a cache of weapons was found, including a well-made spearhead and several arrowheads.

One of the most surprising finds from the Bar-Kokhba Revolt, found inside the Cave of Letters, was a cache of papyri written by Bar-Kokhba himself. One letter is dated to the outbreak of the war in 132 CE and urges Yehonathan "to get the young men and come with them. And I shall deal with the Romans." Another, from a later year, asks Bar Menachem to have his friends and followers bring myrtle, citrons, and palm branches, items needed for a Jewish Passover meal. The rebels expected a long-term confrontation but were bent on observing Jewish religious traditions, especially Passover, which celebrated freedom from bondage.

Another set of documents reveals less about that revolt but much about ancient Jewish families and women. As archaeologists were excavating one of

the caves sheltering the Jewish rebels, they came upon a set of rolled papyri tucked inside a leather pouch. These were the personal documents of Babatha, a Jewish woman who hid in this cave, and apparently died in the revolt or was enslaved afterward. These papyri provide a gold mine of information about gender relations and women's roles, issues that are also of primary concern in the latter epistles of the New Testament.

The Babatha archives paint a portrait of a Jewish woman who lived at the end of the New Testament period. She was born in the Roman province of Arabia at the end of the first century CE to well-to-do Jewish parents. She married a man named Jesus (*Yeshua*), had a son whom they named Jesus, and after her husband died she married a man named Judas. But he was already (and remained) married, to a women named Miriam, who had a daughter. Much of the archives relate to the disputes between Babatha and Miriam after Judas's death; aspects of those disputes are helpful for understanding common attitudes toward women as the first Christians tried to determine the role of women in the church. There are nineteen men mentioned by name in the papyri but only four women. Another eleven wives are noted in Babatha's papyri, but none by name. That contrasts with Paul's closing greetings in Romans, which include twenty-seven names, among them ten women and seventeen men. Of those singled out for special praise, there are five women and six men.

Women in the Babatha archive, for the most part, are defined in relation to men, either their husband, father, or son. They needed a male guardian to function in the legal system. After Babatha's first husband dies, she

> "...the real widow, left alone, has set her hope on God..."
>
> 1 TIMOTHY 5:5

depends on court-approved male guardians to conduct her legal affairs until the son comes of age and serves as Babatha's legal guardian. The male lineage, from father to son, is what counts; women's lineage is either ambiguous or ignored. This contrasts with Luke's matrilineal genealogy of Jesus. Marriage in these documents is clearly considered an exchange between the father and the husband-to-be. Judas's two wives, Babatha and Miriam, wrangled over possessions, but it was their relationship to him and his will that constituted their essential legal claims. Babatha was per-

sistent and not passive in her legal maneuvers, but her archives, indeed all papyri, reinforce the fact that the world of the New Testament was a man's world.

At the end of the Bar-Kokhba Revolt in 135 CE, the New Jerusalem had come. But it was neither what Jews had hoped for — the rebuilding of the Temple — nor what Christians had hoped for: the new city from heaven. It was renamed in Latin Aelia Capitolina, after the emperor Hadrian's family name, Aelius, and dedicated to the chief Roman god, Jupiter Capitolinus. Jews were no longer permitted inside the city, which was rebuilt with the aid of Roman troops who were stationed there. The Temple of Jupiter was built on the old Herodian Temple Mount. After the Bar-Kokhba Revolt, Judaism changed its focus from the Temple to the book, especially the Torah but also other writings in the Hebrew Bible and their interpretation. At that time Christianity adopted the Hebrew Bible, called it the Old Testament, and began the work of assembling its own new book from a set of Gospels, letters, and visions that would eventually be called the New Testament.

opposite page

Bar-Kokhba Letter (132–35 CE)
Statue of Hadrian (117–38 CE)

this page

Exploration of Caves
Babatha Archive (125 CE)
Jewish Silver Shekel (132–35 CE)
Spear from Revolt

A rare bronze statue of Hadrian, the Roman emperor from 117 to 138 CE, was found not by archaeologists but by a tourist in Israel who was searching for coins with a metal detector in 1975. Hadrian was known to love all things Greek and is shown in statues as vigorous and muscular. He traveled widely and crushed the Bar-Kokhba Revolt, whereupon the statue was set up in a Roman fort south of Scythopolis.

The second Jewish Revolt was led by Bar-Kokhba, "Son of the Star," and lasted from 132 to 135 CE. Many Jewish fighters hid in caves in the Judean Wilderness, from which they staged guerilla warfare against the Romans. In these caves, archaeologists have discovered letters written by Bar-Kokhba himself. More recently, aerial photography and electronic surveillance equipment have helped excavators identify this almost inaccessible cave where his spear tip was found.

The status of women in antiquity was clarified greatly by a fortuitous discovery inside a cave used by the Bar-Kochba rebels. The so-called Babatha archive preserved the legal documents relating to a Jewish woman named Babatha, who died in the revolt. The archive spells out in great detail her dependence on males to negotiate through life and the legal system, seemingly at odds with her initiative and persistence.

MASADA AND THE ZEALOTS

The siege of Masada is well known from Josephus's dramatic story of the suicide of the Jewish defenders, who chose to die free rather than be enslaved by Rome. But that story might not resonate in the archaeological record. Masada was first identified in 1838 by the American explorer Edward Robinson, who never actually visited the site but viewed it though a telescope. In 1867 Charles Warren surveyed the winding Snake Path that leads from its eastern side to the top. In the early twentieth century, more thorough surveys, including some of the first aerial photographs, mapped out the surrounding Roman camps, the siege wall, and the basic structures of the site.

In 1963–65, however, the great Israeli archaeologist and statesman Yigal Yadin extensively excavated the site. His excavations uncovered the Herodian palaces, storage facilities, water system, and casemate wall, as well as evidence of the Jewish Zealots who fought the Romans. He also found evidence for how and where the Romans broke through the walls, and believed he had found the skeletal remains of some of those defenders. After Yadin's excavation, which occurred right before the 1967 War, Masada became a metaphor for the state of Israel, and "Never again will Masada fall" became a national refrain.

While most of the work done by Yadin and his now-prominent students is not in doubt, the case for Josephus's story of a mass suicide as well as the initial excavators' ready

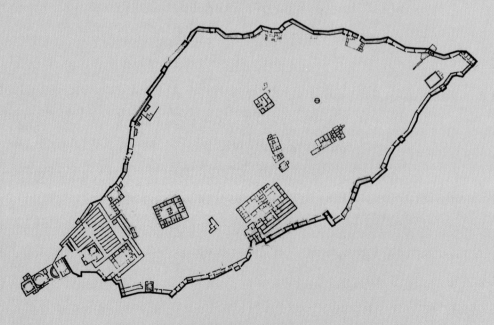

identification of skeletal remains as the defenders of Masada have been questioned. The basic Herodian architecture is well documented, as is the evidence that the Romans besieged a small group of Jews atop Masada from 70 to 74 CE. But the bones of a man, a child, and a woman found with braided hair and a sandal, along with about twenty skeletons in a cistern, were probably not defenders, in spite of receiving a reverent state burial after their excavation in the 1960s. They were probably the remains of Romans who later occupied the site until 111 CE. Joe Zias, a physical anthropologist for the Israel Antiquities Authority, has conducted an extensive analysis of the matter and questions the connection between the bones and the defenders. There are problems with the identification. Why would the Romans leave the zealot bodies to rot when they planned on occupying the site with a garrison for another forty years? How could pig bones be found among Jewish skeletons — a serious problem, since Roman burial ceremonies commonly included pig sacrifices. Because of so many predatory tooth marks on the bones, Zias suggests

that instead of the defenders' final resting place, Yadin may have found the temporary den of a hyena family who scavenged bones from the Roman garrison's burial site decades after the fall of Masada.

The problem of Masada is similar to the problem faced when relating archaeology to the new Testament. On some issues, such as how and where the Romans breached the wall, Josephus's texts and Yadin's excavation are in agreement. Text and archaeology go hand in hand in a complementary way. At other times, however, there is a tension between text and artifact. For example, Josephus tells of the defenders drawing lots to determine who will kill whom in their final suicide pact. Ostraca have been found with names on them that might have served as lots, including the name of the man Josephus says was the group's leader, Ben Yair. But other ostraca, in fact most of them, seem to have served as a kind of rationing system. In this case, it is hard to tell the extent to which a prior reading of Josephus distorts an objective interpretation of the archaeology. That is equally true of the New Testament.

8

THE CHRISTIAN WORLD AFTER THE NEW TESTAMENT

By the beginning of the second century CE, the New Testament books and letters had been written and were being copied and distributed in Christian communities from western Rome to eastern Syria. But it took several more centuries before they were assembled between two covers in what we would recognize as the New Testament, after Constantine the Great (ruled 321–37 CE) legally recognized Christianity. Constantine not only legalized Christianity but sponsored church councils to sort out theological concerns, paid for large-scale church-building, and produced several high-quality biblical manuscripts, with the books of the Old and New Testaments in their current order. We conclude this book on archaeology and the New Testament with a brief look at what excavations and discoveries reveal about Christianity in the second through fourth centuries CE, between the time the New Testament texts were written and the time they were officially canonized. In particular, we examine some of Christianity's religious competitors, the so-called mystery religions; trace the emergence of a Christian material culture beginning in the late second century CE; and sketch the diversity of Christianities as revealed by manuscript discoveries in Egypt. We conclude with a look at the making of the Christian Holy Land and the transformation of Jewish villages like Bethlehem and Nazareth into Christian pilgrimage sites.

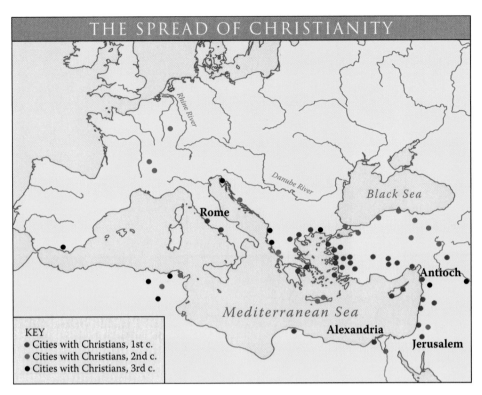

KEY
- Cities with Christians, 1st c.
- Cities with Christians, 2nd c.
- Cities with Christians, 3rd c.

CHRISTIANITY AND ITS COMPETITORS

In this book, we have examined the archaeological evidence for the Roman emperor cult and noted that the first followers of Jesus, whether Paul or the author of Revelation, took a subversive stance regarding the caesars as gods. It is unlikely, however, that Christianity posed a serious threat to the imperial cult; it simply could not compete. In the first century CE, the imperial cult was public and pervasive, while Christian communities were private, subversive, and hardly noticed. In the early second century CE, according to correspondence between the emperor Trajan and the provincial governor Pliny the Younger, Christians are noticed because they refuse to support sacrifices to the emperor, but Trajan's dismissive tone shows little concern for the potential threat posed by Christianity. Less than 1 percent of the population was Christian at that time; there were several Eastern-inspired religions that had attracted many more adherents than Christianity; and none viewed their devotion as conflicting with the older civic or imperial gods.

There is considerably more archaeological evidence for meetings dedicated to Dionysos, Isis, or Mithras than those devoted to Jesus. Scholars call these groups mystery religions, of which the most notable worshipped the Greek wine-god Dionysos, the Egyptian goddess Isis, or the Persian god Mithras. These groups did not keep their devotion secret, but are called mystery religions because their devotees' religious experience was considered so profound as to be unspeakable to non-initiates. Perhaps people were attracted to these mystery religions because they offered a more personal touch and more communal fellowship than did the civic or imperial cults. They offered a package not unlike Christianity, including personal devotion to and attention from

opposite page

Dionysos Mosaic (Sepphoris, 3rd c. CE)
Coin of Caracalla (211–17 CE)
Detail of Coin

this page

Isis (Pompeii, 1st c. CE)
Isis with Horus (Alexandria, 2nd c. BCE)

Victorious Dionysos sits on his chariot in this third-century CE mosaic found in Galilean Sepphoris. Dionysos was one of many gods popular in the second through fourth centuries. The devotion to the wine-god is open to question; perhaps many enjoyed his gift more than the giver.

A Christian stamp on Caesar is found on this coin. A later Christian stamped a *chi rho* Christogram just behind Caesar's bust on this coin originally minted by the emperor Caracalla (211–17 CE). Coins were in circulation for some time, so we cannot be sure when this was done, but it is perhaps one of the earliest instances of a symbol popularized in the early fourth century CE.

The "Mistress of Heaven" was one name for the Egyptian deity Isis. She was the goddess of maternity and infancy, and is often depicted breastfeeding Horus as he sits on her lap, apparently a model for later Christian depictions of Mary nursing the baby Jesus. Isis's popularity grew steadily and reached its apex in the second century; she was certainly more prominent than Jesus and attracted devotion because of the personal attention she is said to have granted devotees.

the deity; the promise of an afterlife; a social setting where people from various backgrounds could find fellowship; and the satisfaction of intellectual curiosity about the workings of the world and cosmos, albeit at a crude level.

In earlier chapters we looked at some archaeological evidence for the cult of Dionysos, whose mysteries can be traced to the ancient cult center at Eleusis near Athens. This cult experienced a resurgence in popularity in the second century CE. More popular than Dionysos was the Egyptian goddess Isis, whose rise archaeologists date to the second century BCE, when she acquired a reputation for personal solicitude. On the Greek island of Delos, an Egyptian

émigré transformed his house into a shrine for communal worship by constructing a small altar in his courtyard and a room for communal dining. Excavators found an inscription that recounts how some Delians sought to shut down the meetings, until Isis "paralyzed these wicked-minded men . . . making their tongues incapable of uttering a single word, . . . and the whole community marveled with dread at your miracle on that day." That kind of personal attention came to be expected of the Egyptian goddess, who is called "-Isis the Savior" or "Isis who lends an ear" in other inscriptions. By the first century CE, Isis was called the dispenser of life, the protector of families, the

guardian of the fields, the healer and deliverer of those who sought her, and above all, the protector of sailors and travelers. Her cult was widespread, reaching key cities where Paul traveled, like Thessalonica, Philippi, Ephesus, and Corinth. Like Judaism and later Christianity, archaeological evidence for her cult is most common along sea lanes, especially Mediterranean ports, and along rivers like the Rhine and Danube. She was popular in Italy among the wealthy, and at Pompeii her temple was the first structure, after the amphitheater, to be reconstructed following the earthquake of 62 CE. By the end of the first century CE, Isis was prominent in the heart of Rome, and the emperor Domitian (81–96 CE) renovated and greatly expanded Isis's temple in the Campus Martius with a colossal statue of her and exotic Egyptian features like obelisks, papyrus ornamentations, and relief-carved baboons and crocodiles.

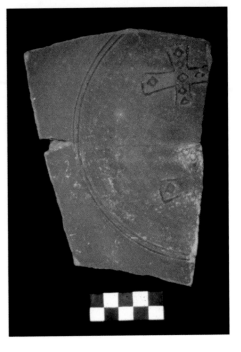

But Isis's life-affirming qualities attracted adherents from all levels of society, a point well documented in epigraphic finds. There are Isis-related graffiti from a small group composed mostly of slaves who met in a modest house on Rome's Aventine Hill. There is epigraphic evidence of devotees who were soldiers and veterans, freedmen and municipal officials, as at Pompeii. At least one member of the imperial family, an in-law of Nero, kept depictions of Isis on her family shrine. Initiates included men, women, and children, Romans and Egyptians, foreigners from all the provinces; a wide variety of people found the personal demands of Isis more rewarding than the traditional civic cults.

The mystery religion that left behind the most archaeological evidence, however, is Mithraism. Little is known for sure about its beliefs, since it had no known scriptures, but archaeological finds relating to Mithraism are so profuse that we have some idea about the essential beliefs and practices of the cult. Worship took place in a *mithraeum,* which are found, among other places, wherever Roman legions were stationed. These *mithraea* were small rooms, usually subterranean or, if above ground, windowless, and were rectangular in shape under an arched ceiling, with benches for reclining on two sides and an apselike altar at one end. On the altar, there was often a depiction of the *tauroctony,* the slaying the bull by Mithras. The craftsmanship of these altars varied greatly. In some places, like

Rome, they were full marble statues carved by skilled stonemasons; in other places, like Dura-Europos in Syria, they were simple relief carvings in a folk style. In other places, like Marino near Rome, they were simply frescoes painted on the wall.

Given the numerous depictions of astrological phenomena and constellations, it's possible that Mithraic theology explains the fate of the soul by analogy to the astronomical procession of the equinoxes. Mithras's slaying of the bull might represent the movement of the constellations at the equinox from Taurus (the bull); Mithras may have been thought to rotate the heavens and control the fate of souls. Most scholarly explanations are so complicated, however, that one wonders if the rank and file would have understood them, and their theology remains shrouded in mystery. We do know that Mithraism was exclusively male and that adherents were divided into a hierarchy of grades. A black-and-white mosaic at one of Ostia's seventeen *mithraea* preserves the names and order of the ranks, from an initiate, called a Raven, through Bridegroom, Soldier, Lion, Persian, Runner of the Sun, and ultimately to the highest rank, Father. Although Christianity was more egalitarian and was open to women, the size of Mithraic meetings may have been similar to early Christian meetings in the first few centuries. The benches on both sides of most *mithraea* accommodated around a dozen for a meal; some of

opposite page

Mithras Slaying Bull (Rome, 2nd c. CE)
Fresco in *Mithraeum* (Marino, 3rd. c. CE)
***Mithraeum* in Warehouse (Caesarea)**

this page

***Mithraeum* under Church (Rome, 3rd c. CE)**
Ossuary with "Cross" (Jerusalem, 1st c.)
Cross on Plate (Sepphoris, 5th c. CE)

The slaying of the bull is the classic iconography of Mithraism, the greatest competitor of Christianity. The so-called *tauroctony* depicts Mithras slaying the bull Taurus. Mithraism was an all-male religion that attracted soldiers, lower-level bureaucrats, and imperial officials who met in cavelike *mithraea,* such as this one found at Caesarea Maritima in Israel, which had been converted from a storehouse near the harbor. Evidence for Mithraism can be found all over the empire, especially where Roman soldiers were stationed.

Christ's triumph over Mithras is readily apparent in the location of many churches, which were built on top of *mithraea,* like this one under the Church of San Clemente in Rome.

No crosses on objects existed before Constantine, though some ossuaries from Jerusalem before 70 CE had such a cross etched on them. But these marks and others, including Greek letters, triangles, and zigzag lines, appear to have been masons' marks to note where the lid best fit the box. Later, after the fourth century, the cross was common on *terra sigillata* pottery.

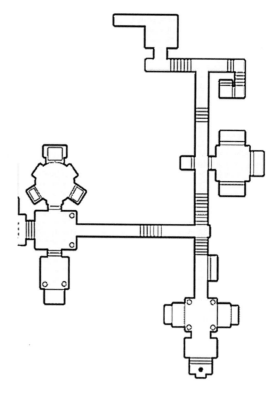

in Rome underneath the Church of San Clemente signals the triumph of Christianity following Constantine, after which churches would be built systematically over *mithraic* meeting places and other pagan holy sites. Nevertheless, the legacy of Mithras or Sol Invictus, the invincible sun whose day was December 25, would survive in the Christian rite of Christmas.

THE EARLIEST CHRISTIAN ARTIFACTS AND IMAGES

Unlike Mithraism, Christianity had no established architectural structure during the second century CE, and most presume that Christians met in houses that are archaeologically indistinguishable. In fact, there is almost no Christian evidence of any kind until Christians developed a distinctive set of artifacts around 150 CE, which increased in frequency in the 200s CE. Of these, the overwhelming majority are from Rome.

As we saw in chapter 1, the cross is surprisingly absent during this period.

the larger ones, like the converted warehouse at Caesarea Maritima, could have held as many as thirty to forty adherents.

One reason archaeologists have discovered so many *mithraea* is because so many were built underground in chambers with only a single entrance. Ironically but probably intentionally, many *mithraea* were covered over by Christians who built their churches over them in the fourth century CE — for instance, at Hawarti in modern Syria, which was discovered when the fifth-century mosaic floor of a church caved in. The well-known *mithraeum*

It would not come into use until the fourth century CE, after Constantine the Great adopted it for his soldiers' shields before the battle at the Milvian Bridge in 312 CE. It does not appear in Christian art or iconography before that time, in spite of attempts to see crosses in places like Herculaneum, as we saw in chapter 1. Some have identified crosses on ossuaries in Jerusalem that date to before 70 CE, and one of these even includes the Greek phrase *Iesus Aloth* —

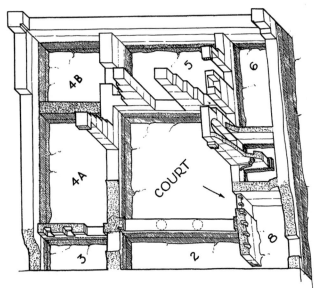

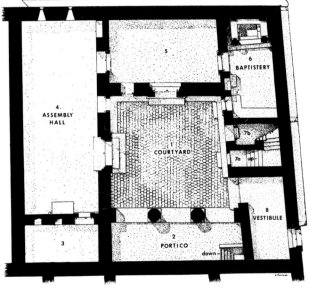

pagan times, like the image of the good shepherd, which was found in a pre-Christian Athenian statue. Christians adopted this youthful shepherd and re-interpreted it as Jesus the good shepherd. When archaeologists encounter one of these symbols alone, they cannot be certain that it is, in fact, Christian. But in context with Christian graffiti or inscriptions, these symbols can confidently be considered to refer to Christian meals or worship practices. The most common Latin phrase in early

allegedly a Christian plea for the dead, "Jesus, alas!" But Jesus was a very common name, one of the most common on ossuaries from the time, and *Aloth* was the man's family name and not an exclamation. The inscription contains, like all ossuary inscriptions, the name of the deceased, and the cross marks on this and other ossuaries are suspicious. They are usually in black charcoal and almost always occur in pairs, on an adjacent lid and box. Archaeologists believe that they served as markers to help line up the lid with the box for the best fit. One finds, in addition to "crosses," Greek or Aramaic letters, in addition to zigzag lines and triangles with no apparent meaning. These were not Christian crosses.

The overwhelming majority of archaeologists are confident that the earliest Christian use of the cross occurs in the fourth century; by the fifth century, it is ubiquitous. The cross appears frequently on Eastern *terra sigillata* pottery, which was widely distributed in North Africa, the Near East, and Tur-key. Many of these crosses, by the way, were stamped off-center on the bottom of plates or bowls, as the identifying stamp of a Christian workshop. More ornate and stylish crosses appear on the front of plates probably intended for use by Christians. Also common at this time were *chi rho* monograms, which combined the first two letters of the Greek word *Christos* to mimic the shape of a cross. It appears for the first time on a sarcophagus from the mid-fourth century found near the Vatican, and is common in Christian inscriptions from the time.

Archaeologists date only a few Christian symbols to the end of the second century CE, but their use grows steadily throughout the third century CE and mushrooms during the fourth century CE. The evidence is almost entirely from the catacombs and sarcophagi of Rome. Symbols include lambs, cups, doves, fish, anchors, and the *orante* — a standing figure, usually female, with arms stretched upward as in prayer. None of these is uniquely Christian; most date to

opposite page

Burial Inside Catacomb (Rome)

Plan of Jewish Catacombs (Rome)

Fish and Anchor (Rome, 3rd c. CE)

Peter and Paul (Rome)

Fresco of Jesus (Rome, 10th c. CE)

this page

Walls of Dura-Europos (Syria)

House at Dura-Europos (3rd c. CE)

Church at Dura-Europos (3rd c. CE)

Earlier and later Christian symbols have been found in the catacombs of Rome. By the late second century CE, some were Christian, like the Domatilla catacombs, and others were Jewish, like those on the Via Latina, whose plan shows how underground chambers typically connected. Among pre-Constantinian symbols were the fish and the anchor. At a later time, the *chi rho* (the first two Greek letters of *Christos* formed as a cross) became common, when Peter and Paul were considered the two key leaders of early Christianity. Depictions of Jesus, like this one, date to centuries later.

The oldest Christian church archaeologists have ever discovered in full is at Dura-Europos on the Euphrates River, at the eastern edge of the empire. It was transformed from an earlier house and later filled in to reinforce the city walls against enemy attacks. To form the assembly hall, a wall was knocked out and a podium set up on one side of the house. In another corner, a baptistery was built, which could accommodate only a small crowd.

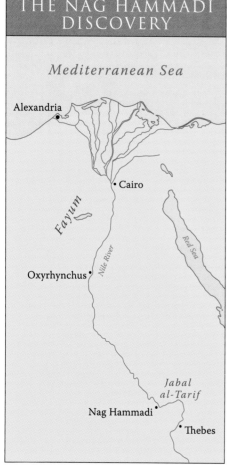

Mediterranean Sea

Alexandria

Cairo

Fayum

Nile River

Red Sea

Oxyrhynchus

*Jabal
al-Tarif*

Nag Hammadi

Thebes

Christian catacombs is *in pacem*, which is similar to the modern "rest in pace" but also echoes the Jewish *shalom* and the first-century CE Pauline greeting.

In the latter part of the third and into the fourth century CE, there were a number of wealthy Christians who commissioned carved stone sarcophagi. The themes that adorned such Christian sarcophagi came mostly from the Hebrew Bible and not the New Testament, which had yet to be established. The most frequent stories tell of God's comfort in a time of crisis: the three Jewish youths saved from the fiery furnace, Daniel's miraculous survival in the lions' den, and Noah safely aboard the ark. Each is suggestive of persecuted Christians finding comfort in a hostile world. This was, after all, a time when Christians were undergoing persistent persecution at the hands of Roman authorities. On frescoes inside the catacombs, depictions of New Testament scenes begin to appear; chief among them are the disciples and Jesus eating together or the feeding of the thousands. There are also frescoes of contemporary Christians gathering for meals and implements or objects used in meals, like chalices and wine, fish and bread. In Rome there were many *marytria,* memorials for the notable dead, whose structures accommodated a shared Christian meal in honor of the dead, including great saints like Peter and Paul and local martyrs. A long-standing Roman pagan practice commemorated the one-year anniversary of a relative's death with a meal at the grave. Libations of wine were often poured onto the ground to please the departed spirit. Wealthy Roman families constructed elaborate tomb complexes where such meals could be held, and the lower classes often banded together in burial societies to purchase such complexes and vowed to attend each others' commemorations. It seems that Roman Christians adopted similar practices; most prominent churches there have a crypt underneath the sanctuary for one or more prominent dead. In that sense, much of Roman Christianity appears to be a cult of the dead, in which Jesus's resurrection took on particular poignancy.

The Roman catacombs do not, however, provide evidence for Christian activities above ground in the second and third centuries CE. For that, only two sites from before Constantine the Great are of much relevance: the House of Saint Peter at Capernaum and a house church at Dura-Europos on the Syrian side of the Euphrates River. We looked at Saint Peter's House in Capernaum earlier in some detail, but I want to stress here that the architecture of the second- to third-century CE house church tells us little about Christian worship at the time. It was a single room converted into the centerpiece of a complex, but we do not know how it was used. It might be an absolutely unique site that marked a Gospel event

simple: a wall was knocked out between two of the southern rooms to create a long rectangular room of five by twelve meters, which could accommodate at most seventy people. A small platform was built on the shorter eastern side, so that the congregants faced the rising sun, as in most temples or *mithraea*. Just to the left of the platform, there was an opening into a chamber, presumably used for storing items, perhaps scrolls or other implements for the service. The assembly room had a single door to the courtyard, but during renovations another window was added that opened onto the courtyard, which had plaster seats added along three sides. It is tempting to think of those seats as either a waiting area or overflow seating for larger services.

The room that received the most thorough renovation had been a small storage room in the southwest corner. To convert this room to a baptistery, the floor was dug out and a ledge built up and plastered, so that the initiate stepped up and then down into the basin. The ceiling was lowered to create a more enclosed, cavelike feel; two columns and an arch helped create a canopy, which was painted dark blue with bright stars. The other scenes in the baptistery, which was the most decorated room, were biblical; their connections are unclear, but they included David and Goliath, Jesus with the

opposite page

Gospel of Philip (Egypt, 4th c. CE)

Muhammed Ali, Discoverer of Codices

Nag Hammadi Codices (Egypt, 4th c. CE)

this page

Jung Codex (4th c. CE)

Fragment of Romans (3rd c. CE).

The Nag Hammadi Codices count as the greatest single manuscript discovery for understanding early Christianity. Found by Muhammed Ali and his brother in 1945, they were only assembled and housed in the Coptic Museum in 1956, and it wasn't until the 1970s that they were fully published. Among the most important texts was a complete copy in the Coptic language of the *Gospel of Thomas*. As a whole, the collection testifies to the diversity of early Christianity.

An early parchment fragment of Romans from Egypt dates to the third century. Most early New Testament manuscripts were written on papyrus, which is inexpensive, but this fragment of Romans 4:23–5:3 is on vellum, the most expensive writing material. The scribal quality is meticulous; this may well represent the most faithful copy of the passage.

or remained in Peter's family. The case is very different at the third-century CE Dura-Europos church, which is remarkably well preserved because its rooms were filled in to reinforce the city wall against imminent attack in 256 CE. At the Dura house church, there is nothing like the complex stratigraphy at Capernaum. Instead, we have a snapshot of the church as it was in the mid third century CE. The most telling characteristic is that it had been transformed from a private house. It provides the best archaeological evidence, coupled with Capernaum and a few Egyptian papyri mentioning houses as places of meeting, that the first church buildings were developed directly from those house churches that we read about in Paul's letters.

The original house was square, measuring approximately eighteen meters on a side, and consisted of eight rooms surrounding a central courtyard with benches. The transformation of the house into a church was remarkably

be stored on a shelf and taken down for reading in the synagogue, the book format had two consequences: it forced believers to determine which texts made it into the book and what order those texts would be placed in. The New Testament canon — what went in and what was placed where — would only be finalized with the rule of Constantine the Great.

THE MAKING OF THE HOLY LAND

Beginning with Constantine the Great, Christian emperors systematically transformed the Jewish homelands into the Christian Holy Land. With the Gospels serving as their map, imperial architects backed by the emperors' funding constructed Christian buildings all across Galilee and Judea. Areas occupied primarily by Jews witnessed an increase in traffic from abroad, as an accelerating rate of pilgrims descended on holy sites and their chapels, monasteries, and basilicas. Archaeological strata of the Byzantine period (fourth to seventh centuries CE) bear the indelible marks of Christianization. Every archaeologist in Israel whose work focuses on earlier periods must first cut through the thick deposits of the Christian Holy Land before hitting Roman, Hellenistic, or earlier strata.

The basilica was the Cadillac of holy sites. Originally, a basilica was a Roman architectural form designed for large public gatherings. In its basic form, it had a long hall focused on a semicircular apse. This hall was divided by two rows of columns that supported a high timbered and tiled roof. This type of roof was cheaper than stone vaults and arches, and allowed more effort and funds to be used on internal ornamentation. Basilicas resembled the Hellenistic city's covered porticoes, or *stoa*, which were the setting for many aspects of civic life; the Roman basilica moved all that indoors. They were used for public gatherings, markets, and judicial sessions, and were increasingly connected to the imperial court, as their name implies — *basilica* means in Greek "royal building." Constantine's first basilica was not at all Christian: he built it next to his palace in Trier (in modern Germany), and from there he ruled part of the empire before taking

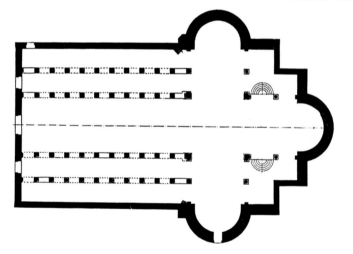

control of it all. Built between 305 and 312 CE, it still stands nearly one hundred feet high, one hundred feet across, and two hundred feet long, and its impeccable acoustics amplified his pronouncements from the apse. High-set windows let in ample light, which radiated off walls that were once multicolored with marble inlays and mosaics made of glass tessarae. In that setting,

there was little distinction between Caesar and god, state and religion. That structure seemed to Constantine the most suitable building for Christian assemblies. They were a far cry from the modest house churches of Paul.

Constantine later built three key basilicas in the Holy Land: the Holy Sepulcher in Jerusalem, the Church of the Nativity in Bethlehem, and the Church

"Gaius Vibius Maximus, the Prefect of Egypt, declares:

The census by household having begun, it is essential that all those who are away from their homes be summoned to return to their own hearths so that they may perform the customary business of registration and apply themselves to the cultivation which concerns them. Knowing, however, that some of the people from the countryside are required by our city, I desire all those who think they have a satisfactory reason for remaining here to register themselves before . . . Festus, the Calvary Commander, whom I have appointed for this purpose, from whom those who have shown their presence to be necessary shall receive signed permits in accordance with this edict up to the 30th of the present month . . ."

of the Annunciation in Nazareth. These became the three main destinations on any Christian pilgrimage. Unfortunately, very little remains from the original Constantinian strata, since most were almost totally destroyed by invading Persians in 614 CE. They were variously rebuilt, torn down again, rebuilt by the Crusaders, and then constantly repaired and renovated up to their present collagelike state. Visitors today can barely recognize anywhere in the Holy Sepulcher the remains of a Jewish cemetery and tomb.

Finally, let us return to Nazareth for a look at what remains of the basilica built on the spot where, according to tradition, the angel Gabriel announced to Mary that she would bear the Messiah. We do so mainly to contrast the stratigraphy of Byzantine Christian Nazareth with the earlier stratigraphy of Jesus's Jewish village. When the Franciscan Order of the Catholic Church rebuilt the Church of the Annunciation in the center of Nazareth in the 1960s, they did considerable archaeological

work under its foundation, exposing a Crusader church and the walls of an earlier Byzantine church and monastery. The first church's focal point was the so-called Grotto of the Annunciation, which contained plaster and stone etched with Christian symbols, prayers, and invocations. Hundreds of dislodged mosaic stones, white and black tessarae, and pieces of painted frescoes that had chipped off when the church was rebuilt by the Crusaders reveal that the first basilica's architecture was monumental and imperial. Patrons from afar made generous donations to replaster the walls or repave its mosaic floors, and some recorded their donations in stone. In one corner of a white and black mosaic, a Greek inscription reads "Gift of Conon, Deacon of Jerusalem." A fifth-century CE mosaic, still in place and intact, is decorated with a red and black wreath or crown in three concentric circles with what look like ribbons hanging from the base. In the center is a *chi rho* abbreviation for the victorious Christ.

The Nazareth of later pilgrims was very different from the tiny hamlet that Jesus would have known and that archaeologists have uncovered. The first-century Jewish peasant from Nazareth would not have recognized the fourth-century imperial religion that transformed his hometown. Jesus's Nazareth was thoroughly Jewish. Debris in the stratum under the first church included architectural elements that may have been the remains of a Jewish synagogue

opposite page
Church of the Nativity (Bethlehem)
Plan of Basilica (Bethlehem)
this page
Census Record (Egypt, 104 CE)

The birthplace of Jesus? The Church of the Nativity commemorates Jesus's birth with a basilica whose template was Constantine's first basilica in Trier, Germany. There are serious doubts that the Church of the Nativity was built in the right spot, on top of a cave. Some scholars have even doubted that Jesus was born in Bethlehem in Judea — there is also a Bethlehem in Galilee. The idea of a worldwide census by Augustus is suspect, although this Egyptian papyrus preserves a local Roman official's request in 104 CE that each person return to his or her own home.

and that are similar to other third-century CE Jewish synagogues in Galilee. A third-century synagogue inscription from Caesarea Maritima confirms Nazareth's Jewishness. Written in Hebrew on a dark gray marble fragment, it contains the earliest mention of Nazareth in non-Christian sources — on a list of locations where Jewish priests resettled after the Roman emperor Hadrian banned all Jews from Jerusalem in 135 CE. Among the twenty-four priestly families who had rotated weekly service in the Temple, a family by the name of Hapizzes moved to Nazareth. The inscription underscores Nazareth's Jewishness for the priests, a Jewishness that is also clear from a Jewish ritual bath in an even earlier layer.

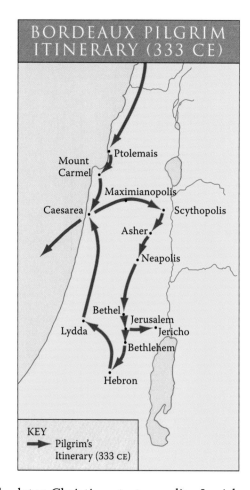

BORDEAUX PILGRIM ITINERARY (333 CE)

Ptolemais
Mount Carmel
Maximianopolis
Caesarea
Scythopolis
Asher
Neapolis
Bethel
Jerusalem
Lydda
Jericho
Bethlehem
Hebron

KEY
→ Pilgrim's Itinerary (333 CE)

If we look at the archaeological evidence from the first century CE, stripping away the Christian architecture and especially the wealth that pilgrims brought to the new Holy Land, we find that Nazareth was a relatively poor and tiny Jewish village. A series of now underground tombs have been found, between two churches and running toward the Well of Mary. They are typical of those used by Jewish families, with chambers and *kokhim* shafts, as we saw in Jerusalem. These tombs delineate the shape of the village as an ovoid settlement covering less than ten acres, with two hundred to four hundred inhabitants. Very little evidence from first-century houses has been found, an indication of Nazareth's poverty. Unlike the discoveries from later Christian strata, earlier Jewish houses had no frescoes, no mosaics, no roof tiles, and no paving stones. There were no arches or columns; instead, houses were made of stacked field-stones. Doorjambs and lintels were hewn, but the rest of the walls were packed tightly with small stones, ceilings were covered with thatched roofs, and floors were of beaten earth probably covered with wicker mats. Some houses had cisterns hewn into bedrock, while others were built against caves that provided living space and storage. Smaller artifacts were also universally modest: there was a handful of bronze coins but no silver or gold, and the few tombs that had decorative items contained only cheap jewelry and little glass, as is common elsewhere. The pottery consisted of locally made wares, coarse cooking pots, casserole dishes, water jars, and storage jars without any fine wares or wine amphorae from abroad.

When we think of the archaeology of first-century Nazareth, it is difficult not to marvel at the subsequent spread of Christianity across the empire. Christianity returned to its peasant roots in Galilean Nazareth but in the form of an imperially sponsored basilica. Earlier in

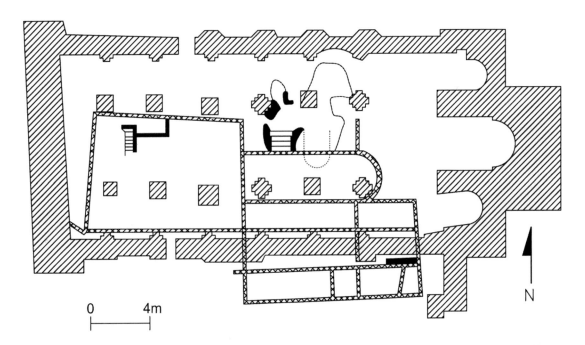

> ". . . can anything good come out of Nazareth?"
>
> JOHN 1:46

stantine the Great. In this sense, Jesus's impact on the archaeological record was delayed by a full three centuries but was certainly just as lasting as the impact either Alexander the Great or Caesar Augustus had on the archaeological strata of antiquity.

opposite page

Church Incense Burners (Israel, 6th c. CE)

View of Modern Nazareth

this page

Plan, Church of the Annunciation

Grotto under Church of the Annunciation

The Holy Land was shaped in the Byzantine period, when Christian pilgrims flooded biblical sites. A pilgrim from Bordeaux traveled there in 333 CE and recorded his itinerary. He did not visit Galilee, but traveled through Samaria down to Jerusalem, Bethlehem, and the Dead Sea area. Galilee at the time was still thoroughly Jewish, with many Judean Jews having fled there after the Bar-Kokhba Revolt. By the end of the Byzantine period, however, all of Israel, from north to south, was covered with churches richly decorated with mosaics, frescoes, incense burners, and hanging lamps, like these from around Scythopolis.

The Basilica of Nazareth today dominates the landscape of the large Arab city. Built in the early 1960s atop two earlier Christian structures — a large Crusader church and a smaller Byzantine church and monastery — the Church of the Annunciation marks the spot where the archangel told Mary she was to conceive Jesus. The impressive modern church is built directly over the remains of a grotto, around which archaeologists found evidence of a small and poor Jewish settlement in the first century.

this book, we used the results of archaeological excavations to sketch the humble context of Jesus's ministry in Galilee; we asked whether he would have ministered in the recently established cities of Sepphoris and Tiberias, which were at best marginal by Greco-Roman standards. We speculated on the impression that the grand Herodian architecture of Jerusalem, and especially its Temple, would have had on him and his disciples. We surveyed how the message of Jesus's Aramaic sayings was heatedly applied in Paul's Greek letters written on papyrus to small Christian communities in the greatest cities of the Roman Empire, including Rome itself. Alexander the Great's Hellenism allowed Paul's Greek letters to be understood everywhere, and Augustus's *Pax Romana* and Roman roads made it possible for him to travel all over the empire. But Paul and other Christians challenged Rome's vision of peace and prosperity, and refused to participate in the imperial cult. That small Christian minority postured against the empire without leaving a trace in the archaeological record until the middle of the second century, but with persistence Jesus's message, as translated by Paul and others to a wider audience, gradually spread. We see flashes of Christian imagery in the archaeological record of the early third century and increases in luminance over the third century, culminating in the radiant fourth-century Christian imperial culture after Con-

Dura-Europos has been labeled the Pompeii of the East because of its rich finds and colorful frescoes. Like Pompeii, much of the eastern Syrian city had been covered until modern times, and its discoverers found rooms intact from floor to ceiling, with undamaged frescoes. This remarkable state of preservation was the result of Roman occupants of the mid-third century CE filling the houses along the city wall with sand in a last-ditch effort to withstand a Sasanian siege. The Romans were defeated as the invaders broke through the Palmyrene Gate; they abandoned the city, and the site was never again inhabited. For archaeologists, then, the ruins of Dura-Europos provide a snapshot of a cosmopolitan garrison town and its mix of religions, frozen at the moment when the city was defeated in 257 CE.

The excavation of Dura has been an international affair. In 1920, Indian troops serving in the British Army were digging trenches and stumbled onto remarkably well preserved frescoes. Ironically, one fresco showed Eastern troops serving a Western empire — Palmyrene troops in the Roman army — nearly two millennia earlier. The first archaeologist to examine that find was the American James H. Breasted; a French team worked on the site for two years under the direction of the Belgian Franz Cumont, who is primarily known as a scholar of Persian Mithraism. Most of the site was excavated between 1928 and 1937 under the direction of the famous Russian classicist Mikhail Rostovtzeff on behalf of the French Academy and Yale University. These excavations determined that this was the city of Europos (*Dura* means fort and was not part of the ancient city's name) and delineated three stratigraphic phases: the original Hellenistic polis founded by the Seleucid Dynasty (ca. 300–100 BCE), the Parthian town (100 BCE–165 CE), and the Roman garrison town on the eastern frontier (165–257 CE).

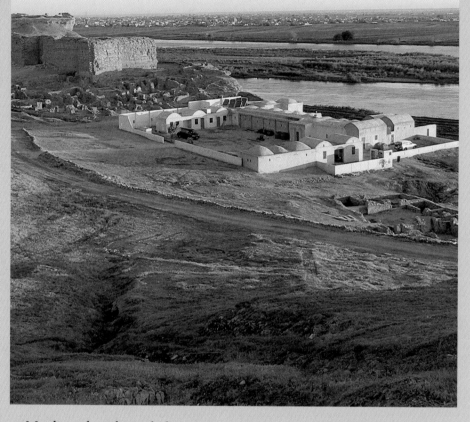

Much archaeological discussion has focused on the most recent stratum, centering on the diverse ethnic and religious aspects of the city at the time. Europos was filled with inhabitants of Persian, Greek, and Palmyrene descent. It had attracted people from inside and outside the Roman Empire, which accounts for the diversity of temples in the forum. As one would expect from a town quartering Roman soldiers, several *mithraea* were excavated. A Jewish synagogue with spectacular frescoes and a Torah niche was also discovered; congregants must have had connections to the thriving Jewish community in nearby Babylon. Of special note is that Jews used local traditions and styles in the synagogue; for example, the Torah shrine is just like the aedicules of nearby pagan temples, but it housed scrolls rather than idols. And there was a Christian church, the oldest

complete place of Christian worship ever found, which had been converted from a private house in the early third century.

Since 1986, modest archaeological excavations have been conducted by Pierre Leriche in a joint French-Syrian effort. Alongside several new probes, this group is working at conserving the site, although many of the finest frescoes were earlier shipped to Yale, Paris, and Damascus, and are in a poor state of repair. This modern project, housed in a nearby dig house, is not only reevaluating the earlier excavation's chronology but also examining numerous artifacts never published by the first excavation teams. This includes a study of Roman military remains by Simon James of the University of Leicester in England and a description of domestic space and private houses by his students, aspects of the site that were of little interest in the 1920s and 1930s.

HOW TO READ A TEMPLE

In the middle of the twentieth century, archaeologists uncovered at Corinth a tetrastyle prostyle pseudodiperal temple, possibly of the Corinthian order, built during the reign of Tiberius (14–37 CE). Labeled Temple G, it faced the forum at the time Paul visited the city. To nonexperts, that dense description is impenetrable, but to scholars of ancient architecture, it communicates the essential shape and form of the temple, which can then be envisioned with considerable accuracy. Roman-inspired temples during New Testament times were modular: they had consistently patterned designs and proportions. To describe those patterns, archaeologists use a set of arcane terms that derive directly from the Roman architect Vitruvius, whose first-century CE textbook on architecture was dedicated to his sponsor, Caesar Augustus.

Though Roman temples were very consistent, those that drew their inspiration from the Near East or the Hellenistic world showed more variety. In Near Eastern cities, typically one temple dominated the urban landscape. Consisting of a set of concentric areas of increasing holiness and ending with the room of the deity, often seated on a throne in the center, the sanctuary can be thought of as the house of the god. This area was surrounded by the *temenos,* a wall that marked the entire area as sacred and enclosed a space where the masses mingled and worshipped during the sacrifice. Typically one entered the *temenos* through a monumental gateway (propylaeum). This is, of course, approximately what was found at Herod's Temple in Jerusalem. Greek temples, like Roman ones, were less clearly demarcated from civic space and were approached by tiered steps on all sides; Greek temples seem more democratic and accessible.

Roman temples, in contrast, were approached from the front; the temple served as a backdrop for sacrifices performed on the altar in front. They usually had only one set of stairs leading up to the porch from an open civic space like a forum. The most visible component of the Roman temple was its front columns. Vitruvius left us an intricate set of terms with which to classify temples, based on their arrangement of columns. Four in front is called *quadrastyle,* six is *hexastyle,* eight *octastyle,* and ten *decastyle.* If there are columns only in front of the temple, it is called *prostyle. Peripteral* or *peristyle* temples have columns on all four sides, and the somewhat rare *peripteral sine postico* has columns along the front and sides, but none in back. Most Roman temples have one row of columns (*monopteral,* so standard that it is often left off in descriptions), others added half-columns attached to the wall (*pseudo-dipteral*), and some of the largest in the empire have two full rows (*dipteral*). Roman temples are further defined by the spacing between the columns, which can be *systyle* (two column diameters apart), *diastyle* (three column diameters apart), or most commonly, what Vitruvius calls *eustyle* (Greek for "the good style"), 2.25 diameters apart.

The orders of columns are perhaps the best-known aspect of Roman temples. They can be Doric or Ionic, which were considered more archaic and typically Greek, or Corinthian, which, in spite of the name, was the latest and most Roman order, with acanthus leaves on its capitals. Roman architects were not averse to mixing the elements of these column orders, taking the column pedestal (sometimes called the plinth) typical of one order and the entablature of another (the horizontal beamlike component that the columns supported, made up of architrave, frieze, and cornice). Above the entablature was a triangular pediment, in which sculptural friezes appropriate to the deity stood. The rectangular room that housed the cult statue, called a *cella* by the Romans and a *naos* by the Greeks, usually had projecting walls (*antae,* which are a bit like the extensions on the letter H) that created a porch on the front side (*pronaos*).

The reconstruction of the typically Roman temple above, built in Rome at the end of the first century BCE by Augustus and dedicated to Mars Ultor, is, then, an *octastyle peripteral sine postico* temple of the Corinthian order. The much earlier Greek Temple of Poseidon built at Paestum in southern Italy during the fifth century BCE is a *hexastyle peripteral dipteral* temple of the Doric order.

Coins provide a wealth of information for archaeologists, and the subdiscipline of numismatics has for more than a century preoccupied professionals and amateurs alike. For the novice, however, identifying the key information contained on a coin is a daunting task. Unlike today, in the Roman period denominations were not obvious, and numerical values were not marked on ancient coins. Instead, the value of a coin in antiquity was based on its metal and weight, so individuals had to have some familiarity with various weights derived from Greek, Latin, or Near Eastern languages, and had to be able to correlate them in gold (abbreviated AU by numismatists), silver (AR), and bronze, copper, or other base metals (AE). Silver coins were debased with added metals of lower quality, especially in later periods, but are still referred to as silver coinage. Thus a Greek drachma is a Roman denarius and half a Jewish shekel. Rome reserved the right to mint all gold coins, and minted most silver coins as well, but other cities or rulers could be granted the right to mint other metals.

Numismatists distinguish between the obverse, which we call "heads" and which in the Roman era usually had the emperor's depiction on it, and the reverse, or "tails." The type refers to the image or symbols on the coin, and the legend refers to the inscription. On all Roman coins, the obverse contains a legend, usually in Latin, although coins minted in Eastern cities were often in Greek. The emperor's name is almost always abbreviated, with *Aug* for Augustus, *Tib* for Tiberius, *C* for Caius/Gaius, or *Cl* for Claudius. The obverse type refers to the portrait of the emperor (or his wife or relative); if the portrait is from neck up it is called a head, and if the shoulders are included it is called a bust. Imperial heads are usually wreathed with laurel or radiating sunbeams. *Laur. hd. r.* is the abbreviation for "laureate head facing right."

The reverse side of the coin varies greatly and includes more information that the emperor wishes to commemo-rate or pronounce. The type is much more varied than it is on the obverse, and it is often used for propaganda. Coins were, after all, the earliest form of mass media. The space beneath the reverse design, called the *exergue,* included some description of the coin's symbols, a workshop and mint location with a single letter, and a series mark. Herodian and Jewish coins had fewer abbreviations and a more limited set of images that excluded pagan images. The Herodians often depicted a helmet instead of a head, and Jewish coins of the revolt had items like chalices, pomegranates, and depictions of the Temple.

For example, the top coin, a sestertius minted by Claudius in 41 CE, would be described on the obverse as a *head laur. r.* (head, laureate, facing right). The obverse legend begins TI(berius) CLAUDIUS CAESAR AUG(ustus). The reverse represents the goddess Hope, SPES, and is called the Augustan Hope (SPES AUGUSTA). SC in the reverse legend notes that it was minted by decree of the Senate.

The bottom coin of Caligula would be described in full as an AE sestertius dating to 39/40 CE. The obverse type would be described as follows: "Pietas, veiled, draped, seated l., holding patera in r. hand and resting l. arm on a small draped figure; the legend is C(aius) CAESAR AUG(ustus) GERMANICUS P(ontifex) M(aximus) TR(ibunica) POT(estas) with PIETAS in the exergue." P M indicates that Caligula held the title of high priest, *pontifex maximus,* and TR POT (*tribunica potestas*) means that he held the Tribunician Power, which gave the Julio-Claudians the right to veto and convene the Senate. The reverse type is "front view of hexastyle temple surmounted by quadriga before Caligula, veiled and togate, sacrifices with patera over altar; one attendant leads bull, second holds patera; reverse legend is DIVO AUG, with S — C large, l. and r. in field." SC stands for *Senatus Consulto,* by decree of the Roman Senate.

	Phoenician	Greek	Roman	Jewish
25			*Aureus* (AU)	
4	*Tetradrachmon* (AG)	*Tetradrachmon* (AG)		*Shekel*
1		*Drachmon* (AG)	*Denarius* (AG)	*Half shekel*
1/4			*Sestertius* (AE)	
1/8			*Dupendius* (1/2 Sest; AE)	
1/16			*As* (1/4 Sest.; AE)	
1/128				*Lepton/Pruta* (AE)

HOW TO READ POTTERY

Pottery is the sine qua non of archaeology. As modern archaeologists dig through the soil, they collect, wash, and examine numerous pottery shards, from fingernail- and palm-sized shards to whole pots. While initially used only for dating stratigraphy, the study of ceramics is increasingly used to describe room function, cooking habits, and the extent of trade.

Archaeologists typically describe four aspects of pottery: ware, form, type, and decoration. Ware refers to the clay used, which in the New Testament period encompasses a great variety. Most clay used by potters in the Roman period was mixed with some kind of temper, either sand, straw, shell, or reground pottery called grog. Tempering the clay lessens warping and shrinkage as the pot dries and is fired. Some well-levigated clays used for fine wares in the Roman period, like *terra sigillata,* contain almost no temper, so they must be fired in highly controlled and sophisticated kilns. They were sought-after and expensive vessels due to the clay's luster. Less well-fired pots needed more temper. Once broken, such vessels reveal a darker-colored core in cross section. Since most past archaeological publications are black-and-white, the ware's color is usually described according to a Munsell Chart, a standardized format used by geologists. Thus, instead of saying a fragment's color is "orangish," a ceramicist calls the exterior color "5YR 7/6," according to its location on the chart.

Form refers to use of the vessel and usually defines its basic shape. There are several utilitarian vessels that are common in the Roman period: closed cooking pots, open cooking pots, storage jars (of which amphorae are a particular kind), jugs, and jugletts. Among serving dishes, there are bowls, plates, and cups. As each particular form develops over time within a potter's assemblage, the rims, bases, or handles develop slight variations. These variations over time are considered typological developments; type refers primarily to the date of a given form. Pottery is usually given some designation based on where it was excavated or on the assemblage produced at a particular kiln.

The components of a vessel are its base, body, neck, rim, and handle. Bases are usually either rounded, flat, pointed, or have a disk shape that projects out from the body. Body shape is usually described as globular, ovoid, pyriform (egg- or pear-shaped), or conical. Rims are most intricate, and their verbal description is quite complex. Their direction can be either vertical or flared outward, their stance either incurving, everted, inverted, pendant, or horizontal. Handles are numbered and described in terms of the location of their attachment. There are a variety of decorations, such as incisions, ribbing, burnishing, or application of a slip to add color.

The above pot, found at Sepphoris but produced at the kilns in nearby Kfer Hananya, would be described as follows: globular ribbed cooking pot with rounded base, short vertical neck, flat rim with a single internal groove and two vertical handles from shoulder to rim. This type is called Kfer Hananya 4A (4 refers to the form, a cooking pot, and A indicates that it is the earliest type of this kind of vessel). It is the most common cooker in Galilee at the time of Jesus. It belongs to the assemblage from Galilee, on the bottom left, which is more utilitarian than the finer wares from Jerusalem, on the bottom right.

HOW TO READ AN INSCRIPTION

The study of ancient inscriptions is called epigraphy. Once a subfield of archaeology, epigraphy has become a discipline in its own right, owing to the abundance of texts from the ancient world written on stone. Over half a million Greek and Latin inscriptions are at the disposal of historians, falling into three categories: (1) public inscriptions commissioned by civic bodies or imperial officials; (2) private inscriptions commissioned by individuals, usually wealthy; and (3) unofficial and usually unapproved scratched letters, called graffiti. The first two categories, both stone inscriptions by professional masons, provide not only invaluable information about historical events but also clues about ancient legal matters, social structures, religious devotion, and demographics.

By the time of Jesus and Paul, professional stone carvers had developed a complex system of abbreviations to save space on stone surfaces and squeeze more text in less space. The system is standard in Greek and Latin inscriptions, much more so than in Hebrew or Aramaic inscriptions from New Testament times. In the Hellenistic period (third to first centuries BCE), inscriptions did not have spaces between letters, and only some inscriptions had either spacing or dots to indicate word divisions. This, coupled with the abbreviated words, makes most inscriptions unintelligible even to those who know Greek or Latin well. Thankfully, the sheer number of inscriptions has given experts enough parallels to decipher almost all inscriptions with considerable certainty.

Key abbreviations in Latin and Greek included references to months, which differed between the Greek East, the Near East, and the Roman West, as well as many names and titles. Lacking a universal calendar, dates on inscriptions were reckoned either by local rulers or Roman caesars. Roman imperial names are present on the bulk of inscriptions from the New Testament era, and their names are typically abbreviated, often to a single letter, which can frustrate a novice to no end. Tiberius, for example, might appear as *TIB*, *TI*, or even sometimes *T*. Sextus could likewise be *SEX*, *SE*, or *S*.

But Sebastos could also be abbreviated *S*, *SE*, *SB*, or *SEB*. Key names of first-century emperors: Augustus is *AUG* or *AUGUS*; Gaius is *G*, *GA*, or *GAI*; and Claudius, luckily, is only *CL*.

One of the most readily apparent features of ancient inscriptions is that many professional stone engravers appear to have been illiterate at worst or inattentive at best. The numerous mistakes, coupled with damage to letters over time, have meant that epigraphers spend much of their time emending texts — that is, reconstructing the intended reading. For standard abbreviations, their reconstructions can be trusted, but any emendation or deletion must be viewed critically and with a healthy dose of suspicion. The following are the most common sigla:

|	line division (in the original inscription)
[. . .]	lacunae with one period per illegible letter
( )	elaboration of common abbreviations
.	doubtful reading
< >	emendation, addition by editor
{ }	suppression by editor

The top inscription is from the Hellenistic period and was found on the island of Delos. It was cut with an unsteady hand (note, for example, that its beginning is not as deep), and there are no word divisions whatsoever. The inscription below, by contrast, is in Latin and was cut by a highly skilled professional, with dots as word dividers. Placed next to the Library of Celsus in Ephesus, built by a wealthy freeman Mazaeus in honor of Augustus and his wife, Livia, it reads:

IMP CAESARI DIVI F AUGUSTO PONTIFICI
MAXIMO COS XII TRIBUNIC POTEST XX ET
LIVIAE CAESARIS AUGUSTI
MAZAEUS ET

"To the Emperor Caesar Son of God Augustus, High Priest 12-time Consul, 20-time Tribune of the People and to Livia Caesar Augustus
and Mazaeus"

GLOSSARY OF ARCHAEOLOGICAL AND ARCHITECTURAL TERMS

Acropolis. Area at the highest elevation of a city, usually with temples and sometimes used as a fortified refuge.

Adyton. Sanctuary of a Near Eastern temple.

Agora. Greek name for the open area of a city, usually used as a market; similar to the Roman and Latin forum.

Amphitheater. Arena for gladiatorial games and other entertainment, oval-shaped with tiered seating.

Amphora (-ae). A large storage jar with a narrow neck, two handles, and a pointed base; stacks well in boats and initially used for wine or olive oil.

Andronikon. Room of a more public nature reserved for men in a Greek house; room between two peristyles.

Anta (-ae). Symmetrical projection extending a wall beyond the façade of a building, usually in pairs on a temple.

Apodyterium (-a). The changing room of a bathhouse.

Apse. A semicircular projection from the side of a public building; often vaulted and designed to house a statue or speaker.

Aqueduct. A slightly sloping water conduit typical of Roman architecture, often spanning depressions in the topography with arched bridges.

Arch. Distinct masonry construction in which stone blocks are arranged to span two supporting elements, like walls or columns.

Architrave. The horizontal beam atop a row of columns; the lowest tier of the entablature, often decorated with patterned sculpture.

Arcosolium (-a). A burial niche, designed to hold a body, ossuary, or sarcophagus. Cut into the side of a cave, with a ledge below and an arch above.

Asclepion. Healing shrine of god Asclepius; usually included a temple, rooms for incubation and dining, and strewn with votive offerings.

Ashlar. Any stone hewn to carefully fit a construction project.

Atrium (-a). The unroofed, rectangular area at the center of a Roman house; often containing a pool or impluvium.

Balk. The vertical face of an excavation trench; in drawings, called a section; can also refer to the meterwide walkway left between excavation squares.

Ballista (-ae). Heavy, roughly cut, spherical stone used in catapults during sieges.

Balneum (-a). Small bathhouse for private, military, or public purposes, distinct from the large public baths (thermae).

Basalt. A volcanic rock, dark gray and porous, common in the eastern Mediterranean.

Basilica. A rectangular building with least two rows of columns covered by a high ceiling in the central nave and lower ceilings in the side aisles; Greek for "royal building" but used mostly in the Roman period.

Bas Relief. A relief sculpture in which the figures project only slightly from the background and are not undercut; sometimes called low relief.

Bema. Greek for a speaker's platform, usually placed in the agora or forum for civic or judicial purposes.

Boss. The untrimmed central face of a stone after a margin of several inches has been cut along its edges; common in Hellenistic and Herodian architecture.

Caldarium (-a). The hot room of a Roman bath.

Capital. The upper section of a column.

Cardo. Main street running north-south in a Roman city, crossed by the decumanus.

Caryatid. Sculptured female figure used instead of a column or pilaster to support an entablature.

Casemate wall. A city wall formed by a ring of rooms used for various purposes that can be filled in when under siege.

Catacomb. Underground burial chamber, usually connected by corridors; typically used for Christian and Jewish burials in Rome after the first century CE.

Cella. The central room of a Roman temple, usually housing the deity's statue and open to the public; similar to the Greek naos.

Ceramic typology. The development in pottery over time, like rims, handles, or bases that determine the sequence in dating.

Chi rho. Monogram for Christ, with first two Greek letters of *Christos* placed on top of each other and forming a cross.

Circus. Latin word for racetrack for horses or chariots, with tiered seating on one, several, or all sides; Greek hippodrome.

Colonnade. A row of columns supporting an architrave; especially related to stoa or portico.

Columbarium (-a). A Roman burial chamber with numerous niches for placing urns containing the deceased's ashes; also used to describe a pigeon- or dovecote.

Column. A freestanding support in Greco-Roman architecture, composed of a base, a shaft, and a capital; usually of three orders, Doric, Ionic, and Corinthian.

Cornice. The top portion of the entablature (which consists of architrave, frieze, and cornice); often served as an eave to drain rainwater to the side.

Course. Any horizontal row of stones, ashlars, or bricks in construction.

Decumanus. Main street running east-west in a Roman city, crossed by the cardo.

Demos. Greek word referring to the assembly of citizens that serves administrative and political functions; citizens were typically male landowners.

Domus. Latin for "house," usually of a freedman's immediate family; much more modest than a villa.

Domus-ekklesia. Scholarly term for "house church."

Drum. The cylindrical section of a column shaft.

Ekklesia (-a). Greek for an assembly or the structure that held it; used in and after the New Testament for a church.

Entablature. The horizontal component above the colonnade and below the pediment. Usually had three components, from bottom to top: the architrave, frieze, and cornice.

Epigraphy. The study and analysis of ancient inscriptions, typically those carved on stone.

Euergetism. The practice in the Greco-Roman world of the wealthy sponsoring urban architecture, games, or benefits for the whole city; from the Greek for "good works."

Exedra (-ae). A large, usually semicircular recess that provides additional space in a structure.

Exergue. The space on the bottom center of the reverse side of an ancient coin, usually containing an inscription.

Ex situ. Opposite of in situ, refers to an artifact no longer where it was originally found.

Flagstone. Stone of any geological material that is flat on one side and suitable as a paving stone.

Forum (-a). Latin term for a Roman city's open space, often used for civic purposes and markets; similar to the Greek agora.

Fresco. Painting on plaster for decorative purposes; true fresco is painted while the plaster is still wet, called *al secco* when painted after the plaster has already dried.

Frieze. The middle piece of an entablature, usually decorated, with architrave below and cornice above.

Frigidarium. The cold room of a Roman bathhouse.

Gymnasium (-a). Greek school for elite youth in the classical period; from the Greek root *gymnos*, "naked."

Gynaikonitis. The section of a Greek house reserved for women; less visible and either in the rear of the house or on a second story.

Hammath. Hebrew for "hot springs," around which bathing complexes were often built in the Roman period, such as Hammath-Tiberias.

Header. Ashlars in a wall constructed using the header-stretcher technique, positioned with the shorter side forming part of the wall's face; alternates with stretcher.

Herringbone. Arrangement of bricks, stones, or pavers in a series of V-shaped patterns.

Hippodrome. Greek term for a racetrack for horses or chariots, with tiered seating on one, several, or all sides; Latin circus.

Horreum (-a). A building used for storage, very often as a granary.

Hypocaust. The hollow space underneath a tiled floor, supported above ground by columns of stacked tiles, where hot air circulates.

Ichthus. Early Christian symbol; Greek for "fish," an acrostic for Jesus Christ God's Son Savior (*Iesus Christos theos uiou soter*).

Impluvium. Pool in the center of an atrium that collects rainwater from the roof.

In situ. Latin for "in place;" used of artifacts whose exact origin is known and recorded.

Insula (-ae). (1) A multistoried apartment building in Roman cities common after Nero; (2) a block of houses (or a single house complex) surrounded on four sides by a streets or alleyways.

Kafr (**Hebrew** *Kefar*). Arabic for "village," used often for smaller archaeological sites, as in *Kafr Nahum,* Capernaum.

Khirbet. Arabic for "ruins," as in Khirbet Qumran.

Koine. Greek language commonly used in the eastern Mediterranean and Near East in the Hellenistic and Roman periods.

Kokh (-im). Long fingerlike shafts protruding from a Jewish burial chamber in the Hellenistic and Roman periods.

Lacuna (-e). A gap in an ancient text written on stone, parchment, or papyrus, the result of deterioration or destruction; usually emended by modern epigraphers or paleographers.

Lararium. Shrine for household gods, known in Latin as *lares;* varied widely in size and decoration.

Limestone. Any of a wide variety of stones from sedentary geological formations, including chalk, from which ossuaries are made.

Loculus (-i). A general term for the area in a burial where the deceased is laid out or which holds the bones.

Locus (-i). Any three-dimensional unit encountered in excavation; can be either a soil layer or architectural feature.

Macellum. Roman term for a meat market or, more generally, any market.

Marble. Crystallized limestone used for architecture and sculpture; ancient authors called most every polished stone, including granite, marble.

Menorah. Seven-branched candelabrum once housed in the Jerusalem Temple and symbolic of Judaism.

Mikveh (-aoth). Stepped plaster pool of varying size used by Jews for ritual cleansing.

Mosaic. A floor of numerous variously colored, cube-shaped tessarae stones arranged to form decorative patterns or pictures.

Munsell Chart. A chart developed by geologists to assign a precise number and letter combination to the various shades of soil color.

Naos. The central and holiest room of a Greek temple, usually in the easternmost portion; similar to Roman cella.

Nave. The central aisle of a basilica, covered with a high ceiling and flanked by colonnades.

Necropolis. Greek for "city of the dead"; a cemetery on the outskirts of an ancient town.

Neutron Activation Analysis. A method of determining trace amounts of chemical elements by measuring their characteristic levels of radioactive decay; used to study the provenance of artifacts.

Niche. An ornamental recess in a wall; usually semicircular and often holding a statue or icon.

Numismatics. The study and analysis of ancient coins; on excavations, numismatists also use chemicals to clean and treat coins.

Nympheum (-a). A public fountain and pool structure, often with niches and statues.

Obelisk. A typically Egyptian pillar often taken to Rome; made from a single stone, obelisks taper toward the top and are capped by a pyramidal shape.

Objet d'art. A French term for an object of artistic worth or curiosity, often unprovenanced.

Obverse. The "head" side of an ancient coin, usually with the ruler's portrait.

Odeum (-a). A small theater-like structure, typically roofed, used for public speaking (Greek Odeion).

Opus reticulatum. A standard Roman style of constructing walls characterized by a face of small square blocks laid in diagonal lines.

Opus sectile. A Roman floor (or wall) made of geometric patterns from variously shaped and colored marble tiles.

Orante. Representation of a (usually female) figure with raised arms and palms forward in a gesture of prayer of adoration, common in early Christian art.

Order. A distinctive style of columns, bases, and entablatures (Doric, Ionic, and Corinthian) used in Greek and Roman architecture.

Ossuary. Burial box that could contain the bones of a deceased; generally used to refer to burial boxes used by Jews in the first centuries BCE and CE

Ostracon (-a). A piece of pottery that was secondarily used to write upon with ink.

Paleobotany. The analysis of plants and their use by ancient cultures.

Paleography. The study and analysis of ancient writing; typically refers to the examination of letters and their dates written in ink on papyrus or parchment.

Palynology. The analysis of pollen collected in excavation that sheds light on agricultural practices.

Patina. A thin film that appears over time on some materials, especially stone and metals, created by a slow chemical reaction.

Pediment. The triangular gable underneath a temple's roof; made up of the tympanum and cornices.

Pentelic marble. White marble quarried at Mount Pentelicon east of Athens and used for its acropolis; considered ideal for architecture.

Peristyle. A courtyard surrounded on all side by columns and a portico, often with a garden and pool.

Petrography. In general, the study and analysis of rocks; often refers to the examination of tiny rocks fragments in ceramic wares to determine provenance.

Phase. In archaeological excavations, a subdivision of a site's stratum.

Pilaster. A pseudo-pillar protruding from a wall; looks like a half-column attached to a structure.

Plateia. Greek word for a wide boulevard or avenue in a city; often leads directly to an important urban monument.

Polis (-eis). Classical Greek city with appropriate urban institutions and independent rule by wealthy males; after the Hellenistic period, can refer to any Greco-Roman style city.

Porphyry. A purple (or rarely green) granite from Egypt used especially for column shafts; though geologically different from marble, it is often considered a marble by ancient authors.

Portico. Roofed walkway with columns on one side and buildings on the other; colonnade that opens onto a street (Greek stoa).

Pozzolana. Volcanic sand that Romans used to make concrete, including a kind that hardens under water.

Pronaos. Area in front of the naos in a Greek temple.

Propylaeum. A gate complex at the entrance to the temenos of a Near Eastern temple; more generally, any civic area.

Proseuche. Greek for "place of prayer," used especially in Hellenistic Egypt for Jewish synagogues.

Provenance. The origin of an artifact that helps assess trade patterns; for ceramics, can be determined by petrography or Neutron Activation Analysis.

Pyriform. Refers to the shape of a ceramic or glass vessel; pear- or egg-shaped.

Quadriga. A four-horse chariot, often depicted on a tympanum and emblematic of the Roman emperor.

Radiocarbon dating. Technique used to date organic objects, based on the predictable rate of decay of isotopes of carbon 14.

Reverse. The "tails" side of an ancient coin; the reverse type refers to the depiction and inscription on the other side of the obverse.

Sarapeion. Shrine, temple, or meeting place for those worshipping the Egyptian god Sarapis and his consort Isis.

Sarcophagus. A body-sized coffin, usually decorated, common after the first century CE; Greek for "flesh-eater."

Scanning Electron Microscope. An electron microscope that forms a close-up three-dimensional image (abbreviated SEM).

Section. The vertical side of a balk, which reveals a site's stratigraphy; can also refer to the balk drawing in archaeological publications.

Shards. Fragments of pottery found and collected on excavations and used especially to date loci.

Stele. A large inscribed stone slab used for public inscriptions.

Stoa. A long covered walkway with columns on one side in a Greek polis; Roman portico.

Stratigraphy. The sequence of layers at an archaeological site created over time by repeated destruction and rebuilding.

Stratum (-a). The architecture, soil layers, and artifacts associated with a discreet time period at a site; can be further divided into phases.

Stretcher. Ashlars in a wall constructed using the header-stretcher technique, positioned with the longer side forming part of the wall's face; alternates with header.

Stylobate. The ground-level course of masonry on which columns or colonnades stand.

Synagogue. Greek word used for a Jewish place of gathering/worship; can also refer to the gathering itself and not necessarily the structure.

Tell (Arabic). Hebrew *Tel.* From Arabic, a moundlike site made up of successive layers of occupation due to destruction and rebuilding.

Temenos. A sacred area often enclosed by a wall that contains a temple; usually used for Near Eastern temples.

Temper. Elements added to clay to avoid cracking or warping of vessels during the production process; can include sand, shell, straw, or ground pots.

Tepidarium (-a). The warm room of a Roman bath.

Terminus ante quem. The latest possible date of an archaeological artifact of excavated layer (Latin for "time before which").

Terminus post quem. The earliest possible date of an archaeological artifact or excavated layer (Latin for "time after which").

Terra cotta. Fired clay used for various objects, including bricks, household pots, and figurative representations.

Terra sigallata. The finest quality pottery during the Roman period; there were both Western and Eastern workshops that produced various serving vessels.

Tessara (-ae). Small cube-shaped stones of various colors that are pieced together to form mosaics.

Thermae. Large public bath with numerous rooms during the Roman period; could include a gym, massage parlor, or library; much larger than a *balneum*.

Tholos. A circular colonnaded pavilion; often used as a temple or to commemorate a heroic dead.

Travertine. A distinctive limestone quarried in central Italy and used widely for construction after Augustus; not technically marble in a geological sense, but considered so by ancient authors.

Triclinium (-a). The dining room of a Roman villa, in which guests sat in a U-shape around an ornate mosaic; Greek for "three benches."

Tufa. Any of several drab-colored volcanic stones used for construction in central Italy, especially Rome.

Tympanum. The triangular face of a pediment under the roof of a temple; usually contains sculptures in relief.

Unguentarium (-a). A small glass or ceramic vial holding perfume or other costly liquids.

Unprovenanced. An artifact whose origins are unknown, often appearing to the public through the black market of antiquities traders.

Villa. The large Roman-style home of a wealthy person; initially part of a country estate but later built inside cities.

Vomitorium (-a). The exit of a theater or amphitheater that "spews out" the spectators after an event.

Votive. Any number of artifacts dedicated to a deity, either in fulfillment of a vow, symbolizing a prayer, or offering thanks for granting a wish.

Wadi. From Arabic for "gulch"; carries torrents during the rainy season, but is dry at other times of year.

Zooarchaeology. The study of animal remains found on archaeological excavations; examines especially the diet of ancient cultures.

coin of Augustan Temple, *47*
coin of Caracalla, 141, *141*
coin of Helena, 7, *7*
coin of Mattathias, *54*, 55
coin of Older Nero, 127, *127*
coin of Young Nero, 127, *127*
coins, 3, 7, 24, 32–33, 34, 35, 37, 38, 41, 43, 47, 49, 55, 61, 66, 67, 70, 79, 85–86, 89, 101, 102, 107, 117, 121, 127, 129, 132, 133, 134, 135, 137, 141, 152; how to read, 157; Temple tax, 85, *85*, 86, 89
coins of Alexander, *34*, 35, *36*, 37, 38
coins of Antipas, *66*, 67
coin with Artemis, 107, *107*
coin with Roma, *134*, 135
Coliseum (Rome), 132–33, *133*
Colossae, 109
computers, 18
Constantine's Basilica (Trier, Germany), 149, *149*, 150, 151
Constantine the Great, 4, 6, 7, 14, 97, 140, 141, 143, 144, 146, 148, 149, 150–51, 153
Coptic language, 147, 148, 149
Corbo, Father Virgilio, 74
Corinth, 15, 19, 22, 28, 44, 47, 100, 105–106, 109, 111, 113, 114–15, 117, 118, 120–21, 128, 142, 156; excavations, 120–21; New Testament and, 120–21
1 Corinthians, 114, 115, 120; **7:4,** 115, 116; **9:24–27,** 106; **10,** 121; **10:20,** 106; **11:21–22,** 114; **12,** 121
2 Corinthians: **11:25,** 118, 119
Cos, 119
Crete, 117
crocodile, mummified, *124*, 125
cross, 8, 9, 93, 123, 143, 144–45
"cross" (Herculaneum), *8*, 9
cross on plate (Sepphoris), 143, *143*
crucified ankle (Jerusalem), 93, *93*
crucifixion, 92–93
Crusaders, 151, 153
Cumae, 113
Cumont, Franz, 154
Cyprus, 13, 117

Damascus, 50, 86
Daniel, 78; **8:5,** 21, 35; **11:31,** 40, 78; **12:11,** 78
Dan Inscription (Israel), *38*, 39
David, King, 78
Dead Sea, 6, 23, 32, 41, 51
Dead Sea Scrolls, 6, 23, 32–33
Decapolis, 59, 60, 63, 64
Decimus Valerius Dionysios, 108
decoration, Temple, 87, *87*
Delos, 42, 43, 44, 86, 108, 110, 112, 113, 115, 119, 142
Delphi, 109, 111; Oracle at, 111, *111*
de Saulcy, Louis Félicien, 98
de Vaux, Roland, 32, 33
diagnostic shards, 18, *19*, 20
diaspora Jews, 41–44, 55, 70, 84, 100; excavated synagogues, 109–10
Dion, 110, 113
Dionysiac fresco, *112*, 113
Dionysos, 72, 113–14, 141, 142; Temple Phallus, 115, *115*
Dionysos mosaic (Sepphoris), *140*, 141
disease, 69, 124
Domatilla Catacomb (Rome), *144*, 145
Dome of the Rock, 98
Domitian, 88, 132, 133, 134–35, 142
Domitian's Temple (Ephesus), 134, *134*, 135
Dor, 40, 43
drain at Siloam Pool, *82*, 83
Dura-Europos, 108, 143, 145, *145*, 147, 148, 154–55; excavations, 154–55; house worship and, 154–55

Early Hellenistic period, 21, 39
Early Roman period, 12, 62
Ecce Homo Arch, 89, *89*, 90
economy, Galilean, 66–69, 73
Egypt, 7, 26, 27, 29, 34, 37, 38, 45, 49, 54, 59, 60, 69, 70, 111, 117, 123, 125, 126, 135, 140, 147, 148, 149, 151; Fayum and, 123, *123*; papyri, 123–28; Workmen in, 17, *17*
ekklesiai, 109
Eleusis, 142
Ephesus, 9, 15, 28, 81, 88, 100, 107–108, 109, 110, 113, 114, 117, 118, 123, 134–35, 142, 149
Ephesus theater, 107, *107*
epigraphy, 159
Erastus, 4
Erastus Inscription (Corinth), 112, 113, *113*, 114–15, 121
erotic bas relief (Pompeii), 115, *115*
eroticism, 115–17
Essenes, 6, 23, 32–33, 41
et-Tell, 20
Euphrates River, 145
excavations, *see specific sites*
excavations at Scythopolis (Israel), *16*, 17, 59, *59*
excavation square (Sepphoris), 9, *9*
excavation trench at Troy, *18*, 19

Fayum, 123, *123*
female personification, *116*, 117
field archaeology, 16–20
fieldwork at Pisidian Antioch, *17*
First Pompeian Style, 131
fish, 8, 9, 20, 24, 55, 68, 69, 123, 145
"fishhooks" from Capernaum, 11, *11*
forgeries, 3, 4, 5
fortress at Herodium (Israel), *130*, 131
fragment of John 18 (Egypt), 123, *123*
fragment of Revelation (Egypt), 135, *135*
France, 103
frescoed room (Pompeii), 27, *27*
frescoes, 27, 51, 67, 68, 91, 92, 107, 110, 113–14, 115, 127, 131, 143, 145, 146, 149, 154, 155
frescoes in Golden House, 127, *127*
fresco Fragment (Tiberias), *66*, 67
fresco Fragments (Sepphoris), 67, *67*
fresco from Upper City, 91, *91*
fresco in *Mithraeum* (Marino), *142*, 143
fresco in Northern Palace (Masada), 51, *51*
fresco of Fish (Ephesus), *8*, 9
fresco of Isis Temple (Pompeii), *106*, 107
fresco of Jesus (Rome), *144*, 145
fresco of Priapus (Pompeii), 115, *115*
funerary bust (Palmyra), *26*, 27

Gadara, 57, 60
Galatia, 49, 105
Galatians: **2:2,** 106; **6:11,** 6
Galilean house, 23, *23–24*
Galilean Jar, *2*, 3
Galilean Pottery, 19, *19*
Galilean valley, *55*
Galilee, 3, 4, 5, *5*, 6, 8, 11, 19, 22, 23, 24, 37, 39, 42, 49, 50, 51, 54–73, 78, 80, 87, 100, 122, 129, 136, 151, 152, 153; archaeological periods in, 56; archaeology, 54–73; changes after Jesus, 71–73; economy, 66–69, 73; excavations in, *56*; Jews, 54–73; language, 70–71; regions of, *54*; synagogues, 65–66, 72–73, 74; territory and terrain, 54–59; urban life, 54, 58, 59–64, 66–70, 76
Gallio, 4
Gamla, 57, 59, 63, 65, 67, 77, 129; ruins of, *58*, *59, 59*

Gamla synagogue plan, 65, *65*
Gaul, 50
Gaza, 37
gender, 24–27, 92, 136; sexuality and, 115–17
Genesis: **49:29,** 93
geology, 19–20, 21, 24, 56, 80
geometric mosaic, *90*, 91
Gerasa, 37, 54, 57, 60
Germany, 149, 150
Gezer, 18, 40
Ginnosar, 57, 69
glass, 92
glass drawings (Tel Anafa, Israel), *60*, 61
glossary, 160–63
Gnaeus Egnatius, 44
Gnosticism, 6, 148–49
Goddess on *Ara Pacis,* 103, *103*
God-Fearer Column (Aphrodisias), 109, *109*
Golan, 57, 59, 63, 129
gold, 19
gold bridge (Italy), 69, *69*
gold coin with Alexander, *34*, 35
Golden House, 127, *127*, 128–29
Golgotha, 81
Gospel of Judas, 6, *148*, 149
Gospel of Mary Magdalene, 149
Gospel of Philip (Egypt), *146*, 147
Gospel of Thomas, 6, 124, 147, 148, 149
grains, 57, 69
Great Britain, 125, 127
Greece and Greeks, 4, 8, 19, 34–44, 45, 54, 86, 100, 111, 113, 120; Alexander the Great and, 34–37; Jews and, 34–44; urban life, 36–37, 38, 40, 41
Greek language, 34, 35–36, 37, 38, 39, 41, 42, 43, 44, 70–71, 73, 84, 124, 132, 144, 145, 159
Grotto under Church of the Annunciation, 153, *153*
Gush Halav, 25

Hadrian, 72, 89, 90, 105, 135, 137, 152; statue of, *136*, 137
Half-Shekels, 85, *85*, 86
Hammath-Tiberias, 73
Haram al-Sharif, 98
Hasmonean dynasty, 39, 40–41, 42, 43, 45, 49, 50, 56, 65, 76, 81, 87; expansion, 6, *41*
Hawarti, 144
Hazor, 18
Hebrew, 70, 71, 84
Hebrew Bible, 137, 146
Hebron, 31
Hefzibah Inscription, 38
Helena, Queen, 4, 6, 7, 84, 97, 98
Hellenes, 42
Hellenism, 34–44, 45, 46, 49, 51, 57, 60, 66, 72, 86, 93, 130, 153; Jewish revolt against, 37–44
Hellenistic Kingdoms, 37–38, *38*
Hellenistic period, 6, 20, 21, 22, 34–44, 54, 60, 71, 79, 95, 97, 123, 150, 153, 154, 159
Heracles, 72
Herculaneum, 8, 9, 68, 110, 111, 115, 144
Herm, 39, *39*
herms, 39
Herod Agrippa, 81
Herodes Atticus, 113
Herodes Theater (Athens), 113, *113*
Herod Family Tomb, 95, *96*, 97
Herodian bathhouse (Masada), 131, *131*
Herodian masonry, *80*, 81
Herodium, 49, 65, 95, 97, *97*, *130*, 131, *131*, 132
Herod Philip, 20, 49, 57, 59, 73
Herod the Great, 6, 29, 30, 31, 49–53, 66,

78–79, 80, 81, 82, 92, 93, 95, 97, 130, 131, 132, 156, 157; building projects, 50, 79–80, 81, 86–90, 95, 97; Caesarea and, 52–53; divided kingdom, 50; palaces, 51, 51
Hezekiah, King, 81
hieroglyphics, 37
Hippos, 37, 57, 59, 59, 60
Hizma, 92
Homer, 19
homosexuality, 116
Hormu, 7
house at Dura-Europos, 145, 145
house churches, 109–15, 146–48, 154–55
Household Shrine (Delos), 112, 113
House of the Bicentenary (Herculaneum), 8, 110, 111
Hyrcanus, 45

Idumea, 39, 49
imperial cults, 103–106, 121, 134, 135, 141
imperial inscription (Ephesus), 134, 135
incense burners (Israel), 152, 153
India, 34, 35
inscribed Temple stone, 80, 81
inscription (Modern Forgery), 3, 3, 4
inscription and phallus (Pompeii), 115, 115
inscription from Temple, 78, 79
inscription on Campus Martius, 102, 103
inscriptions, 3, 4, 5, 12–14, 24, 34, 35, 37, 38, 39, 42, 43, 44, 70–71, 79, 81, 83–85, 87, 89, 91, 94, 103, 107, 108, 109, 111, 113, 115, 135, 145; how to read, 159
in situ, 8–10
insulae, 110–12
interpretive archaeology, 16, 24–31
Iobacchoii Hall, 113, 113
Iobacchoii Inscription (Athens), 113, 113
Iraq, looted site in, 8, 9
Iraq el-Emir, 38, 41
Irenaeus, 149
Isaiah: 9:1, 55
Isfiya, 85
Isis, 119, 141, 142–43
Isis (Pompeii), 141, 141
Isis Statue (Delos), 118, 119
Isis with Horus (Alexandria), 141, 141
Israel, 9, 20, 21, 23, 39, 49, 51, 52, 61, 63, 131, 153; modern excavation, 18, 19
Israel Antiquity Authority, 4, 5, 10, 31, 52
Issos, 135
Isthmia, 106
Isthmian Games, 106
Iturean settlements, 60
Iudea Capta Coin, 132, 133

Jabal al-Tarif, 148
James, 3, 4, 6, 18, 69, 124
James, Simon, 155
James ossuary, 3, 3, 4, 4, 5, 9
Jericho, 18, 49, 61, 65, 66, 92
Jericho synagogue plan, 64, 65
Jerusalem, 4, 8, 10, 19, 28, 29, 31, 37, 38, 41, 42, 43, 48, 54, 61, 66, 73, 80, 100, 129, 130, 143, 144, 150, 153; archaeology of, 78–99; crucifixion and Jewish burial practices, 92–97; evidence for pilgrimage to, 82–86; excavations in, 98–99; First Temple period, 78; landscape and cityscape, 80–82; Lower City, 80, 81, 82; New, 135–37; in New Testament, 98; priestly aristocracy in Upper City, 90–92; Second Temple period, 64, 78, 81, 82, 83, 94, 98; Temple, 3, 29–30, 30, 31, 31, 32, 41, 49, 63, 66, 78–79, 79, 80, 80, 81–90, 86–89, 95, 98, 99, 107, 122, 132, 135, 137, 153, 156; topography, 81; Upper City, 80, 81, 82, 90–92, 95, 99

Jerusalem pottery, 19, 19
"Jesus" Boat (Ginnosar), 68, 69
Jesus Christ, 3, 4, 6, 8, 10, 11, 12, 14, 18, 24, 27, 28, 34, 42, 50, 57, 63, 70, 73, 100, 105, 122, 141, 145, 146, 149, 151, 153; burial of, 93, 97; crucifixion of, 78, 81, 93, 95; Galilee and, 54–73; Jerusalem and, 78–99
Jewish Silver Shekel, 128, 129, 137, 137
Jewish Wars, 50, 72, 79, 122–39; first, 6, 41, 50, 65, 79, 117, 122–23, 129–34; second, 6, 72, 79, 123, 135–37
Jews, 3, 4, 5, 8, 15, 19, 23, 30, 32, 34–51, 100, 117, 145, 146, 149, 150, 151–52, 153, 154, 157; archaeology and, 34–51; burial practices, 63, 64, 84, 92–97, 145; diaspora, 41–44, 55, 70, 84, 100, 108–109; excavated diaspora synagogues, 108–109; first Christians and Jewish Wars, 122–39; Galilean, 54–73; Jerusalem and, 78–99; purity practices, 5, 44, 61, 62–64, 79, 82, 83–85, 89, 92, 100, 130, 132; revolt against Hellenism, 37–44; sexuality, 116; synagogues, 65–66, 72–73, 74, 83, 100, 108–109, 130–32, 151–52, 154
John, 4, 5, 69, 73, 81, 83, 123, 148, 149; 1:46, 153; 2, 5, 98; 2:6, 5; 2:20, 88; 4:46–54, 72, 74; 5:1–9, 81, 83; 7, 98; 9:7–11, 81; 11:55, 84; 12, 98; 18 fragment, 123, 123; 19:5–13, 89, 90; 20:16, 70
John the Baptist, 4, 32, 50, 76
Joint Expedition to Maritime Caesarea, 52
Jordan River, 20, 57, 59
Joseph, 3, 4
Josephus, 4, 10, 30, 57, 58, 59, 76, 104, 129, 138, 139
Joshua, 18
Jotapata, 59, 66, 67, 77, 129
Judah "the Prince," 77
Judas, 6, 149
Judas Maccabee, 39
Judea, 37, 38, 50, 61, 62, 63, 64, 66, 87, 122, 129, 136, 151
Julian Basilica (Corinth), 121
Julias, 20, 57
Julia Severa, 109
Julio-Claudian Emperor, 117, 117
Jung Codex, 147, 147

Kafr Cana, 4, 5, 5
Kathros, 91, 99
Kedesh, 40, 60
Kenyon, Kathleen, 98–99
Kerem al-Ras, 5
Kfer Hananya, 158
Khirbet Cana, 4, 5, 5
Khirbet Qumran, 23, 32–33
Kidron Valley, 95
1 Kings, 18
King's Highway, 54
Kizilburun, 119
Kohl, Heinrich, 74
Koine Greek, 35–36, 37
kokhim, 94, 95, 152

Lachish, 18
lamps, 3, 20, 21, 23, 45, 55, 66, 67, 116, 135
lamp with Cleopatra, 45, 45
lamp stand (Ephesus), 135, 135
language, 70–71
Late Hellenistic period, 60, 61, 65, 70
Late Roman period, 77
Latin, 159
lead weight (Sepphoris), 70, 71
Lebanon, 4
Leriche, Pierre, 155
letters, ancient, 123–28

letter to slave (Egypt), 125, 125
lice, 69
life expectancy, 69
limestone, 56, 62, 80
lion relief (Iraq el-Emir, Jordan), 40, 41
literacy, 7, 159
Lithostrotos Pavement, 89, 89, 90
locus, 17, 20
Lofredda, Father Stanislao, 74
looted site in Iraq, 8, 9
looting, 9
Lower Galilee, 56, 58
Lucius Sergius Paullus, 13
Luke, 12, 49, 137, 149; 2:1, 47; 2:21–52, 98; 4:31, 74; 4:39, 68; 5:19, 12; 7:1–10, 72, 74; 7:25, 66; 10:15, 57; 10:38–42, 27; 13:34, 79; 19–24, 98; 20:20–26, 102; 23:53, 94

Maccabean Revolt, 6, 43, 60
Maccabees, 6, 38, 41–42, 78
1 Maccabees, 38, 41
Macedonia, 34
Machaerus, 50
Magdala, 57, 57, 58
magic, 69–70, 124
magical papyrus (Egypt), 68, 69
male domination of females, 115–17, 149
map of Christian Catacombs (Rome), 15
marble, 44, 47, 53, 67, 80, 92, 114
marble fragments (Tiberias), 66, 67
Marcus Papirius, 111
Marcus Tittius, 108
Marino, 143
Marisa, 37, 40
Mark, 12, 149; 1:20, 69; 1:33, 74; 2:1, 74; 2:4, 11, 12; 2:14, 74; 7:3, 61; 7:26, 63; 8:27, 21; 11–16, 98; 12:13–17, 100, 102; 12:23–33, 94; 13:2, 87
Mark Antony, 45, 90, 103
Martha, 27
Mary, 4, 27, 141, 151
Mary Magdalene, 4, 45, 57, 58, 149
Masada, 49, 51, 65, 86, 92, 129, 130–34, 131–32, 138–39; Zealots and, 138–39
Mattathias, 39
Mattathias Antigone, 55
Matthew, 149; 2:22, 51; 412–22, 55, 74; 59, 129; 8:1–13, 72, 74; 9:1, 74; 10:9–10, 58; 21–28, 98; 21:12, 89; 21:32, 27; 22:15–22, 102; 23:2–3, 43, 44; 27:59–60, 93, 94
Mazar, Benjamin, 99
medicine, 69
Megiddo, 72
Meiron, 23, 63, 69
Melos, 39
menorah from Upper City, 79, 79
menorah on a lamp (Sepphoris), 54, 55
menorah on Arch of Titus, 133, 133
Meyers, Eric and Carol, 76
Middle Roman period, 21, 55, 77
Miletus, 9, 29
Miletus Gate (Berlin Museum), 9, 9
mithraea, 143–44, 147, 154
Mithraeum in warehouse (Caesarea), 142, 143
Mithraeum under church (Rome), 143, 143
Mithraism, 143–44; archaeological sites for, 142
Mithras, 141, 143, 144
Mithras slaying bull (Rome), 142, 143
Mizpe Yammim, 65
mosaic (Pisidian Antioch), 2, 3
mosaic fragments (Sepphoris), 67, 67
mosaic in situ (Pisidian Antioch), 9
mosaics, 2, 9, 35, 55, 67, 72–73, 76, 91, 92, 110, 114, 141, 150, 151; synagogue, 72, 72, 73, 73

STEP INTO THE ANCIENT WORLD OF JESUS AND THE FIRST CHRISTIANS

This one-of-a-kind presentation of the New Testament world and its archaeological treasures provides a new, more complete understanding of the world in which Christianity was born. Through lavish photographs, architectural plans, extensive maps, and detailed charts, you can explore the landscape of Nazareth where Jesus grew up; sit at the shores of Galilee where he preached; and enter the streets and temple of Jerusalem where his ministry was fulfilled. An experienced archaeologist and biblical expert will guide you throughout your journey around Israel and beyond—on the Mediterranean voyages of Paul to the homes and synagogues of the Roman Empire, where he planted the seeds of Christianity. Visit Emperor Nero's "Golden House," witness the desperation of the Jewish revolutionaries at Masada, and explore the magnificent basilicas of Constantine the Great.

The HarperCollins Visual Guide to the New Testament features:

- Rich descriptions of the worlds of Jesus, Paul, and the first Christians

- Full-color photographs of excavations, artifacts, coins, and pottery from New Testament sites

- Extensive maps

- Architectural floor plans of temples, palaces, and synagogues

- Commentary on how archaeology relates to the Bible

- Examination of modern excavation techniques and methods

- A beginners' guide to understanding pottery, coins, temples, and inscriptions

JONATHAN L. REED is a leading authority on the archaeology of early Christianity and has excavated in Galilee since 1987. He has conducted research at the Albright Institute for Archaeological Research in Jerusalem, the American Academy in Rome, and the American School of Classical Studies in Athens. He is author of *Archaeology and the Galilean Jesus* and has co-authored with John Dominic Crossan two bestselling books, *Excavating Jesus* and *In Search of Paul*. He is professor of New Testament at the University of La Verne and is on the research council of Claremont Graduate University's world-renowned Institute for Antiquity and Christianity, where he is directing their Galilean Archaeology and the Historical Jesus project.

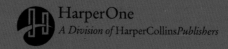
HarperOne
A Division of HarperCollinsPublishers

Cover design: Mark Ong, Side By Side Studios

Printed in the U.S.A.